DEMOCRACY IS SINKING

Think and Act with an Open Mind to Develop a Vibrant Democracy

SRB

Notion Press

Old No. 38, New No. 6
McNichols Road, Chetpet
Chennai - 600 031

First Published by Notion Press 2019
Copyright © SRB 2019
All Rights Reserved.

ISBN 978-1-68466-775-8

Contents

Contents

Appeal to Enthusiastic Readers

Mahatma Gandhi, who got us independence from the mightiest empire by leading a non-violent movement, has shown us how even unbelievable changes can be achieved when ordinary people come together and use their hidden power to do extraordinary things. The first step for using this hidden power of people to achieve a vibrant democracy is to make people aware of (1) the reasons for the sinking of our democracy and (2) the advantages of replacing it with the comprehensive democracy outlined in Article 27 which ensures the aim of people living happily with good quality of life and dignity under peaceful environment and carrying on their activities without hindrance.

The first step to save the sinking democracy is to make as many people as possible aware of the obstacles and possible solutions discussed in these articles so that they can understand and appreciate the need and urgency for innovative ideas to save our sinking democracy. For creating this awareness, understanding and appreciation, people have to spread these ideas through articles in newspapers and journals, e-mail and social media like WhatsApp, face book and twitter followed by group discussions, and debates. This awareness, understanding and appreciation ought to lead to healthy discussions and debates on the comprehensive democracy outlined in Article 27. These will help to arrive at a preliminary general consensus about advantages of comprehensive democracy (paragraph 87 of Article 27). During these discussions and debates constant attention is required to avoid getting bogged down by (1) any point other than advantages of comprehensive democracy and (2) distracting details, both deliberately and cunningly focused upon by opponents. To make all this possible, conscientious regional and national leaders, who can lead a well organized peaceful movement for replacing our sinking democracy with comprehensive democracy, have to come up and act with commitment.

As a prerequisite for kick starting a peaceful movement, people with vision should act to (1) strengthen mass awareness by suitable dialogues, discussions and debates on Articles 24 to 27 at least and (2) arrive at a preliminary general consensus about advantages of comprehensive democracy (paragraph 87 of Article 27). For reaching this general consensus, constant attention is required to avoid getting bogged down by any point other than advantages of comprehensive democracy or distracting details, both deliberately and cunningly focused upon by opponents.

Organizers of the peaceful movement have to constantly keep in mind that any radical and crucially needed reform will meet with fierce opposition from the entrenched vested interests in India and possibly in some other countries also. On the other hand, they should not lose hope and should be constantly guided by the fact that India got independence by a peaceful movement against a mighty empire, which had put up a series of obstacles and taken many cruel and violent steps. They should be encouraged by the fact that peoples' power and patience ensured that these obstacles and violent steps could only prolong attainment of success. With adequate precautions to neutralize opponents' obstacles, commitment, determination to fight against persistent obstacles and patience success can be achieved and will confirm the invincibility of peoples' power. It is pertinent, encouraging and reassuring that the mass awareness already created by the first step will ensure that peoples' power will be forthcoming to support adequate precautions needed from time to time.

Creation of mass awareness and support for a peaceful movement to have a democracy managed by professionals without distorting supervision by unqualified elected leaders (Article 27) has become easier now because "65% Indians say a system in which "experts" rather than elected officials make decisions would be good" (India Today dated 06.11.17, page 9).

The peaceful movement should then demand setting up of a new Constituent Assembly to (1) discuss this consensus and all pertinent articles which discuss some details, (2) work out full details of comprehensive democracy taking into account suggestions in this series of articles and (3) make changes in the Constitution to make comprehensive democracy a reality.

As stated by Lao Tse *"The journey of a thousand miles begins with just one step."* I appeal to you to take at least the first step to set the ball rolling to ensure wider appreciation of the manifold benefits of this comprehensive democracy. This will lead to the next steps of acceptance of comprehensive democracy with suitable modifications (if necessary) and its implementation. You can be proud that, for the benefit of your country you have made this praiseworthy contribution to replace our sinking democracy by the comprehensive democracy outlined in Article 27 which will have 27 outstanding achievements (paragraph 87 of Article 27) which include fulfillment of the aim of people living happily with good quality of life and dignity under peaceful environment and carrying on their activities without hindrance. ***A special appeal: Click NOTA option in coming elections.***

Introduction

Any attempt to develop a true and vibrant democracy has to first understand the history of democracy. Democracy was intended to get rid of despicable monarchy, in which all power was concentrated on one individual, and give power to people. In the type of democracy which was developed, people (who according to the definition of democracy are the masters) shifted (or were indoctrinated to shift) power to their elected representatives. Often, power became concentrated on one leader of these representatives who became a crafty monarch. This violated the reason for starting democracy viz., prevent concentration of power on an individual. Even after this happened, hardly any attempts were made to reverse the retrograde step of people giving away their power to elected representatives. In this manner, the process of developing true democracy was stopped midway. This series of articles attempts to restart the process and develop a system (Article 27) which restores power to people by enabling them to have a direct say in all matters, which ought to be a real aim of true democracy.

To overcome this situation, a first step is to find out why the process of developing true democracy was stopped midway and why no attempts were made to restore power directly to people. The process of democracy was initiated by politicians and their supporters. After it reached the stage when they had complete control of government, they enjoyed power and gloated over it and decided not to go ahead with any steps to complete the process of attaining true democracy. Thus, historically, power hungry politicians were responsible for stopping mid way the process of developing true democracy.

People were not capable of objecting to this because commitment to ideology of democracy was confined only to a minority of the population. They were overwhelmed by another minority of dominant sections of population who alone used to exert their voice. For the same reason, no attempts were made to restore power to people. An additional reason could have been that they were not able to come out with an alternative plan because of lack of innovative thinking. To come out of the rut, this series of articles has attempted to revive this process and restore power to people. Those who are keen to complete the process of attaining true democracy and restore power directly to people have to start a long peaceful fight against the present system. Fortunately, the environment seems to have become more and more favourable to them in most parts of the world now because of increasing dissatisfaction with the present system.

The second step is to study the defects in the present system so that these can be eliminated. A serious problem is that the parliamentary system which was adopted is fundamentally defective because the political party, with majority membership of parliament, controls both government and parliament (Article 6). This defective system allows dictatorial attitude in the party and the government and defeats the very purpose of having parliament as an independent pillar of democracy. Article 19 has highlighted this fundamental defect and some other serious problems and demanded abolition of parliament. Keeping these in view Article 27 has suggested a system without parliament, which directly gives power to people.

Another fundamental defect in the present concept of democracy is to consider that democracy is needed only for good governance (Article 18). Many more aspects have influence on quality of life. To live happily with good quality of life and dignity under peaceful environment and carrying on activities without hindrance all these aspects require careful attention and proper direction. Sad to say, present democracy ignores the fact that conflicts relating to some of these aspects have been responsible for many unhappy situations and disturbance of peace and harmony. For example, conflicts due to religion have lead to disharmony, fights, riots and even wars many times in many parts of the world. Tackling such problems is outside the jurisdiction of present democracy. Ignoring these is not a solution. Article 27 has evolved a comprehensive democracy which can tackle, in a democratic manner, all aspects which have influence on living happily with good quality of life and dignity under peaceful environment and carrying on activities without hindrance.

India had a literacy rate of 12% only at the start of democracy. Awareness of and commitment to principles and processes of democracy were negligible. People were overjoyed by attainment of independence and continued to be preoccupied with that emotion. There were hardly any discussions about principles and processes of democracy. Even after India made tremendous progress in economic development, influence of literacy and education on review of principles and processes of democracy was negligible. Therefore, hardly any attempt was made to study in depth the real situation of democracy in India. This series of articles attempts to do so.

When India became independent after 200 years of colonial rule grave doubts were expressed about having a sustainable democracy.

Miraculously, despite low literacy and immense diversity, India had phenomenal success in sustaining a democracy for about 70 years. In addition to this, the tremendous efforts of Election Commission in conducting large scale elections without any serious anomalies received high praise.

But, these two creditable successes and the fact that Indian democracy has closely followed the time old system in UK led to a sense of complacency. This is another reason why no attempts were made to study in depth the real situation of democracy in India.

This series of articles is an attempt to fill the serious gaps in knowledge about the real situation of democracy in India and to study in depth how a truly vibrant comprehensive democracy can be developed.

As a part of this attempt, this series of articles identified thirty-two obstacles which caused a distorted and ineffective democracy and suggested possible solutions for these. These are presented in separate articles for pointed attention and easier assimilation. Article 24 sums up the preceding articles for a quick recapitulation or quick reading by anyone who faces shortage of time. Article 25 spells out the basic principles which should guide formulation of a reformed system of democracy and Article 26 describes some basic issues. Based on all these, Article 27 gives an outline of a system of comprehensive democracy for public discussions and debates. Hope these articles will lead to spreading of awareness and facilitating point by point discussion and debate on each of these obstacles and possible solutions for these to arrive at a consensus for replacing our sinking democracy with the comprehensive democracy outlined in Article 27.

Articles 21, 22 and 23 emphasize the need for urgency to start a peaceful movement to usher in the comprehensive democracy outlined in Article 27 which has many advantages including 27 outstanding achievements listed in paragraph 87 of Article 27. These include the following five distinct and praiseworthy achievements which deserve special mention: (1) Enables people in each block and urban ward to have a direct say (once in six months instead of indirectly once in five years) in all matters – which is a real aim of true democracy. (2) Drastically reduces injustices, inequalities and greed which according to Mahatma Gandhi and the Pope is destroying the earth, (3) Tackles, in a democratic manner, many aspects other than governance which have influence on living happily with good quality of life and dignity under peaceful environment and carrying on activities without hindrance, (4) Provides houses to millions of homeless people who had to live along roads, on railway platforms and under flyovers and (5) Avoids continuation of a nation of dishonest people trying to evade tax and eliminates black money and corruption.

To achieve these lofty and noble aims, without further waste of time, <u>people with vision</u> should take keen interest, study all aspects of developing comprehensive democracy and <u>lead a peaceful movement</u>. Organizers of the peaceful movement have to constantly keep in mind that any radical and crucially needed reform will meet with fierce opposition from entrenched vested interests in India and possibly in some other countries also. On the other hand, they should not lose hope and should be constantly guided by the fact that (1) India got independence by a peaceful movement against a mighty empire which had put up a series of obstacles and taken many cruel and violent steps and (2) peoples' power and patience ensured that these obstacles and violent steps could only prolong attainment of success. With adequate precautions to neutralize opponents' obstacles, commitment, determination to fight against all obstacles and patience success can be achieved and will confirm the invincibility of peoples' power. It is pertinent, encouraging and reassuring that creation of mass awareness by the first step will ensure that peoples' power will be forthcoming to take adequate precautions needed from time to time.

Creation of mass awareness and support for a peaceful movement to have a democracy managed by professionals without distorting supervision by unqualified elected leaders (Article 27) has become easier now because "65% Indians say a system in which "experts" rather than elected officials make decisions would be good" (India Today dated 06.11.17, page 9).

Though this series of articles is based on the situation in India, some of the comments, discussions and suggestions therein are likely to be applicable to other countries also with suitable modifications. Moreover, all countries are likely to benefit from discussions and debates on the Outline of Comprehensive Democracy (Article 27).

Article 1

Eligible Voters

For good reasons, only adults are allowed to vote in elections to parliament and assemblies (two pillars of our democracy). But this leaves out a large percentage of population which unfortunately includes many teenagers who are (unlike in the past) more capable of balanced thinking and energetic action to safeguard democracy because of modern (technological) advances in education and knowledge environment. It is pertinent that these excluded teenagers who are more capable of responsible voting than a much larger number of adults, particularly lakhs of illiterates, already included as voters. Further, there are errors in voters' lists (both human and manipulated) which distort elections. For example, during last 50 years, number of women left out from electoral roll increased fourfold from the already large 15 millions to 68 millions.

Irresponsible voting among most eligible voters was forcefully brought out by the Press Council of India Chairperson Justice Markandey Katju's statements: "Ninety percent Indians vote in droves like sheep and cattle,"…many are "voting along caste and religious lines."…many say "I won't vote because my vote is meaningless." (Deccan Chronicle dated 31-03-13, page 6). What is worse, many voters are only interested in selling their votes and making a mockery of democracy. This has been emphasized by anti-corruption crusader Anna Hazare: "It often happens that after facing injustice, people decide to teach [parties] a lesson in the elections. However, they forget to do so after being treated to a party at a dhaba or after getting Rs. 200 or a Rs. 500 note." (The Hindu dated 18-03-14). In a sample survey in 2013 across Karnataka, as many as 41% had stated that caste was very important in deciding who to vote for (The Times of India dated 01-11-14, page 6).

A large proportion of educated adults do not vote because their votes are meaningless in the context of overwhelming 90% voting in droves or selling votes without any intention of safeguarding democracy. Callousness also may play a part.

Absence of the truly democratic and sensible right to reject all candidates when none are suitable had swelled the group of uninterested voters. The "None Of The Above" (NOTA) option recently allowed by Supreme Court (SC) order may not change the situation. Those who do not vote because they feel their vote is meaningless (due to the reasons explained above) may not come forward to exercise NOTA option. They cannot be blamed because the SC order does not lead to rejection of the election even when NOTA voters form majority!! In other words NOTA option, which should have been respected as peoples' voice, has become meaningless because of the defective SC order. Only a guarantee from Election Commission (EC) that such a clear expression of rejection of all candidates when none are suitable by majority of voters will lead to fresh election, in which the rejected candidates cannot take part, will help to get over the feeling of meaninglessness of NOTA option.

While non-voting group may or may not exercise NOTA option, those who vote in droves or sell their votes will not exercise NOTA option because they are influenced by other factors and are not bothered about safeguarding democracy. The fact is that both these voting groups together form a large proportion of actual voters and will vitiate aim of elections even with NOTA provision.

Sad to say, effective attempts have not been made to overcome this dismal state of voting, even after 70 years. To sustain a vibrant democracy, quality of voters is much more important than extent of coverage of adult population.

Inability to confine voting to only voters who are interested in safeguarding democracy and to make them vote is the <u>first obstacle</u> which has resulted in a distorted and ineffective democracy.

The main reason for including irresponsible and uninterested voters is blind enforcement of the adult franchise requirement, even when majority of adults are not capable of making proper independent choice or are not interested in voting. To overcome this to a large extent, while preparing voters' lists, it should be ascertained from each adult whether he/she wants to exercise his/her right to vote or not, after the responsibility of a voter is explained to him/her. Those who do not want to vote should be considered ineligible for voting by their own choice and asked to sign an affidavit in a prescribed form as a record of their voluntary rejection of their right to vote. A copy of the affidavit should be given to such persons to avoid doctoring of the list. However, chance should be given to withdraw this affidavit during any subsequent revision of voters' lists.

The remaining interested voters with confirmed eligibility should be told that voting is not only their right but also their responsibility to elect suitable representatives and that if they do not perform their responsibility without valid reasons their right will be withdrawn. Similarly, if there is sufficient reason to believe that a voter has "sold" the vote or has voted in droves, he/she should be educated about the harmful effect of this wrong action and warned not to repeat it. In both cases, the relevant fact should be entered in the list and his/her signature obtained. In case they repeat either of these twice (i.e., the third time), their names should be deleted when revising the voters' lists. However, they should be given a right to appeal to safeguard against misuse or genuine mistakes.

The above modifications are based on two principles: (1) no right can be thrust upon an uninterested person and then blame him if he does not exercise it and (2) no right is absolute and can be withdrawn if the responsibility arising from this right is not fulfilled or the manner of exercising the right invalidates the reason for giving this right. However, any voter should have the truly democratic and sensible right to really reject all candidates when none are suitable (not notionally as per SC judgment). Till then non-voter's name should not be deleted.

As stated earlier, confining eligibility to adults only will exclude a large number of younger persons who are capable of balanced thinking and energetic action to safeguard democracy because of modern (technological) advances in education and knowledge environment. To reduce such illogical exclusions, eligibility should be extended to all those who have completed 15 years of age (United Nations, World Health Organization, China and Australia have fixed lower limit of age for youth as 15 years). A better alternative is a lower limit of 14 years because a child is defined as below 14 years for child labour. Among the so defined age group (15+ or 14+), eligibility should be confirmed only for those who have expressed their interest in voting, after the responsibility of a voter is explained to them.

It is a pity that even after 70 years, most voters do not have the bend of mind and capacity to use their right to vote independently and effectively to develop a sound democracy (resulting in

90% voting in droves or large numbers selling votes – see paragraph 2 of this Article). Most likely, they will not be able to develop these capacities for many more years, in the absence of any mission to rectify matters. Therefore, should we not seriously think with an open mind about other options for exercising peoples' voice effectively? This aspect is explored in later articles.

Article 2

Representation of People

At best, an average of about 70% of eligible adults vote during elections to parliament and assemblies. Most elected persons receive much less than 50% of the total votes cast. Therefore, at best, most elected persons represent less than 35% of adult population, often much less. This proportion will be negligible if we exclude votes of about 90% irresponsible voters who do not really contribute to a proper choice of representatives because of selling their votes or voting in droves (Article 1).

Voting figures show that those who did not vote formed more than 30% of the electorate. Large numbers voted in droves; some others made the serious mistake of selling their vote; some others have allowed themselves to be intimidated even though their vote was secret; some others had preferred persons of their own caste. In a sample survey in 2013 across Karnataka, as many as 41% had stated that caste was very important in deciding who to vote for (Article 1). Thus, those who did not vote and those who voted on caste basis together form more than 70% of the electorate. No estimate is available for the other three groups of irresponsible voters. With their addition, percentage of voters who did not consciously fulfill their responsibility is likely to exceed 90%. This is also confirmed by the statement in second paragraph of Article 1 that about 90% vote in an irresponsible manner. Because of this grave failure by people, most of our elected representatives had the support of only a negligible minority (may be less than 10%) of voters who had voted consciously to fulfill their responsibility!! In other words, most of them do not really represent people.

A member of parliament (MP) and assembly (MLA) elected by people is considered as a representative of people. But, to *really represent people they have to be elected by more than 50% of the electorate.* Claim of most MPs and MLAs that they are representatives of people is void because they had support of much less than 50% of the electorate only (preceding paragraph). *Consequently the parliament and assemblies they formed were void.* It is shocking that EC and SC have overlooked this fact. Sad to say, EC did not exercise its responsibility under the Constitution to elect representatives of people despite having the relevant data to judge which candidates had secured votes of more than 50% of the electorate.

Most candidates failed to satisfy this requirement because votes were shared by large number of candidates in each constituency. To overcome this illegality problem and satisfy the Constitution requirement, EC ought to have introduced a two stage voting system. The two candidates who secure first and second positions in number of votes at the first stage only will become eligible for the second stage of voting. Winner of second stage will then have valid majority support and satisfy the Constitution requirement.

It is a matter of serious concern that out of 543 MPs elected in 2009, vast majority of 78% had approval of only less than half of the electorate (The Times of India dated 23-03-14) and their claim of being representatives of people is void. If irresponsible voters who form large majority as mentioned earlier and in Article 1 are excluded, 100% of MPs may have approval of only less than half of the electorate. Even with 78% of MPs having approval of only less than half of the electorate, 2009 parliament was void. The situation is likely to be the same among MPs elected in 2014 also resulting in 2014 parliament also being void.

Even after the spectacular success in 2014 elections, BJP has the support of only 31% of the electorate!! (The Times of India dated 17-05-14, page 1). In other words, it does not have support of 69% of the electorate. This proves beyond any doubt that BJP's claim that it represents people is void!!

A representative of people has to perform important functions of governance. It is naïve to expect that voters (including millions of illiterates) have the capacity to understand these functions and their significance and recognize and elect persons who can perform these functions efficiently. This contemptible expectation is a grave fundamental defect of the election system. To overcome this to some extent people should be asked to select only from a list of candidates who have the requisite qualifications and experience. Though this stipulation is essential for good governance, the Constitution could not lay down requisite qualifications because of shortage of such candidates 70 years back. But the fact is that voters have still not been provided an opportunity to elect suitable representatives by taking steps to remove shortage of candidates with the requisite qualifications and experience. Sad to say, such steps have not even been thought of during a long period of 70 years because of hardened callousness and laissez faire attitude.

As a result, people are often electing not only persons without adequate qualifications and experience required for good governance but also persons with criminal background. As many as 30 MPs elected in 2009 and 127 MLAs have themselves declared in their affidavits to Election Commission that they have been involved in electoral malpractices. These include corrupt ways to win votes, threatening voters, tampering of electronic voting machines and preventing voters from exercising their franchise (DNA dated 22-1-13, page 9). The Association for Democratic Reforms, which examined the sworn affidavits of a total of 4,827 MPs and MLAs, found that 14% (i.e., as many as 676) had declared serious criminal charges against themselves (The Hindu dated 26-09-13). A study by Association of Democratic Rights has shown that "money, muscle and criminal background are sure-fire qualifications to ensure a victory in the elections" (DNA dated 30-07-13).

A petition was filed in SC in 2005 stating that Sections 8, 9 and 11A of the Representation of Peoples Act, 1951 (RPA) allows convicts to be legislators even though these violate Articles 84, 173 and 326 of the Constitution which had expressly put a bar on criminals getting registered as voters or becoming MPs/MLAs. SC had then issued a notice to the Attorney General on the petition. After a long lapse of seven years (i.e., in 2012) SC woke up and agreed to examine this important petition and in July 2013 (a year later) it struck down Article 8(4) which had protected elected representatives with criminal background from disqualification, despite conviction, if they filed an appeal within three months. This order had only prospective effect. Thus, SC allowed convicted legislators to continue till a High Court takes a decision about their disqualification, which normally takes many years. The High Court decision can even be distorted because witnesses may be afraid to depose freely against such powerful persons with criminal background. According to newspaper reports, SC did not order quick disposal of their cases. Neither did it allow disqualification when the High court takes a prima facie decision that the charges are sustainable, considering long delays in final disposal. Moreover, there are no reports regarding orders of SC about (a) preventing criminals from registering as voters, as required under the Constitution and (b) other subsections of Section 8 and Sections 9 and 11A questioned in the original petition. It is not clear whether these provide loopholes which can be exploited for non-application of the modified Section 8. Lack of interest and commitment of SC is clear.

As a result, 162 Lok Sabha members and 1,268 MLAs who had declared criminal records were allowed to continue to function (DNA dated 12-07-13). What is most damaging is that neither SC nor Government was sincere about quickly removing such perverted representation of people even though it is forbidden by the Constitution.

Association for Democratic Reforms has observed that 86% of Rajya Sabha members were crorepatis and Lok Sabha 2009 had 58% crorepatis (The Times of India dated 06-02-14). This shows a highly imbalanced and unhealthy representation of people in parliament.

All these prove the utter inefficiency of the election system to have a balanced and healthy representation of people in parliament and having MPs with required qualifications and experience. Should we continue to be hoodwinked by this system and hide it under the carpet or should we seriously consider an alternative system for giving voice to people? This aspect is further explored in later articles.

Such grossly inappropriate, questionable and perverted representation of people is the <u>second obstacle</u> which resulted in a distorted and ineffective democracy.

If the changes in the system suggested in Article 1 are implemented, those who are not interested in having a representative will be excluded from the denominator for calculating representativeness. Because voting will be considered as a responsibility for the remaining confirmed eligible voters and those not voting repeatedly will lose their eligibility, only very few among them will not vote. Those who mock at democracy repeatedly by selling their votes or voting in droves also may lose their eligibility and, therefore, may not pervert the election. These three situations will result in the elected person representing more than half of those who are interested in having a representative.

As stated earlier, one reason for the low proportion of votes for the winning candidate is that there is no limit to the number of persons who can compete in elections for any constituency. To ensure that the elected representative has majority votes conduct election in two stages. Though this two stage voting will increase the burden for conducting elections it will satisfy representativeness – an important requirement of a democracy – and **give legal validity to parliament and assemblies**. Further, one way to reduce this burden is suggested in Article 3.

To ensure that voters are asked to select only from a list of qualified persons, aspiring candidates should qualify themselves as graduates or post graduates in political science or social welfare, with a managerial component for which recognized colleges should start suitable courses. A reasonable time frame has to be given for acquiring these qualifications by sufficient number of persons. RPA has to be amended to ensure that, after a fixed date, only persons who have the requisite qualifications and experience will be eligible to become peoples' representatives because the important functions of enactment of laws and governance should not be left to persons who do not have the required qualifications and experience.

NOTA should be considered as a clear expression of peoples' rejection of all candidates when none are suitable. Fresh election, in which the rejected candidates cannot take part, should be held if NOTA option is used by large number of voters.

These steps will lead to elimination or at least reduction in the number of unqualified persons and criminals getting elected as representatives.

The need for electing representatives will not arise if a way can be found for people to directly exercise their voice. Such a system is discussed in detail in later articles.

Need for a Flexible Election System

The aim of elections is to have pillars of democracy (parliament and state assemblies) which can (1) represent people truly and effectively and (2) manage governance with efficiency and accountability. With regard to the first aim of selecting true representatives of people the election system has failed miserably as clearly pointed out in Article 2. With regard to the second aim of an efficient and accountable system of governance also this system has failed as explained below.

When elections are carried out once in five years (or sometimes even earlier), number of efficient representatives, who are contributing admirably to an efficient and accountable system of governance, are unnecessarily weeded out along with the inefficient and the tainted ones, unlike the management infrastructure which has continuity because it is not broken up completely and reassembled. This lack of continuity in top levels of governance leads to avoidable distortions and distractions in governance and in functioning of democratic and other institutions. Those representatives who are functioning efficiently should be continued beyond five years to have the benefits of continuity of efficient service and save a substantial part of the huge amounts of tax payers' money spent on electing another full set of representatives once in five years. This flexible procedure will also motivate some of the other representatives to perform more efficiently and reduce cost of election further.

Moreover, there is no guarantee that representatives from a new election will be better. They can even be worse. Obviously, election is a costly gamble using huge amounts of public money. Why should we not seriously think of a better method for giving voice to people, not just once in five years as an ineffective ritual as at present, but more frequently and effectively? This is examined in later articles.

Another defect of the present system of elections is that it diverts attention of government from governance to securing re-election and results in lack of efficiency, transparency and sincerity in governance, particularly during pre-election months. Further, the need for large amounts of money for participating in election leads to undesirable and illegal activities and generation of black money. All these harm the economy, besides distorting governance to satisfy fund providers. If elections are made flexible as explained earlier, these two dismal situations can be mitigated, besides saving enormous public funds.

Moreover, a fixed five year period is likely to allow inefficiency and lack of transparency to continue for five years. When these are happening, instead of allowing these to continue, we should replace the representatives responsible for these failures. This will also serve as a warning to other representatives who have not justified the faith placed on them by people, besides saving expenditure.

Another definite advantage of the flexible system of elections is that the management infrastructure, which has adjusted to a political power system, will not have to waste time and energy to readjust to another political power system once in five years or even less.

All these justify a flexible election system.

To avoid distortions and distractions in functioning of parliament, assemblies and management infrastructure, it is better that this flexible election system is guided solely by the need for improvement in governance.

Neglecting these aspects is the <u>third obstacle</u> which resulted in a distorted and ineffective democracy.

These problems can be solved by having flexible durations for MPs and MLAs based on an efficiency approach for making desirable changes. The present governing system has yearly efficiency assessments for all officials of the management infrastructure except legislators who occupy the most crucial positions. To remove this serious anomaly, at the end of each year, efficiency of MPs and MLAs (including ministers) should be objectively ascertained and those not performing efficiently should be given a warning to improve. Those who do not show improvement after one year should be disqualified and their seats filled up by new election. Other efficient representatives should be allowed to continue till they happen to become inefficient in later yearly evaluations or cross a prefixed age limit or voluntarily retire. This flexibility will ensure continuity of governance and inject a sense of responsibility and accountability among the representatives who, sad to say, are not being assessed now because there is no system of evaluation for this top level of governance!! An appropriate election system should avoid discarding efficient representatives along with inefficient and tainted ones, particularly because the former are rare to find.

This new system of flexible elections based on yearly assessment will, besides ensuring continuity and efficiency of governance, reduce expenditure on elections to a much smaller number of seats every year and on life time payments to smaller number of retired MPs and MLAs. A small part of the enormous amount thus saved can be used to have two stage elections (refer Article 2) to ensure that persons elected as per the new system of elections truly represent majority of people.

Election Commission

Under the Constitution, it is the duty of EC to carry out free and fair elections to pick up true representatives of people as members of various legislative bodies in the country. Articles 1 to 3 have shown that the main aim of electing true representatives of people has not been achieved because, on an average, only a minority of the electorate (estimated as less than 35% in Article 2) had supported the elected persons. It is a matter for serious concern that this resulted in void representation. Even worse, these low levels of representation were of dubious nature because many had voted irresponsibly in droves due to caste or other considerations or sold their votes. (Refer to Articles 1 and 2 for details).

Sad to say, 78% of MPs elected in 2009 had approval of only less than half of the electorate (The Times of India dated 23-03-14) and were void. Therefore, the 2009 parliament was void. The parliament elected in 2014 also is likely to be void for the same reason. It is shocking that EC and SC accepted these void parliaments. What is worse, EC did not exercise its responsibility under the Constitution to elect true representatives of people.

During last 50 years, number of women left out from electoral roll increased fourfold from the already large 15 millions to 68 millions (Article 1). EC did not act to rectify this serious mistake of increasingly denying right to vote for millions of women.

Moreover, candidates for election and political parties who sponsored them were eager to spend enormous amounts on election (often even secretly exceeding the limits fixed by EC) mainly because of two reasons: (1) money is one of the "sure-fire qualifications to ensure a victory in the elections" (refer Article 2); and treating voters to a meal or giving Rs. 200 or a Rs. 500 note influences voting (refer Article 1) and (2) the system gives elected persons unfair opportunities to amass wealth. This attracted criminal mafia also to get elected, or get their stooges elected, by using money power and/or intimidation. Thus, the election system not only failed to elect representatives having support of majority of people, despite wasting huge amounts of public money, but also is the root cause of unlimited corruption and control by mafia. EC did not even try to remove these anomalies. By conducting election in two stages, as suggested in Article 2, EC could have removed one anomaly by ensuring that the elected representatives had majority support and are legally valid representatives.

Political parties need enormous amounts of money to fight elections. They get substantial amounts from corporate bodies. When they form a government they are obliged to give special favours to these rich bodies, which are often detrimental to people. This practice is antidemocratic. EC was well aware of this but did not do anything to overcome this anomaly also.

Article 3 had also stated that election is a costly gamble using huge amounts of public money and emphasized the need to seriously think out of the box for a better method for giving voice to people, not just once in five years as an ineffective ritual (as at present), but more frequently and effectively. EC did not apply its mind to develop a better method.

Elections are to be conducted according to constitutional provisions, supplemented by laws made by parliament. Election laws are to be based on the basic values of constitutional democracy. In order to protect these values from legislative and executive influence, the Constitution had incorporated these values as constitutional provisions. SC has held that where the enacted laws are silent or make insufficient provision to deal with a given situation in the conduct of elections, EC has the residuary powers under the Constitution to act in an appropriate manner. SC has further clarified that the jurisdiction of EC is wide enough to include all powers necessary for smooth conduct of elections. EC did not make use of these powers to improve election.

Because of this, the election system failed miserably to elect true representatives of people (Article 2). Moreover, it threw up some challenging situations which EC did even try to tackle. Three examples are given below:

1. Number of times a political party which had higher share of votes (showing higher peoples' support) had a lower share of elected representatives as happened in the recent assembly elections in Karnataka in which a party which had a 2% higher vote share (peoples' support) got 26 representatives less than the party with lower vote share. This is a mockery of the support given by people which ought to be a backbone of democracy. Repeatedly overlooking this important fact exposes a major defect of the system.

2. Another example relates to complaints about "horse trading" to secure majority in assembly. Opposition parties claimed that the party in power at the centre paid enormous amounts to those who agreed to defect. EC failed to verify the facts and take action, if necessary. It did not also try to remove loopholes in the system if any to stop such corrupt practices.

3. Recently, Central Bureau of Investigation (CBI) became unusually super active and filed large number of cases mostly against political opponents of government. The opposition parties claimed that the government is misusing CBI for a political witch hunt to spoil their image and have focused on the selection of the state, victim and time chosen for these attacks to give credence to their claim. EC failed to verify the facts and take action, if necessary. It did not also try to remove loopholes in the system if any to stop such antidemocratic practices.

According to the spirit of the Constitution, the sole purpose of election was to give voice to people. Sad to say, even when the election system repeatedly failed to give voice to people, EC continued to focus on this faulty system and did not apply its mind to develop a better method for giving voice to people that too not just once in five years as an ineffective ritual as at present, but more frequently and effectively. EC had also not applied its mind to the fact that it is empowered to adopt any better method which fully supports the spirit of the Constitution.

The main reason seems to be hesitation or omission on the part of EC to exercise the powers vested on it by the Constitution to give voice to people, even though EC had powers to act in an appropriate manner, which is insulated from legislative and executive influence.

This failure to act is probably because EC became too complacent after receiving kudos for conducting the herculean task of organizing elections on a massive scale. It is also possible that the Election Commissioners felt a soft corner or obligation to the government for appointing them to this coveted post without undergoing a rigorous system of selection.

All these repeatedly show that EC has not applied its mind to develop a proper system to ensure democracy by exercising the powers vested on it by the Constitution.

This is the <u>fourth</u> and very serious <u>obstacle</u> which resulted in a distorted and ineffective democracy.

The functions of EC also include looking after all problems connected with elections besides conducting elections. This function has not been satisfactorily executed as shown by the following examples:

1. When violations of the mode of conduct occurred, EC did not give any serious punishment to the violators and violations continued unabated because of this soft approach of barking but not biting.

2. Only after repeated criticism, EC expressed concern about criminalization of politics instead of acting to prevent it by using its constitutional powers. For example, as the statutory custodian of democracy (not for conducting elections alone), it could have forcefully demanded suitable amendments to the Representation of Peoples Act, 1951 (refer Article 2). It is not clear what prevented EC from being more assertive in taking suitable actions against criminalization of politics by exercising its wide powers instead of expressing concern or making recommendations.

3. EC had recommended (<u>not ordered</u> using its powers) the inclusion of NOTA as an option for voters. SC allowed NOTA but did not agree to carry out fresh elections even if those using NOTA form the largest group. If many voters have rejected all candidates it is a clear indication that fresh election is the will of the people. EC has been silent about this and did not appeal

against this anti-people decision by SC. Moreover, EC did not protest against SC interfering with its powers as the Statutory Authority for conducting elections.

4. EC had proposed to the government that its administration should be a "charge" on the Consolidated Fund of India like for other constitutional authorities. A bill for this purpose which was introduced in 1994 is still pending. EC did not forcefully demand restoration of this need as for other constitutional authorities (not as a special case) but only meekly reiterated this need from time to time, for the last 24 years!!

5. EC suggested poll reforms instead of ordering these using its powers. Government has been sitting on these for more than 10 years. There may be administrative and financial bottlenecks also which EC had to face. This step motherly attitude of a democratic government towards EC, which is the statutory body set up to ensure democracy, is against the spirit of the Constitution and deserves to be condemned outright. But EC is silent about these, instead of using its powers under the constitution to act in an appropriate manner.

All these show that EC has been acting like a modest advisor to government instead of a statutory authority with wide powers, despite the strong support from SC judgments!! Whereas SC (another statutory authority) has been passing strictures against government whenever called for, EC has closed its eyes when government put spokes in its functioning as a statutory body which is essential for democracy.

These aspects depict the <u>fifth</u> and very serious <u>obstacle</u> which resulted in a distorted and ineffective democracy.

The manner of functioning of parliament and assemblies has clearly shown that political party system may be more a hindrance than help to democracy. Sad to say EC, the statutory custodian of democracy (<u>not</u> for conducting elections alone), had closed its eyes to the fact that political parties had repeatedly stalled functioning of parliament or distorted it to serve their interests. EC has not cared to apply its mind to retrieve the situation e.g., by warning political parties about disqualifying them for undemocratic and undisciplined behaviour. Shockingly, it did not even react against such undemocratic and undisciplined acts by political parties which led to huge wastage of money and time. Neither has it insisted that political parties should have effective internal democracy which is essential for true democracy.

Absence of such important actions by EC is the <u>sixth</u> and very serious <u>obstacle</u> which resulted in a distorted and ineffective democracy.

To overcome all these serious drawbacks, it is essential to have an EC which constantly applies its mind and powers to ensure a truly vibrant democracy and passes necessary orders for the sustenance and growth of democracy, which are binding on government and political parties, similar to orders passed by SC.

As pointed out earlier, EC has been acting like a modest advisor instead of a statutory authority with wide powers, despite strong support from SC judgments. The reason may be appointment of unsuitable persons. To safeguard against this possibility, suitable qualifications and experience (including demonstrated capacity for innovation and taking strong decisions when needed) should be prescribed for Election Commissioners, and the field should be thrown wide open and not effectively restricted to civil service officers alone. Appointments should be made directly by President of India on recommendation of a committee consisting of Lok Sabha Speaker, Minister of Parliamentary Affairs, Chief Justice of India, Chairpersons of Human Rights Commission and Union Public Service Commission, two eminent social activists and representatives of two outstanding NGOs providing welfare services to people.

An independent reviewing body has to be set up immediately to ascertain the reasons for EC not functioning as a constitutional authority but as a modest advisor (as at present) and to recommend directly to the President steps which are essential to ensure that EC exercises the powers vested on it by the Constitution instead of shirking these as at present.

Meanwhile, EC ought to do the following immediately, keeping in mind that it has powers under the Constitution to act in an independent and appropriate manner to solve all problems connected with elections besides conducting elections.

Instruct all political parties to carry out elections using secret ballot to restore internal democracy at various levels within a fixed period (may be about three months), failing which their registration should be cancelled.

Develop a system for assessment of functioning of MPs and MLAs (including ministers) and conduct such annual assessments, starting with immediate effect, followed by further actions as suggested in Article 3 to reduce frequency of elections.

Prescribe qualifications and experience required for candidates for election as MPs and MLAs to be enforced after a prescribed gap for acquiring these.

Lastly, no amount of praise is adequate to acknowledge the tremendous efforts of EC in conducting such large scale elections without any serious anomalies. However, sad to say, because of the faulty election system these laudable efforts could not produce desired results.

Article 5

Government Formation

Selection of Prime Minister (PM)/Chief Minister of a state (CM) is often based not on capacity for governance but on extent of popularity and other extraneous considerations like faction leadership. PM/CM should have the capacity to (1) manage even a heterogeneous team without curbing their enthusiasm like a dictator, (2) resist pressures from vested interests and (3) listen to suggestions from the management infrastructure, leaders of people, journalists and social activists. It is naïve to believe that every popular hero or faction leader will have these capacities.

Moreover, PM/CM is seldom elected by the winning party in a democratic manner. Two methods are followed. (1) A dominant leader manages self selection. In this case he tends to become a sly dictator. (2) A coterie of most influential leaders of the party (or parties) which forms government makes the selection and a farcical election is conducted to give pretence of democracy. In this case, the PM/CM is not able to function effectively because of lack of firm majority support and domination by other power centre(s). PM/CM has to support ministers who are corrupt, inefficient or acting against national/state interest, instead of taking action against them. Non-government members of the coterie will exercise powers without accountability.

PM/CM and the coterie of influential leaders then select ministers and allot portfolios to them. Experience and efficiency in carrying out required functions are supposed to play a part.

But, in reality, there are number of extraneous considerations and power play which are not conducive to forming an efficient team of ministers.

All these actually result in a type of subtle and concealed dictatorship rather than a democracy.

These aspects depict the <u>seventh</u> and serious <u>obstacle</u> which resulted in a distorted and ineffective democracy.

To overcome this obstacle and enable the PM/CM to be able to function effectively with support of peoples' representatives and without interference from other power centres, they should be directly elected by parliament/assembly, preferably through secret ballot. PM/CM can then select the team of ministers from MPs/MLAs. Efficiency assessments of MPs/MLAs suggested in Articles 3 and 4 will immensely help to form an efficient team without extraneous considerations.

Another aspect is that a government can function only for a maximum period of five years even if its performance has immensely benefited the country. Why should the country gamble by spending enormous amounts of public money to replace such a desirable government with a new government every five years when there is no surety that a new government will be better than this efficient government? It can even be worse. Moreover, lack of continuity leads to avoidable distractions and distortions in functioning of government. Unfortunately, continuity of governance or desirable changes in governance when required are not given importance because of lack of commitment and feelings such as public "business" is "nobody's business." Will a corporate body or private enterprise change an efficient CEO merely to have a change at regular intervals? Will it wait for years to dismiss an inefficient CEO? Why are we not applying such thoughts to decide on change of government?

This undesirable convention of unnecessarily changing even efficient governments is mainly due to linking government formation with parliament/assembly formation. Why dismiss an efficient government just because a new parliament/assembly has to be constituted? All that is necessary is that the efficient government team should automatically continue as MPs/MLAs and should continue to be efficient and answerable to the new parliament/assembly.

On the other hand, a five year period can allow inefficiency and/or lack of transparency to continue for five years and ruin the country. In such a situation, why should we not immediately change that undesirable government without wasting lot of time to dissolve parliament/assembly after completing the five year period, wait for completion of election processes, form a new parliament/assembly and then form a new government? Keeping in view the importance of having an efficient and accountable government, the parliament/assembly (not the coterie of influential leaders) ought to first seriously consider selection of another set of members to form government. Efficiency assessments of MPs/MLAs suggested in Articles 3 and 4 will immensely help to form an efficient team without extraneous considerations. Any obstacles to this should be removed in order to ensure quick dismissal of an inefficient or corrupt government without wasting time and incurring massive expenses for re-election of parliament/assembly.

In either situation mentioned above, interests of the concerned political parties may come in the way of taking suitable action with independence to (1) have an efficient and accountable government and (2) avoid spending enormous amounts of public money to form a new parliament/assembly when not required. It seems that the only tangible reason for regular change of parliament/assembly and government even when these are working efficiently is felt need or ambitions of politicians who did not get a chance to become MPs, MLAs or ministers. If there are no valid reasons for the rigid five-year change, is it appropriate to have a governance system tutored to the felt needs and ambitions of politicians?

Need for change of government should be based only on a regular system of assessment of efficiency of governance (Article 3). Providing the option to either continue or change government based on efficiency assessment will also increase efficiency and accountability of some more members of the government team.

Should we not think seriously about removing the linkages mentioned above which come in the way of continuity of efficient and accountable government or quick dismissal of an inefficient or corrupt government?

These aspects depict the <u>eighth</u> and serious <u>obstacle</u> which resulted in a distorted and ineffective democracy.

Overcoming this obstacle requires flexibility in choosing periodicity of elections (as suggested in Article 3) and de-linking parliament/assembly formation from government formation. These will help in two ways: (1) either continue an efficient government even after five years or dismiss an inefficient government whenever required and (2) save huge election expenses. What is urgently required is to start a regular system of assessment of efficiency of government to decide on change of government. This ought to be organized and conducted by a statutory body like EC as suggested in Article 4.

Article 6

How Government Works

In a democracy, government has to function by giving utmost attention to feeling pulse of people. To do this, government has to keep an open mind and obtain information and feed back by making full use of different sources available in the country such as MPs, MLAs, media, social activists, intelligentsia, Panchayat Raj institutions, resident welfare associations in urban areas, special groups of people who speak up about their problems etc. But, government does not have a systematic proactive approach to make use of all these multiple agencies to feel pulse of people. What is worse, it is not inclined to have this.

When government's actions are questioned or suggestions for improvement are made, usual reaction is to ignore these on the faulty premise that listening to these will be considered as a sign of weakness. Such intolerant attitude shows a know-all dictatorial approach and is anti-democratic. This clearly shows that government gives only lip service to democracy and do not care for democracy, while ironically boasting that it functions as a democratic government. It has not realized that the real strength of a democratic government lies in its ability to (1) listen to people, (2) accept useful ideas and (3) act on these with vision and commitment. This attitude and expertise are sadly lacking.

A democracy has also to ensure that public funds are used efficiently and for the intended purposes. For this purpose, Constitution has set up an authority called Comptroller and

Auditor General of India (CAG). Sad to say, government has not acted to remove the large number of anomalies about misuse and enormous losses of public funds pointed out by CAG. This attitude of not acting on important information provided by even a constitutional authority is another instance of a dictatorial approach and is a serious blow to democracy.

Faced with other problems of faulty governance, a strategy of escapism and/or buying time is chosen by referring these matters to Commissions, Standing Committees of Parliament etc. The findings of these top expert bodies are mostly put in cold storage and not acted upon. Even worse, sometimes, actions contrary to their recommendations are taken. For instance, in 2005, Parliament's Standing Committee on Energy had urged government to reduce its reliance on petro-taxes. This was not only ignored but revenue from petro-taxes was repeatedly increased, showing not only a dictatorial approach but also scant respect for parliament. This recommendation is still relevant and blatantly ignored.

The fact that government has scant respect for parliament is further confirmed by repeatedly breaking promises given during replies to questions in parliament and discussions on bills and motions. During the last 10 years, this immoral action was repeated 1,024 times, as reported by the Ministry of Parliamentary Affairs (DNA dated 16-09-13)!! Over a longer time period many more instances of similar disrespect could have happened. This speaks volumes about (1) government's gross lack of credibility and disrespect for parliament, (2) the latter spinelessly tolerating disrespect more than thousand times, without the dignity expected from the august supreme body of democracy and (3) failure of parliament to exercise the responsibility of having a check on functioning of government.

A main reason for these shocking situations is a basic defect in the parliament system. The political party which forms the government also controls the parliament because of having majority. Evidently, **parliament cannot function as an independent pillar of democracy.** This faulty system allowed a subtle dictatorial attitude in the party and the government towards parliament which led to these shocking situations.

Another attitude towards listening to people is also lamentable. Who said is more important than what is said. As a result, many useful and innovative ideas had no chance of being heard, because these were told by persons who were not important people or known persons or sycophants.

Considering listening to people, expert groups set up by government (even constitutional authorities) and parliament as a weakness instead of strength is the <u>ninth</u> and very serious <u>obstacle</u> which resulted in a distorted and ineffective democracy.

To partly overcome this obstacle, an organization has to be set up to

(1) encourage people to freely express their views (particularly innovative ideas), (2) analyze these and (3) sort out and accept important/useful ones for implementation with commitment. If an important idea selected by that organization or any recommendation of an expert group or constitutional authority is rejected by government, it should approach parliament/assembly for ratification. The latter should either ratify the rejection if there are valid reasons for it or disallow the rejection.

Government is obsessed with GDP growth and revenue collection. It becomes upset if GDP growth rate falls but it does not feel concerned if people continue to suffer!! Sad to say, the fact that high GDP growth resulted only in widening the gap between the rich and the poor is not its concern. Even its obsession with money seems to be selective because government has not taken any tangible action against the multiple scams which have resulted in enormous losses of public money which, otherwise, could have been used for welfare of people. General tendency is to initiate action against scams etc. quickly and publicize it, if opposition party is involved, so that it can be discredited. After this, interest in follow up action is lacking and punishment is pending for many years.

Another problem is questionable use of public funds with a lopsided mindset. For example, a scheme named Sonia Gandhi Go Shiksha Yojana "has been running for over eight years and almost Rs. 8,000 crores of tax payers' money has been spent in the name of teaching traffic rules to cows!!" (DNA dated 6-10-12).

Thousands of crores are being enthusiastically spent (planned to be spent) on statues of historic figures; seems to be for political gain because people do not benefit. An example of such lopsided priority is the budget provision of Rs. 200 crores for a statue of Sardar Patel and only Rs. 100 crores for women's safety, ignoring that the whole nation is crying hoarse for the latter. Besides being a lopsided priority, this is also another example of ignoring peoples' voice!!

Almost every year audit reports caution about large scale wastages and surrendering of budgeted amounts because of lack of commitment. But, these reports gather dust and hardly result in suitable action. Late Prime Minister Rajiv Gandhi had stated that 85% of money spent on rural projects do not reach beneficiaries. Such colossal wastages depict not only inefficiency and lack of transparency but also a callous mind. These and other undisclosed wastages of tax payers' money still continue without even a semblance of efforts to reduce or stop these. To cover up resultant increase in deficit due to these inefficiencies, tax burden on people has been callously increased.

The more efficient officers specially allotted to Finance Ministry have been super active to collect additional revenues which are, sad to say, allowed to be wasted or mis-utilized by all ministries. Serious thinking for devising clever methods for collecting additional revenue is laudable if these funds are used for welfare of people. But, realities are disgusting. To reduce fiscal deficit, emphasis has been on taxing more. The more healthy options of reducing fiscal deficit by preventing wastages and postponing projects with less priority hardly get attention.

Low priority and insufficient funds for alternate sources of power are matters for serious concern because shortage of power is a serious problem. Moreover, inefficient utilization of even the meager funds allotted for various modes of power generation is another matter for more serious concern. For example, capacity addition target for power generation was not utilized by 47% in 8th Plan, 54% in 9th Plan, 49% in 10th Plan and 30% in 11th Plan. Lack of commitment leading to the large number of instances of non-utilization and mis-utilization of public funds ought to be disconcerting but not so for government.

All these show that government is happy with its lopsided priorities and inefficiencies. The above aspects depict the <u>tenth</u> and serious <u>obstacle</u> which resulted in a distorted and ineffective democracy.

This obstacle can be overcome only with a change in mindset to avoid lopsided priorities and inefficient implementation. In a democracy, welfare of people (not GDP growth rate) should be the main guiding factor unlike at present.

Successful governance requires qualified professionals to be completely in charge of activities which can be properly handled by them only. But most technical departments are headed by Indian Administrative Service (IAS) officers. This illogical positioning allows professionals to be supervised by administrators and leads to disputes and lack of cohesion. These have also resulted in heads of departments withholding required funds and other necessities for projects for welfare of people. Control of funds and facilities for professionals by administrators has hindered them in performing professional activities. All this hinders progress as well as accountability. The emphasis is on administration of professional departments and not on facilitating effective performance of activities required for welfare of people. One reason given is that professionals have no training in administration. This flimsy reasoning attaches more importance to administration of departments than to activities to be performed for welfare of people!! Moreover, the obvious solution to improve efficiency of professional services to people is to arrange for management training for professionals. Smothering their work by illogical supervision and control of resources by administrators is damaging and should be stopped.

This illogical positioning is the _eleventh_ and serious _obstacle_ which resulted in a distorted and ineffective democracy.

To overcome this obstacle, highest priority should be given to various professional activities which are essential for welfare of people and not to administration of departments as at present. All departments carrying out professional services to people should be headed by professionals with training in management to organize effective professional services. They should be assisted by qualified administrators for tackling problems in administration within the department.

Article 7

Management Infrastructure

It is a matter for serious concern that the management infrastructure (MI), consisting of ministers and government officials at all levels, ***has eleven basic faults*** in functioning. Some of these are continuing only because no one has questioned these and some despite being questioned.

To sustain a vibrant democracy, ministers and all officials at all levels of MI should have (1) a mind set to comply with principles of democracy and (2) proper perceptions about (a) framework of democracy and (b) different aspects of management of democracy. If there is no uniformity in mind set and perceptions about principles and management of democracy within MI, it cannot function as a well-knit unit with full focus on democracy. Disruptions and working at cross purposes are bound to occur frequently and smooth functioning of governance according to principles of democracy cannot be achieved. Sad to say, no specific efforts have been made to create these basic requirements among ministers and all officials so that they can work in unison. Only a detailed study of the situation, changes needed in it and implementation of its recommendations can help to develop these basic requirements of mind set and perceptions among all members of MI.

In this context, a rough idea about mind set and perceptions of government officials can be obtained by asking a sample of them, after assuring them of confidentiality, why they prefer a government job. It is likely that the most common reply will be that they feel assured of having a reasonably good salary, can work leisurely, enjoy number of holidays and have the security of a pension. These depict that they are working with a selfish mind set without idealism about democracy.

If pressed further about why they prefer leisurely work, the truly honest among them may admit that by delaying work they can enjoy people running after them saying "sir," "sir" and paying some money under the table – exposing an unworthy mind set for democracy.

It is very likely that no one will give a reply that they like to work for a democratic government which gives high priority to welfare of people – exposing lack of required mind set and perception about democracy.

Even if a few give a proper type of reply, absence of proper mind set and perception about democracy among the remaining majority of officials will be obvious. It is likely that most of the ministers also do not have proper mind set and perceptions about democracy. Because of this basic fault MI cannot function as a well-knit unit with full focus on democracy.

A <u>second basic fault</u> arises from ignoring the indisputable fact that most efficient governance can be provided only by professionally qualified and experienced persons, without hindrance from persons without required qualifications (For details refer to "Illogical positioning" in Article 6). To overcome this, Article 6 has suggested: "All departments carrying out professional services should be headed by professionals with training in management to organize effective professional services. In addition, they should be assisted by qualified administrators for tackling problems in administration within the department"

Senior officers prepare drafts of policies, projects and solutions to problems of infrastructure and administration after a thorough study of all aspects based on their qualifications, training and long experience. When these are submitted to the minster for approval, quite often these are modified or rejected by the minster in a dictatorial manner to uphold party interests or selfish interests or vested interests. This dictatorial decision making practice makes a mockery of the "officer selection system" in which some of the brilliant and energetic minds in the country are selected through competitive examinations and interviews and given long training!! Dictatorial decision making practice and allowing extraneous factors to score over merit is the <u>third basic fault.</u>

Such obviously dishonest and dictatorial practices destroy the belief of all the officers of the department in honest functioning, in addition to belittling their expertise and much longer experience compared to those of the minister. As a result, many of them lose their sense of commitment and/or become cynical – both detrimental to efficient functioning. Even worse, some of them are tempted or forced by circumstances to form a nexus with the minster for undemocratic and non-transparent activities. These result in mis-governance and even scams. The destruction of belief in honest functioning, belittling of expertise and formation of nexus are the <u>fourth basic fault.</u>

Management infrastructure is not people friendly and has developed arrogance and a negative approach in using their powers. These have put spokes in almost all activities for development and welfare of people. The resultant red tape has given a bad name for bureaucracy in the country. Even worse, when tackling any problem faced by people, an arrogant and negative attitude of denial of help to people has been all pervasive in a government for the people!! People, whose welfare is of utmost importance in a democracy, have been ironically made to run from pillar to post with anxiety for months. This <u>fifth basic fault</u> is continuing even though it has faced criticism.

Due to various reasons including scope for amassing wealth, lack of transparency has increased. Rules and a protective approach stood in the way of taking deterrent actions against those indulging in such activities. Even more shocking, some dishonest officers have been given promotions or choice postings!! This situation has emboldened many officers to continue to misuse their powers and indulge in undemocratic and non-transparent activities, besides amassing more wealth. This <u>sixth basic fault</u> is continuing despite criticism.

Curbs on positive actions to safeguard democracy are quite common in the guise of enforcing discipline, leading to harassment of honest officers. This has been supplemented by an environment of fear and subservience which prevent honest performance. Officers who were honest and sincere were either sidelined or transferred frequently with some officers being transferred 40 times or more!! The message of encouraging dishonesty is loud and clear. This <u>seventh basic fault</u> is continuing though these facts have led to criticism.

A majority of about 66% of IAS officers had very short average tenures of 18 months or less, 24% between 18 months to two years and *only 10% more than two years* (The Times of India dated 01-01-14). This was detrimental to efficient governance because a minimum tenure of two years is required to do justice to any job and about 90% officers did not have it.

The demoralizing brief tenures could not have been productive; more so because these harassed officers would not have been in a mood to put in their best efforts. There were also instances of

52 transfers in 31 years, 50 in 36 years and 46 in 30 years, in which the officers did not have time even to settle down!! How can they have mental peace to do good productive work? This has resulted in development and welfare of people getting sidelined or even ignored. The absence of stability and peaceful work environment is the <u>eighth basic fault</u> which is continuing though these facts have led to criticism.

Some officials tend to identify themselves with one political party or the other. They give more importance to the interests of that party and national interests are sidetracked or abandoned. On the other hand, when a political party which is not of their choice forms government, these officials drag their feet to slow down development activities and thereby try to discredit the party which has formed the new government. Ministers are often afraid that such officers will become a hindrance to their activities and prefer to have officers whom they can trust. Therefore, deliberate transfers of officers are made with a vindictive mind or to help favorites. This results in the "favorite" officials misusing their powers and those not favoured dragging their feet. Both create distractions and emotional problems which affect proper functioning of MI. In the process, development and needs of people get sidelined or even ignored. This is the <u>ninth basic fault</u>.

Another problem which retards progress in development and delivery of services of good quality to people is inter-service rivalries and tendency of some officers to withhold support for progressive action in order to show off their importance and status. Even technical departments are headed by IAS officers and allow professionals to be supervised by non-professionals. This has increased inter-service rivalries which hinder progress as well as accountability. Not preventing such rivalries and negative attitudes are the <u>tenth basic fault</u>.

When faced with problems of faulty governance, strategy of escapism and buying time is chosen by referring to Commissions, Standing Committees of Parliament etc. Findings of these top bodies are seldom acted upon.

Some archaic acts, rules and procedures and undemocratic attitudes of officials are not conducive for healthy development and attending to welfare of people, particularly for ensuring maximum benefit to people. No serious attempts have been made to rectify the above situations. This is the <u>eleventh basic fault</u>.

The above aspects depict the <u>twelfth</u> serious <u>obstacle</u> which resulted in a distorted and ineffective democracy.

To overcome this obstacle, a thorough study has to be undertaken to ascertain what stands in the way of MI (1) functioning as a well-knit unit with proper mindset, perceptions about (a) democracy and (b) different aspects of management of democracy, (2) complying with democratic principles and (3) developing an attitude of helping people instead of denying services on some pretext or the other. This should be followed by action to remove these bottlenecks.

All ministers and officials should attend a specially conducted course which emphasizes the need for a proper mindset, perceptions about (a) democracy and (b) different aspects of management of democracy as well as compliance with democratic principles and developing an attitude of helping people instead of denying services on some pretext or the other. This will enable them to function effectively as a part of a well-knit organization with focus on democracy. New ministers and officials should attend this course soon after joining service.

Article 8

Law and Order

One of the most important expectations from a democracy is that people can live happily with good quality of life and dignity under peaceful environment and carry on their activities without hindrance. Sad to say, these expectations remain a woeful dream in many ways.

Rape and violence against women have rocked the whole country. An analysis by Commonwealth Human Rights Initiative showed that 2,64,130 rapes were reported between 2001 and 2013 in 28 states – an average of 56 rapes per day (The Times of India dated 28-07-14, page 7). Four rapes and nine molestations were reported in Delhi every day. (DNA dated 04-01-14). Robberies also are daily features. Murders are quite common, that too of senior citizens. Instances of people taking law into their hands and lynching and/or murdering in the name of cow protection or intolerance are causing serious concern. Police are not only ineffective but also callous. When rich or influential persons are involved in crime police tend to take their side. When police somehow manage (or are forced) to file cases against rich and influential persons, the latter threaten witnesses and use delaying tactics to postpone trial. After a long interval, courts do not punish them stating that there is lack of evidence. To overcome these, SC wanted immediate steps to be taken to ensure protection of witnesses who often turn hostile due to threats or other corrupt practices (DNA dated 15-11-13 page 9). But, the situation remains the same. Moreover, possibility of these rich and influential persons influencing court cannot be ruled out.

Police have earned a reputation of being corrupt in dealing with problems faced by people. Most people are afraid to go to a police station with a genuine complaint. Filing of a case is subject to whims of police or the pressures they face. Burking of crime is so common that every year about 60 lakh cases are not registered (The Hindu dated 13-11-13, page 13). A general impression is that persons with money or influence can get away with any crime. Even worse, SC was constrained to remark that policemen are like "criminals in uniform" (Deccan Chronicle dated 14-10-12). Even this castigation from the highest court could not produce results. Continuation of this dismal state of affairs was confirmed by a Chief Minister of a state stating: "It's no surprise that people think twice before visiting a police station. They are scared to talk to police." "How can anyone expect justice from police when they are so corrupt and indulge in illegal activities?" (Deccan Chronicle dated 14-06-13, page 3).

In a TV discussion, a former police commissioner stated that police have now become an "armed militia of politicians in power." (Deccan Chronicle dated 06-02-13, page 8). "Today, our political leaders not only want police to do their dirty work but also collect money for them." "At the centre, the Intelligence Bureau furthers the interests of the ruling party" and the Central Bureau of Investigation (CBI) has been reduced to being a "caged parrot" of government, (as remarked by SC). "We not only need to free police from malignant and suffocating political control but also streamline its organization to ensure a people friendly and highly efficient police force." (Deccan Chronicle dated 22-05-13, page 9).

In connection with a Public Interest Litigation case which alleged that 1,17,480 children had gone missing between January 2008 and January 2010 and of them 41,546 were yet to be traced,

SC remarked that "Nobody seems to be concerned about missing children. This is the irony." (Deccan Chronicle dated 06-02-13, page 1).

All these show that most people are very unhappy with police who have earned the reputations of being "criminals in uniform" and "armed militia of politicians."

Elected representatives of people often close their eyes to all such dreadful realities and allow matters to drift. What is worse and cruel, some of them derive personal benefits from this anarchy or even create such situations for their selfish gains. There are many instances of lawmakers taking law into their hands and demonstrating their contempt for law. This has led to their supporters and friends also taking law into their hands without fear of punishment. Children of politicians also indulge in unlawful activities and escape punishment. These leaders do not realize that not only they are causing harm but they are also setting bad examples as leaders.

"Like any democracy, we have all the laws. But we don't have the courage, the competence or the candour to implement them." (The Week dated 09-06-13). Apathy and callous attitude of government continue, even after multiple failures in law and order are highlighted by media every day. These attitudes have become conspicuous and have resulted in loss of trust on government.

All these have made people unhappy, frustrated and cynical.

One reason for this state of affairs is acute shortage of police officials (policemen and officers). There are only 106 policemen for one lakh people, which is even less than half of the recommended ratio of 222 (The Times of India dated 23-02-14). Government has been callous and has not taken adequate steps to overcome such gross shortages of police officials, even though this would have benefited people and reduced unemployment also. It is surprising that this has not been done even when unemployment is a major problem which hurts government. This is due to low priority and not lack of resources. Inability to ensure that more recruitment will not create more criminals in uniform can be a possible reason for hesitation!! Or, are politicians afraid that this will come in the way of their unlawful activities?

What makes the shortage even more alarming is that available police officials are frequently misused or deputed for non-governmental activities e.g., 700 constables, 120 SHOs and 35 DySPs were put on duty for the marriage of a top politician's daughter, which shockingly was a vulgar display of wealth with Rs. one crore being spent on the main dais alone (CNN IBN news on 3-11-12). Moreover, police yielding to external pressures is all too common. Such misuses are callously rampant. As a result, "In India, there are three policemen for every VIP and just one for every 8,000 people" (DNA dated 08-02-13, page 1). Even after SC passed strictures about misuse, hardly any serious actions are visible.

Democracy also requires equality in application of laws. Violations of this requirement are far too common. Poor people hardly benefit from the law and order machinery. In fact, they are even afraid of the protectors of law. No committed efforts have been made to rectify matters.

Faced with decay in functioning of police, a National Police Commission was set up to recommend reforms. This Commission made many important recommendations. But, these were put in cold storage despite directions issued by SC. A thorough review has to be conducted to ascertain reasons for this and other dismal situations which affect people all over the country. Government should take immediate action on the basis of this review and report to parliament. The latter should question government in case of delay.

Meanwhile, immediate action should be taken to recruit and train sufficient number of police personnel and ensure that they function effectively without hindrance from others. This is so important for welfare of people that adequate budget has to be provided if necessary by preventing wastages and by cutting down budget for projects which are less important for welfare of people. For this a change in mindset and commitment are essential.

Often people are punished on the ground that ignorance of law is no excuse. This shows ignorance of realities. Vast majority of people are not aware of all laws. Even experienced lawyers and judges have to repeatedly refer to law books, showing that even they are not fully aware of all laws. Further they often differ in interpretation of law showing that laws are not clear even to them. Then, why do judges expect that common man will know all laws and their sections and sub sections? Therefore, how can they justify punishment for ignorance of law? Particularly so when even law makers and influential persons get away after breaking laws and only common people are punished for ignorance of law.

The above aspects depict the <u>thirteenth and serious obstacle</u> which resulted in a distorted and ineffective democracy.

To avoid unfair punishment for ignorance of law, crimes should be classified into the following three categories:

1. Crimes like murder, rape, theft, cheating etc. commonly recognized by society even without knowing the relevant laws. For these ignorance of law is no excuse.

2. Crimes which are not likely to be known by all people and was committed because of ignorance of law. For these only a warning is sufficient for the first offence. Repetition should be punished.

3. Other crimes deserving punishment because there is reason to believe that it was committed despite awareness that it was prohibited by law. This includes a second offence under (2) above, a politician taking law into his hands, violence attempted by groups of people to break law to show protests etc. These should be punished.

If instances of (2) above are too many, an education campaign should be carried out to reduce ignorance of the relevant law. If necessary, these laws should be modified to make these unambiguous and clear.

An expert body should make a thorough study of all existing laws to weed out those which are obsolete and to modify the remaining laws to reduce differing interpretations by judges and lawyers and to make these broadly understandable to people.

As stated earlier, people are even afraid of the protectors of law. To overcome this unhappy situation it is necessary to build up a good relationship between police and people. For example, the entire area of a police station should be divided into as many sub areas as number of constables in the police station. Each constable should have frequent interaction with the people living in the sub area allotted to him/her by forming a "Police People Interaction Club" (PPIC). PPIC should regularly meet once a month and whenever there is a special need. In these meetings people should inform the constable about security problems they are facing and ask the constable to inform the police inspector so that action can be taken to solve the problems. In the next meeting, the police inspector should inform people about the status of the required actions and reasons which are standing in the way if action is not complete. This will lead to mutual understanding of the problems faced by both groups. People should make use of the half yearly meetings suggested in Article 18 to question about these and ask for expediting proper action to solve the problems.

In the PPIC meetings, the police inspector should tell what people can do to improve security and request for their cooperation. PPIC can also be used by the police inspector to improve awareness of laws among people and to arbitrate disputes, if any, among residents of the sub area.

All such interactions by police will lead to mutual understanding of the problems faced by both groups and also make police "friends of people" instead of "criminals in uniform" and "armed militia of politicians" as at present.

Article 9

Corruption

People want a corruption free government. It was envisaged that the institutions set up to ensure checks and balances will help to control corruption. But, all these failed miserably for the reasons explained below.

Besides corruption being rampant in every sphere of activity, mega scams have been exposed with alarming frequency. Punishment to persons involved in these is dragging on indefinitely and causing concern and increasing cynicism among people. This lack of interest in pursuing cases shows that these scams were exposed only to gain political advantage and not to end corruption!! This is the <u>first instance</u> which exposes hypocrisy about zero tolerance to corruption. This view is supported by the following 26 additional examples of hypocrisy about highest priority to getting rid of corruption.

Central Vigilance Commission (CVC) was set up, even as an advisory body, only in 1964 (i.e., 14 years after the Constitution came into force), through an ordinance. In 1998 (i.e., 34 years later), government introduced the CVC Bill in Lok Sabha to replace the ordinance. But it was not passed. The Bill was re-introduced in 1999 and remained with parliament till September 2003 (i.e., for another four years). Then only it became an Act after being duly passed in both Houses of parliament. This long delay of 53 years in conferring statutory status to CVC (an anticorruption organization) speaks volumes about the lack of interest of government and parliament to control corruption, though government has been repeatedly proclaiming that it gives highest priority to getting rid of corruption!! This is a second instance which exposes hypocrisy about zero tolerance to corruption.

What is worse, CVC can investigate corruption against government officials only after government permits it, though CVC is a statutory body!!. This is similar to asking a thief's permission to catch him. The reason given for this presumes that CVC (a responsible statutory body) will be frivolous!! Delays and denials of permission are quite common and show government's reluctance to allow proper checks. This check stands deliberately watered down in this manner even now. This is a third instance which exposes hypocrisy about zero tolerance to corruption.

Annual reports of CVC gave not only details of work done by it but also brought out the system failures which lead to corruption in various Departments/Organizations and suggested improvements in the system and various preventive measures needed. Cases in which CVC's advices were ignored were also listed. A government which is keen to get rid of corruption would have welcomed the suggestions for improvement!! But this was not done. Moreover, hardly any action was taken on any of the important recommendations. Government's callousness and lack of commitment are obvious. This is a fourth instance which exposes hypocrisy about zero tolerance to corruption.

CVC has a very small set up with grossly inadequate staff and other resources needed to investigate corruption in more than 1,500 central government ministries and departments. It cannot direct CBI to initiate enquiries against any officer of the level of Joint Secretary and above without permission from the concerned department. It does not have powers to register criminal cases and deals only with vigilance or disciplinary cases. Even for the limited investigations taken up, it can only make recommendations and cannot impose penalties. As a result, CVC has neither resources nor powers to inquire and take action on complaints of corruption that may act as an effective deterrence against corruption. Sad to say, government does not even think about the need to rectify the situation let alone take any action. This is a <u>fifth instance</u> which exposes hypocrisy about zero tolerance to corruption.

CBI is the top investigating police agency in India. Its jurisdiction covers corruption by central government servants and employees of public sector undertakings and nationalized banks. From 1965 onwards, CBI has also been entrusted with investigation of economic offences.

Government appoints Director (CBI) from a panel of candidates based on the recommendations of a committee chaired by the head of a toothless CVC. Even appointment and discipline of lower ranking CBI officers are not handled by CBI but Ministry of Personnel. Control of government on appointments at all levels of CBI is an obvious travesty. This is a <u>sixth instance</u> which exposes hypocrisy about zero tolerance to corruption.

To begin an investigation, CBI must obtain a series of approvals. For corruption investigations CBI needs approval of Ministry of Personnel. Further these are monitored by the toothless CVC. In order to investigate allegations of corruption against senior civil servants, CBI must seek consent of Ministry of Personnel. It must also have permission from chief minister of the state where it wants to conduct an investigation. Restrictions on CBI to start work are a <u>seventh instance</u> which exposes hypocrisy about zero tolerance to corruption.

CBI is dependent on Home Ministry for staffing, since many of its investigators come from Indian Police Service. Likewise, it depends on law ministry for lawyers. Critics of CBI ask: "How can a body dependent on so many departments of government and answerable to them investigate the actions of government officials? Not attempting to remove these suffocating dependencies is an <u>eighth instance</u> which exposes hypocrisy about zero tolerance to corruption.

In 1991-92, in its 13th Report to Lok Sabha, the Estimates Committee of Parliament recommended "enactment of a new law laying down organizational structure of CBI, functions to be discharged by it, types of offences which it can investigate and providing for conferment of powers of police, (laid down in Criminal Procedure Code 1973), on members of CBI." It also recommended a constitutional amendment to provide for extension of CBI activities to any state without consent of its government. No action was taken on this recommendation by a parliament committee.

SC, in a 1996 judgment, said powers of Minister for Personnel, Public Grievances and Pensions does not "permit the minister to interfere with the course of investigation" by CBI. In 1997 SC further intervened to ensure CBI a measure of independence in probing corruption cases. Both orders of SC did not yield any results, forcing another round of court hearings on the same subject in the coal block allocation case.

After the apex court's 2006 judgment on police reforms in the Prakash Singh case were disregarded by most states, contempt cases were initiated but are yet to be settled!! The regularity with which orders and judgments of SC and High Court have been flouted by states is fraught with grave implications for democracy.

Despite repeated recommendations and court orders, CBI continues to be hampered and cannot play an independent role. All these show a ninth (and most serious) instance which exposes hypocrisy about zero tolerance to corruption.

CBI has been dragging its feet while investigating prominent politicians, leading to their acquittal or non-prosecution. CBI has not been allowed to make a dent on the rampant corruption in the country. This is a tenth (and most serious) instance which exposes hypocrisy about zero tolerance to corruption.

Joginder Singh and B.R. Lall (former director and joint director respectively of CBI) have exposed government for engaging in nepotism, wrongful prosecution and corruption. In Lall's book, "Who Owns CBI," he details how investigations are manipulated and derailed by government. Government resorting to manipulations and derailments is a eleventh (and most serious) instance which exposes hypocrisy about zero tolerance to corruption.

Information obtained under Right to Information Act 2005 (RTI) has revealed corruption within CBI. RTI activist Krishnanand Tripathi has alleged harassment by CBI to save itself from exposure via RTI. Instead of setting matters right, in 2011, government exempted CBI from the provisions of RTI Act on the pretext of national security!! This has been criticized by Central Information Commission (CIC) and RTI activists, who said the blanket exemption violated the letter and intent of RTI Act. These form a twelfth (and most serious) instance which exposes hypocrisy about zero tolerance to corruption.

CBI became the subject of ridicule because it allowed a minister and government officials to modify its report on allocation of coal mining licenses. SC then criticized CBI for making changes in its report at the request of a minister and two bureaucrats and remarked that CBI is "like a caged parrot" of government. Because of this and particular mention of manipulation in Lall's book it is reasonable to conclude that government has been making changes in CBI report. Making such manipulations is a <u>thirteenth (and most serious) instance</u> which exposes hypocrisy about zero tolerance to corruption.

The court gave government time till July 3, 2013 to lay out steps to make CBI independent. This order was the latest in a long line of failed efforts to establish a robust anticorruption investigating agency. It is shocking that no steps have been taken to make CBI independent even by 2018 (i.e., more than four years after the time limit set by SC) though this is a contempt of the highest court and a big blow to democracy. This is a <u>fourteenth (and most serious) instance</u> which exposes hypocrisy about zero tolerance to corruption.

Recently, CBI became unusually super active and filed large number of cases mostly against political opponents of government. The opposition parties have claimed that the government is misusing CBI for political witch hunts to spoil their image and have focused on the selection of the state, victim and time chosen for these attacks to give credence to their claim. If true, CBI now deserves to be called a "caged ferocious dog" of government.

The series of raids by Income Tax department (IT) and Enforcement Directorate (ED) during the same time period has led to doubts about political control on functioning of these three state investigative agencies. A disturbing fact, which confirms political control, is that these simultaneous raids were not only carried out on premises of number of political opponents of government but

IT and ED also resorted to a highly objectionable act to spoil the image of these persons viz., giving wide publicity to what it found during the raids, even before establishing that they are guilty.

Referring to a series of raids by IT during the same time period, an editorial in The Times of India dated 04.08.17 stated as follows: "Income tax investigations and raids only on opposition parties can raise questions of partisanship of state investigative agencies…" To avoid this, government should ensure that, besides CBI, agencies like IT and ED are insulated from political control. Else, they could soon be labeled like CBI which was famously called a "caged parrot of government" by the Supreme Court in 2013. It is pertinent that the claim of political witch hunt on opposition parties is supported by this editorial.

All these depict a <u>fifteenth (and most serious) instance</u> which exposes hypocrisy about zero tolerance to corruption.

Following criticisms by SC to ensure "functional autonomy," CBI asked for sufficient financial and administrative powers and a minimum three-year tenure for its director who should be vested with ex-officio powers of Secretary to Government of India, reporting directly to the minister, without having to go through the DoPT. Decisions on these are still pending. This is a <u>sixteenth instance</u> which exposes hypocrisy about zero tolerance to corruption.

Another atrocious event which shows callousness is the missing of files needed for corruption investigation from Ministry of Coal Mines.

Creation of Lokpal to probe complaints against public functionaries in high positions was pending for more than 44 years!! Though a bill for this was passed in Lok Sabha in 1969,

Rajya Sabha rejected it as many as nine times up to 2008!! The bill was revived several times in subsequent years. Each time, after the bill was introduced in parliament, it was stalled using devious methods. A modified bill drawn up by civil society activists (referred to as Jan Lokpal Bill) which proposed improvements to the Lokpal and Lokayukta Bill 2011 was not taken up for discussion in parliament till 2013. These repeated impediments extending over many years show lack of interest in passing such an important bill to provide a check on corruption. This is a seventeenth (and most serious) instance which exposes hypocrisy about zero tolerance to corruption.

At last, The Lokpal and Lokayuktas Act, 2013 was passed and approved by President. But, Lok Pal has not been appointed even in 2018 (after more than four years). This inordinate delay is an eighteenth (and most serious) instance which exposes hypocrisy about zero tolerance to corruption.

Considering the prolonged series of obstacles in passing this important anticorruption bill, it is reasonable to believe that other aspects of implementation of the bill also will have to face lot of obstacles which will cause long delay. This long delay of more than four years in starting implementation is a nineteenth (and most serious) instance which exposes hypocrisy about zero tolerance to corruption.

In 1966, Administrative Reforms Commission recommended setting up of 'Lok Ayukta' for redressal of citizens' grievances. Despite a long interval of 52 years, 10 states do not have Lok Ayuktas. Even in states with Lok Ayukta, proper action has not been taken against persons charged with corruption by it. It has no power to take independent action to penalize those found guilty.

Its capacity has been further downgraded by not providing it with adequate staff and other facilities. Evidently state governments want to avoid such checks on criminal activities by their staff. Central government has not taken any action to rectify this atrocious situation. This is a <u>twentieth instance</u> which exposes hypocrisy about zero tolerance to corruption.

RTI provides to citizens the right to access information under the control of public authorities, in order to promote transparency and accountability in the working of every public authority. Most people are yet to make full use of this Act. But, even after limited use by people, many government departments either employ delaying tactics or refuse to give information. This has resulted in avoidable flooding of appeals to CIC. Moreover, some departments have started feeling uncomfortable about the disclosures, leading to government thinking of how to curtail use of the Act and expressing the need to make changes in the Act. This hostile approach to this important Act is a <u>twenty-first instance</u> which exposes hypocrisy about zero tolerance to corruption.

Many RTI activists, including policemen, have been harassed and even murdered for seeking information to promote transparency and accountability in the working of public authorities. Many face assaults regularly. People seeking information from their gram panchayat and local administration face social ostracism also. A few activists who sought information under RTI Act related to MGNREGA scams were killed. Many threats and attacks (including murder) go unreported by media. Government has not taken any worthwhile action to protect RTI activists. This callous approach of government towards this important check by people which can expose corruption is a matter for serious concern. This is a twenty-second (and most serious) instance which exposes hypocrisy about zero tolerance to corruption.

When CIC ruled that political parties are answerable under the Act about funds given to them, it was reported that government hurriedly planned to introduce an amendment to the Act to nullify this. It will not be surprising if political parties use their combined strength to safe guard their secrecy, although transparency in political funding should be a vital necessity for democracy. They may be afraid that right to information will, in due course, force them to be accountable for the funds they collect. This is a twenty-third instance which exposes hypocrisy about zero tolerance to corruption.

Comptroller and Auditor General (CAG) regularly reports deficiencies observed and system failures and suggests improvements. But hardly any worthwhile action was taken even on serious matters involving corruption. This is a twenty-fourth instance which exposes hypocrisy about zero tolerance to corruption.

In 2009, CAG requested government to amend Audit Act 1971 to bring all private-public partnerships (PPP), Panchayti Raj Institutions and societies getting government funds within the ambit of CAG and to enhance CAG's powers to access information because almost 30% of documents demanded by CAG were denied. Though projects worth millions of rupees are executed under PPP model, these projects are not audited by CAG. About 65% of government spending does not come under scrutiny of CAG!! But government has not cared to amend the Act even after eight years. Thus, the very purpose of having this authority to provide checks has been callously defeated. This is a twenty-fifth (and most serious) instance which exposes hypocrisy about zero tolerance to corruption.

Whistleblowers (persons who expose misconduct, alleged dishonesty or illegal activity occurring in an organization) play an important part in control of corruption. Unfortunately, they had to face many reprisals and devastating situations. There have been multiple instances of threatening, harassment and even murder of whistleblowers. The harsh reality is that vested interests usually triumph because laws are inadequate, media are ineffective and citizens are silent. Peoples' representatives do not care to set things right. Consequently, culprits in influential positions manage to suppress embarrassing facts, discredit whistleblowers and subject them to demoralizing situations. Long delays in disposing of such cases also help them to get away without punishment. Under these circumstances, odds are heavily loaded against whistleblowers and only a few can succeed or lead a stress free life. Many are subject to debilitating anxiety or depression forever. Lack of action to improve the situation is a <u>twenty-sixth instance</u> which exposes hypocrisy about zero tolerance to corruption.

The judiciary has repeatedly directed government to formulate suitable guidelines/regulations to protect whistleblowers. In 2001, Law Commission of India in its 179th report recommended a specific legislation to encourage disclosure of information regarding corruption or maladministration by public servants and to provide protection to informers. Only after ten years, the Whistleblowers' Protection Bill 2011 was passed by the Lok Sabha. But, sad to say, the Bill is pending in Rajya Sabha for more than seven years!! Moreover, the proposed law has no provision to encourage whistle blowing (e.g., financial incentives). Nor does it provide a penalty for those attacking a whistle blower. It has faced considerable criticism because its jurisdiction is restricted to those who are working for central government or its agencies and does not cover state government employees. Corporate and private sectors also are not within its jurisdiction.

Moreover, ministries proposing draft legislation usually involve a process of public consultation but such an opportunity has been denied to the public for this bill. It is shocking that even after a gap of more than 17 years after the Law Commission recommendation, a full-fledged law to protect whistleblowers, drafted with public consultation, is still a long way off. This is a <u>twenty-seventh instance</u> which exposes hypocrisy about zero tolerance to corruption. In the absence of such a law, people have a low level of confidence in fighting corruption because they fear retaliation and intimidation against those who file complaints.

All these also indicate that government is not confident that there is nothing to hide and prefers to have toothless agencies for investigating corruption.

It is shocking that there are at least twenty-seven instances which expose hypocrisy about zero tolerance to corruption. May be there are some more instances of not taking suitable actins to remove corruption, which have not been reported so far. This convincingly proves that government is only fooling people by bluffing that it has zero tolerance to corruption.

Despite strictures from SC, it did not take any action to rectify the atrocious situations and ensure that the anti-corruption agencies have been provided with adequate power and facilities to function smoothly and effectively with full independence without interference from government. What is worse, government put spokes in their functioning. This deliberate misuse of power resulted in wide spread corruption as confirmed by the following studies.

Transparency International ranked India at 79 out of 176 countries in Corruption Perception Index 2016 and 1st among 18 Asia – Pacific nations in bribery rate (India Today dated 20.11.17, page 12). What is more damaging, India slipped to rank 81 in 2017 (The Times of India dated 23.02.18, page 1).

This organisation reported that in 2017 as many as 45% of respondents claimed they paid a bribe at least once in the past year to get work done. What is worse, this proportion had increased from 43% for the previous year (The Times of India dated 10.12.17, page 8).

A survey by Centre for Study of Developing Societies, India in May 2018 found that <u>two thirds</u> of people surveyed were of the view that government is corrupt (Deccan Chronicle dated 24.08.18, page 8).

All these data for three consecutive years undoubtedly show that corruption is widespread now and increasing. This was bound to happen because, instead of providing anti-corruption agencies with adequate power and facilities to function smoothly and effectively with full independence, government had not only put spokes in their functioning but also misused them in number of ways and manipulated their reports as explained earlier in this article. Despite all these, government claims that corruption has been eliminated!! Ironically, sad to say, there are people who blindly believe in this myth.

Article 10

Human Rights

A democracy has to ensure that people are not subjected to violations of human rights. For this purpose, National Human Rights Commission (NHRC) was set up under the Human Rights Commission Act 1993. The statistics during the period from 2006 to 2011 gives a vivid picture of the performance of NHRC. During this period, about 5.4 lakh persons had complained to NHRC that they suffered from human rights violations, at an alarming average of about 90,000 per year!! Many lakhs more are likely to have complained to all State Human Rights Commissions together. Some lakhs more might have suffered but did not complain because of despondency arising from outright rejection of lakhs of earlier complaints by others (explained below). The atrocious fact that such amazingly large number of people had complaints of violation of human rights is a matter for serious concern in a democracy. Any attempt to put these under the carpet as frivolous complaints will only expose callousness and will not have any takers because lakhs of complainants cannot be frivolous. It is shocking and shameful that neither NHRC (a responsible statutory authority) nor the democratic government felt concerned that such amazingly large number of people had complaints of violation of human rights.

In a democracy, how these complaints have been dealt with is very important. Among these, about 1.1 lakhs *(about one fifth)* only were properly "disposed with directions." Alarmingly, NHRC had no feeling of guilt in refusing to examine about 3.4 lakhs *(about two-thirds of the violation complaints)* and "dismissing these in limini" – a deeply disgusting picture of deliberate inaction to remove human rights violations. What is worse and shocking is that this deeply disgusting situation has been continuing for years!! Thus even the last channel of hope was cruelly cut off for many lakhs of possible sufferers from human rights violations. This shameful and atrocious situation arose on account of NHRC (procedure) Regulations 1997 which did not allow NHRC to review judgments by courts and commissions. NHRC did not give the important information about how many of the 3.4 lakh cases not examined were complaints against court judgments. It is reasonable to presume that vast majority of these violation complaints arose from perceived denial of justice by courts and did not arise from recommendations of commissions. It is shocking that NHRC ignored the fact that lakhs of people were complaining to it against court judgments. An obvious reason is that NHRC is headed by retired judges who did not want to open a Pandora's box of injustices to which they and their colleagues might have contributed. This also is the reason for (1) not using its statutory powers to amend the obsolete Regulation 1997 which did not allow NHRC to review judgments by courts and (2) hiding the important information about how many of the 3.4 lakh cases dismissed without examination were complaints against court judgments.

All these show a grossly dismal picture of human rights violations which is a shame for Indian democracy. NHRC was so callous that it never cared to study its own statistics and take suitable remedial actions which were in its power!!

Sad to say, neither parliament (peoples' representatives) nor government cared to take any action to rectify the atrocious situation of enormous number of complaints against human rights violations not being examined for many years. Probably, they did not even care to keep a watch on the human rights situation and were, therefore, not aware of what was happening!! May be, many of these complaints were ignored because these were against political leaders who are known to take law into their hands against people (Article 8).

NHRC is an autonomous body with operational and financial authority and had powers to regulate its own procedure for disposal of complaints. Section 12 of Chapter III of Human Rights Commission Act 1993 lists the functions NHRC shall perform. Among these, 12 (d) and 12 (j) are pertinent in the present context:

12 (d) – review the safeguards provided by or under the Constitution or any law for the time being in force for protection of human rights and recommend measures for their effective implementation.

12 (j) – such other functions as it may consider necessary for protection of human rights.

These two sections specifically empower NHRC and instruct it to carry out all functions necessary to protect human rights. Yet, it did not act to overcome the shameful and dismal picture of violation of human rights in India, shown by its own statistics. NHRC, using its statutory powers, ought to have amended the obsolete NHRC (procedure) Regulations 1997 which forced it to dismiss lakhs of complaints without examination. Failure to do so even when faced with the atrocious situation of lakhs of human rights violation complaints not being examined shows lack of accountability and tantamounts to contempt of the Constitution. The top level officers of NHRC who lacked accountability and were responsible for this contempt deserve to be penalized immediately to restore faith in NHRC to a large extent.

Central and state governments also have not cared to ensure that National and State Human Rights Commissions are well equipped to carry out their functions smoothly and efficiently. Even though vacancies are bound to occur quite often in HRCs, steps were are not taken in advance to fill up vacancies in time and to empower the next junior level officer to act whenever necessary. For instance, Karnataka State Human Rights Commission (KSHRC) could not register suo motto cases because it did not have a Chairperson for some months, as stated by the Registrar of the SHRC (DNA dated 19.11.2012). Despite media pointing out this lapse and a High Court order to appoint a chairperson and government promising to do so, KSHRC has continued headless for over five years (The Times of India dated 09.12.17, page 7). This shows that government has not cared to fulfill its promise and has shown contempt of High Court. All these depict a shocking lack of interest in tackling human rights problems.

The above aspects depict the <u>fifteenth</u> and very serious <u>obstacle</u> which resulted in a distorted and ineffective democracy.

To overcome this obstacle, a thorough review of the working of NHRC should be carried out by an independent non-judicial body with expertise in human rights and its recommendations should be immediately implemented in full. Any rejection of the recommendations by government should be ratified by both houses of parliament. Meanwhile, the top level officers of NHRC, who lacked accountability and showed contempt of the Constitution by not using their powers to rectify the dismal picture of human rights violations for years, should be punished and removed immediately so that they do not interfere in the review. These steps are essential to restore faith in NHRC.

Thereafter, a new set of top officers of NHRC should be appointed to exercise its statutory power to regulate its own procedure for disposal of complaints by overriding any procedural regulations. In particular, the obsolete NHRC (procedure) Regulations 1997 which had repeatedly forced NHRC to dismiss lakhs of complaints (mostly against court judgments) without examination and made it toothless should be amended immediately. This will also act as a check on denial of justice by courts in future – a worthwhile additional advantage.

Once the modified procedure becomes operative, it is certain that NHRC will have to review a back log of lakhs of complaints about denial of justice by courts. Therefore, instead of judges, human rights activists and eminent lawyers should form the top level officers of NHRC.

Top priority should be given to strengthening of NHRC and SHRCs to make these capable of examining lakhs of complaints, without any restrictions.

Article 11

Justice System

In a democracy, fool-proof arrangements have to be made to provide affordable quick justice to all people. Providing faultless justice is another crucial requirement. The present judicial system has failed in both these aspects, as explained below. There are some basic faults which can be removed only by a totally fresh approach.

Lakhs of cases have been pending in courts for many years and denying justice to many millions of people. In 2009, India had the shameful distinction of having largest backlog of cases in the world. A truly democratic parliament and government would have given highest priority to rectify this serious problem. Instead, a callous laissez faire attitude with least importance to provision of affordable quick justice has been adopted for many years, even after knowing that millions of common people suffered most. Because government, politicians of questionable character and influential persons/organizations are defendants in many of these piled up cases, one can even suspect that they have a vested interest in multiplying and delaying cases. For example, it is highly revealing that SC castigated the central government "for repeatedly filing appeals on identical questions of law despite being fined earlier for clogging the justice delivery system with frivolous cases." (The Times of India dated 01.05.18, front page) It is likely that state governments also have similarly clogged High Courts repeatedly with such cases. These deliberate attempts to clog the justice delivery system to satisfy "selfish interests" of those with power and influence have to be condemned outright as a blot on our democracy.

One of the other main reasons for piling up of cases (also attributable to parliament and government) is shortage of judges. India has one of the world's lowest ratios of judges to population. There are only 13 judges for every 1 million people compared to 50 (i.e., four times) in developed nations (Deccan Chronicle dated 23.10.17, page 12). Parliament and government have not been sincere enough to tackle this problem. The meager allocations made are due to low priority and not lack of resources. While government has all along been claiming lack of resources, it had "chosen to forgo tax revenues amounting to Rs. 5 lakh crores a year through tax concessions to corporate entities and the rich in the past two or three Budgets." (Deccan Chronicle dated 1-10-12). A scheme named Sonia Gandhi Go Shiksha Yojana has been running for over eight years and almost Rs. 8,000 crore of tax payers' money has been spent in the name of teaching traffic rules to cows!! (DNA dated 6-10-12). Government has spent/is planning to spend huge amounts to construct statues of historic personalities, which do not contribute to development or removal of hunger and poverty. Government was prepared to spend Rs. 30,000 crores to bail out Air India so that rich people can fly. There are many more examples of spending money on projects of much less priority and on fanciful ideas compared to providing Justice. Spending even a part of the huge amounts given to such schemes would have been more than sufficient to have adequate number of judges to provide quick justice to millions of people. People want a democratic government to spend their money to meet their essential needs (e.g., justice) and not according to its whims or to help the rich!!

Some fast–track courts were set up in 2000 to speed up justice. But, out of 1,734 such courts only 976 are functioning now because of lack of funds (The Hindu dated 17-08-14, page 1). This shows lack of priority for speeding up justice.

SC is partly responsible for the dismal situation of pending cases. As the statutory authority responsible for providing justice, it should have warned government that the low priority given to providing funds and its unhelpful attitude to ensure quick justice to millions of people are against the spirit of the Constitution. It should have demanded appointment of more judges and staff by avoiding wrong priorities like those mentioned above and reducing wastages repeatedly pointed out by auditors. There have been many scams resulting in loss of huge amounts of money. Years back, Late Prime Minister Rajiv Gandhi had cautioned that benefit of about 85% of money spent on projects for rural development has not reached people. All these and more enormous wastages of public money still continue without even a semblance of efforts at least to reduce these. If SC cared, it should have emphasized that all these show that wrong priorities and wastage are the main reasons for lack of funds for appointing more judges and staff to clear backlog of cases to help millions of suffering people.

Recommendations made by Judicial Commission were not implemented and gather dust. Administrative Reforms Commission and the Committee that reviewed the Constitution had stressed on setting up special benches in High Courts for disposing of poll suits within six months. But in August 2012, the Law Minister stated that at least 76 petitions challenging elections to legislative assemblies between 2010 and 2012 were pending disposal. The situation is likely to be the same even now for both MPs and MLAs. Ignoring these and other recommendations questions the sincerity of parliament and government in providing justice. As a result of this unquestioned prolonged callousness there are approximately

13,500 cases of this type pending judicial scrutiny (The Times of India dated 13.12.17, front page). This has resulted in such a large number of lawmakers continuing to function and enjoy privileges without legal justification.

Another matter for serious consideration is the regularity with which orders and judgments of SC and High Court have been flouted by governments. This has grave implications for democracy.

It is universally accepted that justice delayed is justice denied. When lakhs of cases are pending for years and millions of people are suffering from delay of justice, the courts enjoy vacations regularly. They have callously allowed themselves this distorted privilege which no other part of government has. This heartless attitude is anti-people and reminds one about Nero playing the fiddle when Rome was burning!! Lack of commitment on the part of judges is crystal clear.

Because of a laissez faire attitude judges have not applied their mind to identify and remove archaic procedures followed for many years. For example, when there is an appeal against a lower court judgment, the higher court often refers the case back to the lower court for review. This procedure leads to avoidable increases in number of cases at the lower court (which already has huge arrears), besides delaying justice. Moreover, when either of the litigants appeal against the second judgment of the lower court, as often happens, it results in almost double work for the same case in the higher court also. Further delays and additional expenses for litigants occur. These could have been avoided if the higher court had applied its mind in the first instance itself and given orders.

"A study of over 8,000 orders in Delhi high court cases filed between 2011 and 2015 revealed runaway 'inefficiency' that clogs the justice delivery mechanism. To blame mainly are the additional time routinely sought by counsel, often flouting norms, and lawyers' absence from hearings" (The Times of India dated 29.03.17). Counsel seeking time 1 to 3 times occurred for 33% cases, 4 to 6 times for 38% and 7 to 10 times for 24%. In 64% cases the counsel was absent at least once. In 51% postponement was due to absence of judge. Over 3 adjournments were granted in nearly 79% of delayed cases. The situation is likely to be worse in most courts because Delhi high court is one of the top performing courts in the country.

An in-depth study of all procedures followed by different courts and making necessary innovative changes to quicken justice are long overdue. These will speed up justice immensely. But the real problem is that neither parliament nor government nor judges are interested in such studies to make innovative changes!! A change in the conservative mind set is essential.

Most people cannot afford to fight for justice even at one level. Provision of opportunities for repeated appeals is made use of by rich people or organizations. Each time, they employ senior lawyers paying exorbitant fees and matching this is beyond the reach of most people. This makes it almost impossible for most people to get justice. Repeated appeals lead to long delays also. Justice thus delayed or denied becomes a perfect recipe for social and political unrest (DNA dated 02-11-13, page 8). Neither parliament nor government nor judges have sincerely applied their mind to these problems.

The above aspects depict the <u>sixteenth</u> and very serious <u>obstacle</u> which resulted in a distorted and ineffective democracy.

Overcoming this serious obstacle needs a complete change in outlook resulting in a well staffed and reformed judicial system which can ensure quick justice to all people without directly or indirectly favouring the rich. For this, a thorough review of the working of the judicial system should be carried out by an independent body with adequate expertise and its recommendations should be immediately implemented in full. Any rejection should be confirmed by both houses of parliament to make it valid.

Budget should make adequate provision for appointing sufficient number of judges and staff to clear backlog of cases. To avoid budgetary constraints, SC which is a statutory authority, should be empowered to make the budget for the judicial system and present it directly to parliament. Providing quick and affordable justice to all people is so fundamental in a democracy that other budgets should be pruned by parliament/government, if necessary, to ensure adequate funds.

Because justice is now beyond the reach of common people, costs incurred should be subsidized to help poor people to get justice. Alternately, a graded system for court fees and other expenses attuned to income levels and provision of lawyer services of good quality to those who cannot afford to match the lawyer services engaged by the rich should also be thought of. Possibility of a few persons misusing this arrangement should not be an excuse for denying this to people. The resulting loss will be much less than the huge wastages which now occur without being questioned. In this context, justification for some advocates demanding exorbitant fees not comparable to those in other professions should also be examined and corrective steps taken.

Another matter for serious concern is that transparency of courts is being increasingly questioned by people. Moreover, Article 10 has highlighted that, on an average, about 90,000 persons had complained to NHRC every year about violation of human rights and that, in the absence of proper classified data, it is reasonable to presume that majority of this enormous number of violation complaints arose from peoples' perceived denial of justice by courts. It is highly significant that lakhs of people did not have faith in judgments by courts and appealed to HRCs!! This is a serious blot on our judicial system.

The increasing number of reported allegations of judicial misconduct emphasizes the need for investigation. Moreover, "Prized placements in offices of top lawyers are easily obtained by wards of judges." (Such judges will feel obliged to top lawyers). "The most damaging secret is that the legal profession has remained cloistered and oligarchic, and in this the bar is as guilty as the bench."(DNA dated 28-01-14).

Lord Atkin said "Justice is not a cloistered virtue" (The Times of India dated 28-07-14). "It must suffer the scrutiny and outspoken comments of ordinary men." It also quoted Justice Makandey Katju as saying "Now it is the people who are supreme (see Rousseau's 'Social Contract') and all state authorities, including judges, are nothing but their servants." Contrary to these, quite often, behavior of Indian courts tend to show a feeling of superiority and contempt for people.

In the context of reported allegations of judicial misconduct, it is pertinent that there is a general impression that judges are inclined to "listening" to senior advocates while passing judgments. This also needs to be investigated. If true, is it because these advocates are more knowledgeable and incisive than judges and help them to "decide" cases? Can it be that there is a nexus between these advocates and judges? If so, lack of transparency is a necessity for both. Can there be other reasons?

Letters to SC from ordinary people are ignored. This tantamounts to contempt of people who are the masters in a democracy and also results in throttling of feedback information from them which could have helped to improve justice. There are instances of the office of judges blocking/withholding peoples' letters from judges. All these should be investigated.

The above aspects depict the <u>seventeenth</u> and very serious <u>obstacle</u> which resulted in a distorted and ineffective democracy.

Overcoming this very serious obstacle needs immediate action to provide complete transparency of judicial verdicts and to change the attitude that judges are the masters and can do anything without being questioned, where it exists. Reasons for judgments should invariably be given in a language which people can understand and feel convinced. Letters to SC from people should be answered promptly.

The dismal functioning of the justice system is also due to basic defects in the system. A highly respected retired CJI stated: "A radical transformation of the robed brethren has become necessary." "…the law of interpretation that the judiciary adopts tends to favour the haves, not the have-nots. The social structure and the fundamental character of the instruments of the Executive, the Legislature and the Judiciary have political character" (The Hindu dated 29-12-13, page 13). Moreover, "our justice system is a remnant of British rule. It is archaic and complex. It is also not people-friendly." An in-depth review covering these and other aspects discussed earlier is urgently needed to effect the radical transformation required.

Top priority for radical transformation of the judicial system should be given to abolition of the age old conservative court system in which lawyers tell judges about legal aspects, when judges have the special knowledge, ability and experience to take a fair decision themselves, without help from lawyers. Abolition of the conservative system will remove a blur on judges that they do not have the knowledge and ability to take fair decisions without help from lawyers. And equally important, this abolition will not only make justice affordable to most people who cannot afford to engage lawyers, particularly poor people, but also expedite justice. Thus, the change to court-less system will overcome at least some of the most serious defects in the present judicial system which are major blots in our democracy.

Most important, another major defect of the court system is that lawyers are constantly engaged in fighting for their clients (even criminal) and not for justice. This damaging situation is encouraged inadvertently by judges "listening" to senior advocates while passing judgments and a possible nexus between these advocates and judges leading to an increasing number of reported allegations of judicial misconduct discussed in an earlier paragraph. This may be a reason for lakhs of people not having faith in judgments by courts and appealed to HRCs (Article 10). A method for utilizing the services of lawyers to fight for justice instead of for injustice as at present is discussed later on. All these aspects justify beyond any doubt that abolition of court system is essential to improve the justice system and remove injustice.

An aberration in the judicial system which is not in tune with democracy (in which people are the masters) is that judges have to be addressed as "Your Lordship" or with adjectives like Hon'ble or similar terms, while other officers are addressed as "Sir." This is a remnant of British rule. Extending this point further, it is incongruous that people (masters in a democracy) have to address government officers as "Sir" and bow before them as second class citizens. Is not equality in status enshrined in our Constitution? To be truly democratic and to avoid disrespect to the Constitution, should we not agree on a word for addressing each other with mutual respect irrespective of positions held?

Another serious basic defect is that there are number of instances where judgments of courts were ignored without being punished. For example, SC gave government time till July 3, 2013 to lay out steps to make CBI independent. But, no steps have been taken to make CBI independent even by 2018 (i.e., more than four years after the time limit set by SC) though this is a contempt of the highest court.

In case of a hung assembly, SC had ordered that if a group of parties had agreed to join together and form a government they should be allowed to do so. But, after the recent assembly elections in Karnataka the Governor ignored this and invited the largest single party to form government instead of a combined group of two parties who had support of more members of the assembly. Is this not a contempt of SC? Or, is the governor exempted from the law of the land? What is more shocking SC itself ignored its previous order when the aggrieved parties approached it for relief.

Basic defects and complexities in our judicial system is the eighteenth and very serious obstacle which resulted in a distorted and ineffective democracy.

The urgently needed radical transformation of the judicial system can be effected in two ways:

One approach is to think out of the box and ask many basic questions to reform the judicial system and make it simple, quick, faultless and people-friendly. The following are some examples of questions in addition to those raised earlier in this article: When a person wants to seek justice why can't he/she file a petition online or in writing on ordinary paper (with or without help from a lawyer) and send it through post to a judge and save money and time? To file a petition why is it necessary for even a poor petitioner to pay fees when provision of justice is an essential function of democracy which has to serve peoples' needs? Why is it necessary to argue civil cases in a court of law instead of the judge, who is well versed in laws of the country, disposing it off himself/herself, after discussing/seeking clarifications from both parties (with or without help from a lawyer) to clarify matters? Why ask both parties to a case to engage lawyers to argue before a court of law when a qualified judge (with secretarial assistance) is capable of considering all legal aspects of the case and can provide justice without being side tracked or biased or mesmerized by clever lawyers? Does not the court system, in which lawyers tell judges about legal aspects, question the legal knowledge of judges and their ability to take a fair decision themselves, without help from lawyers? If a judge feels a case is complicated and feels the need for more legal opinion to make sure that all aspects have been properly considered, why can't he/she discuss it formally with one or more colleagues and take a joint decision instead of constituting a bench and delaying matters and increasing cost for litigants by bringing in lawyers who charge heavily? Similarly, when appeals are made against a judgment, can't these be disposed of by senior judges without constituting a bench and bringing in lawyers who charge higher fees? Will not abolition of the court system avoid multiple postponements which delay justice? Will not a court less system reduce the cost incurred by people and government?

Why is it that there is no uniformity in interpretation of laws among judges and lawyers? Did these interpretation problems arise due to politicians making changes in the drafts prepared by legal experts? Is it not essential to redraft laws to avoid or at least minimize differences in interpretations?

Why did even experienced judges and legal experts, who know the complex and time consuming nature of the system, adopt a laissez faire attitude and did not think out of the box and ask lot of questions to simplify the system? Were they afraid that simplifying the system will be against their interests? Is it proper to allow professional interests of lawyers to stand in the way of simplifying the system to make it people-friendly? If their legitimate interests are affected by simplification, how can this be compensated?

If the system is simplified based on answers to many relevant questions including those given above, it will speed up justice and drastically reduce cost to make justice affordable to poor people.

Another approach is to replace the British model with one based on democratic principles and our culture. If people are the masters they should be made the jury by giving judicial power to panchayats to form the first level of a reformed judicial system. Such a democratic practice which has been in vogue in many places can be studied and modified to make it more systematic and fool-proof. These can turn out to be qualified peoples' courts delivering quick justice and avoiding back logs. Historically, India had many rulers like Asoka and Akbar who had dispensed justice with equanimity (without help of lawyers) and earned the praise of people. Changes needed at higher levels for providing justice under the reformed panchayat system should be evolved after a careful study of the practices by these rulers and modifying these to suit modern environment and technology. Such a judicial system, which takes into account democratic principles and our culture, will deliver cheap, quick and faultless justice in tune with our culture.

The first approach is likely to be more acceptable to the judicial profession and will take less time to formulate changes and implement these.

National Integration

Ideally, India should have a democracy which attends to the needs and aspirations of people all over the country. But the situation is very complex and intricate because of wide spread diversities. The feeling that we are all Indians with uniform needs and aspirations is lacking in the country. This has resulted in multiple sets of needs and aspirations which have to be satisfied by a democracy. State wise, language wise, religion wise, caste wise and tribe wise alienations in individualities stand in the way of having uniform needs and aspirations. Wide gaps in economic status also divides the country into distinct groups with vastly different individualities, needs and aspirations. This is made worse by activities of politicians which often encourage diversities in individuality by creating group conflicts to serve their selfish interests. All these make the situation very complicated with regard to needs and aspirations to be met by a democracy. Therefore, the needs and aspirations of people can be ideally met only by a federation of multiple democracies and not by a unified democracy. The fact that such multiple units of democracy, if at all they can be made functional, will criss-cross and clash with each other will make the situation extremely complicated and difficult to manage. Therefore, it is more realistic to strive for developing a national democracy which satisfies the needs and aspirations of maximum number of people to the extent possible, with special stress on the "have nots" who need democracy most, unlike the "haves" who manipulate to have a good quality of life. The situation can be assuaged to a large extent only by a well planned and actively implemented national integration programme. This is the way to develop the best possible democracy for the whole country.

But, attempts at national integration have not succeeded even after 70 years because of a bureaucratic approach with least priority and commitment. Attempts made have been sporadic, patchy and ineffective due to lack of vision and commitment. Hardly any attempt has been made to identify institutions which have been struggling to reduce alienations in individualities and support these and to identify and motivate more institutions to do so, because of lack of vision and commitment. State wise, language wise, religion wise, caste wise and tribe wise alienations in individualities stand in the way of uniform needs and aspirations. Sad to say, politicians have not only exploited these situations but also made these worse to serve their interests, instead of trying to reduce these to build up Indian brotherhood and promote national integration. There is an urgent need to systematically plan and actively implement multiple innovative strategies to progressively improve national integration, in a mission mode.

These aspects form the nineteenth and serious and complicated obstacle which resulted in a distorted and ineffective democracy.

To overcome this obstacle, national integration projects with vision should be implemented in a mission mode using multiple strategies. Thinking out of the box and implementing innovative ideas are absolutely necessary.

One way is to have planned interstate migration by identifying people who feel frustrated in achieving their visions or to have a good quality of life and encouraging them to shift to another area. To the extent possible, alternate choices should be offered to them to choose from. Each state should have an annual target for this and systematically identify, educate and motivate persons (e.g., by quoting successful migrations), to meet the target. This planned interstate migration has the additional advantage of reducing tensions in the former areas by relocating frustrated persons. The receiving states will welcome this if it solves their problems like shortage of particular types of labour force and new type of enterprises, improvement in trade, additional cottage industries etc. It is pertinent that such types of migration have taken place to some extent (even without state sponsoring) and have resulted in inter mingling of people from different places, without any serious problems in the receiving states. A happy "give and take" approach among the concerned people has been created. For example, thousands of people from Bihar, Kerala and Tamil Nadu are working for years in some other states and many thousands from North-eastern states can be found in cities like Bengaluru.

A positive approach is to encourage such migration in larger numbers by giving financial and other incentives to settle down after migration. Those who have already migrated should be encouraged to bring their relatives and friends. Another way to identify frustrated persons interested in migration is to search among religious and linguistic minorities and tribal groups. Improvements in economic status and quality of life should be the guiding factors for migration. A systematic proactive approach with patience will yield substantial improvements in national integration soon.

Inter-caste, interreligious and interstate marriages should also be encouraged by giving grants to such couples. Tendency for honour killings and other inhuman and immoral atrocities which stand in the way of such marriages should be tackled through educating people and giving grants to families of the couple and to village panchayats, for each such marriage. Award for panchayats and wards or residential associations in towns and cities with maximum number of such inter marriages should be instituted. People should also be educated about the genetic advantages of such inter marriages.

School children and college students should be regularly taken on "know your country" education trips to areas with a different culture and provided opportunities to understand and appreciate different cultural practices. This will help to develop national brotherhood among children and young people. Incentives should be given to schools and colleges which undertake such specially designed "know your country" education trips which provide opportunities to understand and appreciate different cultural practices (not tourist trips), by way of grants, travel concessions etc.

As stated earlier, state wise, language wise, religion wise, caste wise and tribe wise alienations in individualities stand in the way of uniform needs and aspirations. Attempts should be systematically made to have dialogues with leaders of such groups to motivate them to enthuse a national identity and brotherhood in their groups by educating them and emphasizing that there is no substantial clash between national and group interests. Wherever a perceived clash of interests continues, educative dialogues should be continued to amicably remove the misunderstandings. Prestigious state and national awards should recognize individuals and institutions excelling in promotion of national integration.

There are fields such as sports, arts, music, dance and entertainment in which the above type of alienations are negligible. Priority should be given to encourage interstate activities in these fields to speed up national integration. An additional benefit is that such activities help participating people to forget their worries for some time and feel happy.

Multiple languages in the country complicate the problem. A national script to be used by all languages should be adopted to mitigate this problem. Mastering a new script is the most difficult part of learning a new language. Once proficiency in the national script is achieved, it is easier for people to learn other languages and enjoy the richness of the literature in other languages of their choice. The fact that people knowing the national script will be able to read many words which are common to many Indian languages (particularly because of their Sanskrit origin) makes it even more easy. Making it easier to learn other languages because of a common national script will lead to better understanding of different Indian cultures and thereby promote national identity and brotherhood.

When people travel from one linguistic state to another, they often face difficulties because they are not able to read the names of places, roads, eating places, bus routes and their destinations, travel direction sign boards etc. If these are written in a national script all over the county, these difficulties will not arise and tensions on interstate travelers will be reduced.

Because all people have to learn the national script which will be used by all languages, there will be no complaints about anyone group getting an advantage over others as happened when attempts were made to propagate Hindi as the national language. Having a national script for Hindi also will reduce difficulty in learning it by other language groups using national script and will promote its acceptance as the national language. This is a worthwhile additional advantage.

In addition to the above, if a variety of serious innovative attempts are made with vision and commitment to make it easier for people to interact with each other, they will understand each other better and feelings of nationality and brotherhood will automatically develop.

All these emphasize the need for planning and implementing multiple innovative approaches to promote national integration with determination and a sense of commitment to a mission mode. This will have a definite impact on making the needs and aspirations of people all over the country less complex and reduce obstacles in developing a democracy which satisfies maximum number of people in the country.

It is important to have a change in mind set to provide adequate funds for all national integration schemes on top priority basis in order to achieve the worthy aim of national integration, which is essential to have a successful democracy, besides many other advantages listed earlier. A pennywise and pound foolish approach should be strictly avoided.

Large States – A Hindrance to Democracy

Efficient administration is virtually impossible in large states. For example, a minister or head of department in a large state like Uttar Pradesh will not have time (without neglecting other work) to make adequate number of visits to all districts for discussions, supervision, contact with people etc. even once a year. Many aspects of good governance will suffer in many parts of a large state in the absence of frequent intensive supervision which is essential for efficient administration. Due to inadequate attention by government machinery, people in some parts of a large state feel that they receive only step motherly treatment. As a result of such inadequate interaction between government and people, large states are less efficient in satisfying the needs and aspirations of people which is crucial for success of a democracy. Moreover, people in many parts of a large state are unhappy that they have to waste more time and money to visit the capital of the state to sort out their problems with government.

Diversities are more common within large states. The resulting intra state rivalries between different identity groups have made functioning of democracy more difficult and ineffective in large states.

Dissatisfactions and frustrations within various identity groups are increasing day by day in large states. This has led to increasing conflicts and disintegrating tendencies. Because of pent up dissatisfactions and frustrations people in large states have often resorted to acts of violence even at the drop of a hat. Other law and order problems also become more difficult to handle in large states.

All these show that democracy will function better if we divide the country into optimal small states. USA with much smaller population has many more states!! Following this example of a modern flourishing democracy it is essential for India to have more than 50 states. The situation is so bad that some states have large populations which exceed the population of some countries!! Because of a laissez-faire attitude, parliament and government have not given thought to improving democracy by having optimal small states.

Disgusted identity groups have been mounting pressure again and again for carving out small states of their choice from large states. Government has not realised that such pressures have shot up in many parts of a large state only because of its callousness or inability to carry out investigations throughout the state to ascertain the reasons for these. Hardly any systematic attempt has been made to ascertain the needs and aspirations of people in different areas spread across large states because of a defeatist mentality arising from enormity of the problem. Due to inadequate attempts to tackle or meet needs and aspirations of people, violence and terrorist activities had steadily increased in many parts of large states. After prolonged costly delays which had caused lot of heart burn and violence resulting in destruction of properties and even life, government was forced to ultimately carve out small states out of Uttar Pradesh, Madhya Pradesh, Bihar and Andhra Pradesh. Yet, government is not prepared to see the writing on the wall that such piecemeal approaches will not suffice. It has not cared to apply its mind to ascertain the optimum size of a state to have a successful democracy.

Despite facing many problems, government does not have the vision to carry out studies to understand the emerging needs and aspirations of local people or to foresee possible divisive and destructive developments and act to forestall unhappy events. It often relies on superficial reports of intelligence agencies which do not have the capacity and time required for in-depth studies.

Because of a laissez-faire attitude, it blindly waits for things to happen and adopts in haste only haphazard piece meal approaches, that too after allowing agitations to build up and cause heavy damages. It has not cared to study the advantage of forming small states in a democratic manner before agitations come up. It refuses to recognize the realities and is hanging on to straws (like a drowning man), with a conservative approach.

As pointed out in Article 6, government considers listening to people as a sign of weakness instead of strength of a democracy. This intolerant attitude is anti-democratic and shows a know-all dictatorial approach. It proves beyond doubt that government gives only lip service to democracy and do not at all care for democracy, while ironically boasting that it functions as a democratic government. It has not realized that the real strength of a democratic government lies in its ability to (1) listen to people, (2) accept useful ideas and (3) act on these with vision and commitment, which can be more effectively done only in small states.

Large states have more MPs and are able to put more pressure to derive additional benefits for their states or to block developments in other areas to spite their neighbours and to show off their superiority. This makes people and MPs in smaller states unhappy.

Such biased approaches which give better opportunities to some people and treat others with a step motherly attitude are against the principles of democracy.

Thus, having large states causes dissatisfaction among people in both large and small states and results in a discordant democracy which can explode into violent revolution.

These aspects form the <u>twentieth</u> and most serious <u>obstacle</u> which resulted in a distorted and ineffective democracy.

To overcome this serious obstacle, another States Reorganization Commission should be set up immediately with definite instructions to ascertain the optimum size of a state to have a successful democracy in different demographic situations and carve out small compact states (may be with approximately two crore population each) which can satisfy the needs and aspirations of different identity groups to the maximum extent possible. Emphasis should be on creating homogenous small states to have a true democracy which satisfies people.

Additional expenditure required to set up and maintain homogenous small states should not stand in the way of having a true democracy. People want government to spend public money to meet their needs and aspirations and not according to its whims or to waste as at present. No doubt, having more states will increase over head expenses. But, there will be considerable savings in expenses for travel, administration etc. over a long period of time which will reduce the additional financial burden to a large extent. Most important, it is worthwhile to spend any amount of money to have a successful democracy which meets needs and aspirations of people and removes violent conflicts.

Article 14

Fundamental Weaknesses of Present System of Democracy

The present system of democracy has fifteen fundamental weaknesses.

A <u>fundamental weakness</u> of parliamentary system of democracy is that parliament cannot be an independent pillar of democracy (as it ought to be) because the political party which controls government also controls parliament, having majority of MPs (Article 6). This basically defective system results in a servile parliament which allows dictatorial attitude in the party and the government and defeats the very purpose of having parliament as a pillar of democracy. There were more than thousand instances of government continuously ignoring parliament (Articles 6 and 23). Moreover, ability of parliament to speak for the poor is curtailed because majority of MPs were very rich (Article 2).

In addition, parliament totally failed to represent people because (a) large majority of MPs have support of only less than 35% of electorate (often much less) and shockingly resulted in a void parliament, despite this proportion being pushed up due to irresponsible and influenced voting (Article 2) and (b) majority of MPs were rich crorepatis (Article 2). Therefore their election as` representatives of people is void and the parliament they form also is void. Shockingly, everyone including EC and SC accepted this atrocious situation. Moreover, propriety and efficiency of parliament are doubtful when MPs are elected by people who do not have the knowledge and expertise needed to select efficient persons with specialized qualifications and experience to enact laws, make policies and govern the country. This situation is a <u>second fundamental weakness</u> of the present system of democracy.

As stated earlier, people who elected MPs did not have the knowledge and expertise needed to select efficient persons with specialized qualifications and experience to enact laws, make policies and govern the country!! This lack of knowledge and expertise among people (the selectors) becomes deplorable when large numbers of them (often the majority) are illiterate or do not have even a moderate level of general education. Just imagine what will happen to patients if surgeons are selected by such people; or to dams, bridges and houses if engineers are selected by such people; or to delivery of justice if judges are selected by such people; or to students if the teachers/professors are selected such people; and so on!! Selecting top managers of governance by such people is bound to have similar atrocious consequences. It is significant that such calamities have not occurred only because multiple professionals responsible for governance have been selected by specialized institutions manned by highly qualified selectors with many years of experience. In sharp contrast, shockingly, political leaders who have to supervise these expert professionals are selected by people without requisite knowledge and expertise!! This ridiculous mockery is <u>the third fundamental</u> weakness of present system of democracy.

Successful governance of a country requires multiple professionals with specialized qualifications and experience working at the top levels without hindrance. This basic requirement has been ignored. Functions of policy making, enactment of laws, planning and implementation of projects and overall governance have been usurped from qualified professionals by politicians without the required qualifications and experience under the questionable claim that they are representatives of people!! The situation became worse because they became enemies of democracy and also took damaging decisions (Article 19). This topsy-turvy and dangerous situation is a <u>fourth fundamental weakness</u> of the present system of democracy.

Fortunately, even though people were least competent to select efficient persons to run a democratic government, they had awareness enough to distinguish between the bad and the worse and throw out the latter when they came to know that they had failed miserably to satisfy their needs and aspirations. They also refused to be fooled by the high decibel propaganda about high growth rate which has benefited the rich but not the poor. Such awareness, which had received praise after general elections, has so far saved our democracy from crumbling down further and ruining our country, by cautioning politicians that their misdeeds will not be tolerated indefinitely – the so called incumbency factor which is a reflection of this awareness. Despite their prolonged frustrations, this awareness has also kept in check revolutionary violence for the time being. But, further frustrations may burst the dam because of continued inability to get rid of bad governance before long gaps of prolonged pain and suffering. This is the <u>fifth fundamental weakness</u> of present system of democracy.

A spate of political defections in number of states has led to confusion and disruptions in functioning of democracy. There were allegations that large amounts of money have been paid by the party in power at the centre to manipulate these defections. If true, this party which proclaims zero tolerance to corruption is following this corrupt practice. Therefore, it was very important that Election Commission should verify the facts and take further action if necessary. But, Election Commission shirked its responsibility to verify the facts and take further action. It did not also try to remove loopholes in the system, if any, which stood in its way to verify and stop such corrupt practices. These constitute a <u>sixth fundamental weakness</u> of the present system of democracy.

A <u>seventh fundamental weakness</u> of the present system of democracy is that there is no system to assess efficiency of performance of political leaders in highly responsible positions every year as is regularly done for the qualified professionals involved in governance. Lack of this assessment system is obviously illogical and risky, more so because these political leaders are generally not qualified to govern and are likely to make many serious mistakes. The risk can be very high because they have become enemies of democracy (Article 19).

The only assessment (if it can be called so) for politicians in power is that some people (not even majority) without knowledge and expertise of governance, consider their governance as satisfactory, that too once in five years (not annually), even when they have not fulfilled the needs and aspirations of people!! This has been manipulated by political leaders by making promises and mesmerizing people to blindly believe that they are their benefactors, using power of their oratory. Ironically, this situation has been continuing for such a long time that no questions have been asked.

It may be argued that increased GDP growth rate has proved efficiency of governance. This argument is faulty for two reasons:

It ignores that growth has not been inclusive and poverty, hunger and malnutrition of children continue to be rampant. Food prices are spiraling; infrastructure projects have slowed down; manufacturing sector is in dire straits; unemployment is increasing; petroleum prices are high; the rupee has collapsed; fiscal deficit is high; the rich are becoming fabulously richer (e.g., crorepatis increased by 23.5% in financial year 2015); farmers are committing suicides; and even the high growth rate has fallen steeply from 9.2% in 2015 – 16. Moreover, governance has not only resulted in these shameful situations but also to complete callousness in rectifying these shameful situations. Article 15 gives 100 examples of shameful and shocking situations faced by the country despite GDP growth!! All these clearly show that except for GDP growth rate, which has resulted in a sense of complacency, the government has hardly achieved anything substantial to speak off for welfare of people. The single track pursuit of growth rate and other misplaced priorities have been at the expense of welfare of people. There is a strong possibility that if the qualified and experienced professionals, who formed the back bone of governance for many years, had been allowed to govern the country without interferences by politicians, the situation could have been much better and many shameful and shocking situations could have been avoided!!

Moreover, by contrast, it makes a mockery of the education and training given to qualified professionals and the assessment of efficiency of their performance.

These constitute an <u>eighth fundamental weakness</u> of the present system of democracy.

It is also not realized that the illogical situations explained above are actually proclaiming loudly that politics is a strange profession which can be practiced by anyone, even without basic education or qualification. Yet, shockingly, politicians have been given the responsibility of managing government, even when their claim that they represent people was hollow also (Article 2). Thus they need neither education, nor qualification nor true popular support to hold high positions – a completely farcical situation!! Acceptance of this highly illogical and absurd situation about this profession is a <u>ninth fundamental weakness</u> of the present system of democracy.

Even more damaging, people have even welcomed politicians (often gladly) to occupy any position (including highly responsible positions) without having requisite qualifications or true popular support and without being assessed for efficiency in performance. Why is it that people are so gullible and do not ask any questions? People behaved like slaves when under British rule for about 200 years and, sadly, are not able (or not even inclined) to come out of the slavish mentality to rulers even after 70 years of independence, when they ought to have become masters under a democracy!! This is a <u>tenth fundamental weakness</u> of the present system of democracy.

Political leaders, instead of helping people to come out of this slavish situation, took advantage of it and, by becoming heroes using the gift of the gab, fooled people to believe in number of absurdities about the system without questioning these (Article 23). For instance, they fooled people to believe that they had the super human capacity to effectively supervise and control professionally qualified, specially trained and experienced persons, that too in a variety of disciplines!! Absence of efforts to get rid of absurdities is a <u>eleventh fundamental weakness</u> of the present system of democracy.

By their callousness and repeated, uncontrolled and selfish activities, politicians became enemies of democracy (Articles 19 and 20) – Article 19 has given five solid reasons for this conclusion. This is a <u>twelfth fundamental weakness</u> of present system of democracy.

The parliament they formed did nothing to overcome 100 shameful and shocking situations faced by the country (Article 15). This is a <u>thirteenth fundamental weakness</u> of present system of democracy.

To complete the shock, parliament also brought disgrace on itself because of lack of guts to punish government for breaking promises to it and lack of dignity by spinelessly tolerating such disrespect by government (Article 6 pointed out more than thousand instances of lack of guts and lack of dignity of parliament). This is a <u>fourteenth fundamental weakness</u> of present system of democracy.

Lastly, because of mental slavery to politicians (Article 23) people were so dumb and callous that they tolerated being governed by suspected criminals, justifying the remark that "A nation of sheep gets a government of wolves." This is a <u>fifteenth fundamental weakness</u> of present system of democracy.

These fundamental weaknesses of present day democracy form the <u>twenty-first</u> and one of the most important <u>obstacles</u> which resulted in a distorted and ineffective democracy.

To summarize, fifteen fundamental weaknesses have been pointed out above:

1. The political party which forms government also controls parliament. This defective system results in a servile parliament and allows dictatorial attitude in the party and the government and

defeats the very purpose of having parliament as an independent pillar of democracy.

2. Election of representatives of people is void and the parliament they formed also is void. Shockingly, everyone including EC and SC have accepted this atrocious situation.

3. Because people do not have the required knowledge and expertise, they are least competent to select efficient persons with specialized qualifications and experience to enact laws, make policies and govern the country.

4. Functions of policy making, enactment of laws, planning and implementation of projects and overall governance have been usurped from qualified professionals by politicians without the required qualifications and experience.

5. The system is unable to get rid of bad governance before long gaps during which people had to suffer prolonged pains and suffering.

6. The system is not able to verify complaints that corrupt practices have induced defections from political parties.

7. Lack of a system to assess efficiency of performance of political leaders every year is obviously illogical and risky, more so because these political leaders are generally not qualified to govern and are likely to make many serious mistakes.

8. Mockery of the education and training given to qualified professionals and the assessment of efficiency of their performance.

9. Politics is a strange profession which can be practiced by anyone without having requisite qualifications or true popular

support and without being assessed for efficiency in performance. Yet, politicians have been given the most important responsibility of managing democracy.

10. Inability to overcome the slavish mentality towards rulers despite 70 years of independence, when people ought to have become masters under a democracy.

11. Absence of efforts to get rid of absurdities.

12. By their callousness and repeated, uncontrolled and selfish activities, politicians became enemies of democracy.

13. Parliament did nothing to overcome 100 shameful and shocking situations faced by the country.

14. Parliament brought disgrace on itself because of lack of guts to punish government for breaking promises to it and lack of dignity by spinelessly tolerating such disrespect by government.

15. Because of mental slavery to politicians people were so dumb and callous that they tolerated being governed by suspected criminals.

To overcome all these fundamental weaknesses, parliament and election system should be abolished and an alternative should be found. This is discussed in detail in Article 27.

Meanwhile, all elected representatives should be given the necessary special training before they start functioning as MPs or MLAs so that they can do justice to their work at least in a semi professional manner. It is desirable to train some of them to work as specialists in a field of governance of their choice to qualify as professionals in governance. It is pertinent that, unlike for political leaders, special training is a normal practice for all persons recruited for civil and military services before they are given responsibilities.

At the end of each year, efficiency of all elected representatives (including ministers) should be objectively assessed and those not performing efficiently warned to improve, as suggested in Article 3. Those who do not show improvement after one year should be disqualified and their seats filled up by new election. Other representatives should be allowed to continue till they happen to become inefficient in later yearly evaluations or cross a prefixed age limit or voluntarily retire. Their replacements also should be given the training suggested earlier. Their absence during training period will not seriously affect continuity of governance because majority of political leaders would have been already trained as suggested earlier and will be working more efficiently because of yearly assessment of efficiency.

Change in mind set is also essential to overcome all the fundamental weaknesses by thoroughly overhauling the system using a professional approach which is badly needed. This aspect is discussed in detail in another article.

Article 15

How Parliament Works

The callous and interrupted manner in which this pillar of democracy works is notorious and has resulted in loss of respect for this institution. Attitude of MPs and their actions show that they are always guided by their party's interest and selfish interests only. Peoples' needs and aspirations are often ignored. Disruptions and walk outs are so common that lot of time and public money are wasted. Speakers of both Houses have often felt disgusted and adjourned sessions. For example, Lok Sabha Speaker described the incidents in parliament on 13-02-14 as a shame and said "It is a blot on democracy" (The Hindu dated 14-02-14, page1). Shameful "photographic" exposures of members sleeping or watching porn during sessions speak volumes about their lack of desirable character, dignity and sense of responsibility.

All these show absence of both accountability and commitment to the work for which they have been elected by people. Yet, they quite often greedily and shamelessly vote without conscience to increase their remuneration and perquisites (which are already very high), forgetting that they have neither fulfilled their responsibilities to ensure development and peace in the country nor acted sincerely to reduce sufferings of lakhs of people!!

Neglect of national interests has led to at least 100 shocking and shameful consequences described below:

1. Poverty and hunger continue to be alarming while number of millionaires and extravagant spending by thousands of persons

(including politicians) to show off wealth are shooting up. (These huge disparities are despite the misleading GDP growth!!)

2. In the Multidimensional Poverty Index compiled by UN for 109 countries India ranked one of the worst!! UN Millennium Development Goals Report (2014) states that one-third of world's extremely poor live in India (The Times of India dated 17-07-14, page 7). Yet, government callously boasts about the misleading GDP growth.

3. A World Bank paper also shows that India tops the world for number of poor people and having a miserable 33% of world's poor while China (with more population) has only a 13% share, which is only about one-third of India's share. (DNA dated 11-04-14, page 9). This is despite the misleading GDP growth!!

4. In the latest report on Global Hunger Index, India was ranked 100 out of 119 countries. What is worse, India slipped three places and "ranks among the lowest of the low" (Deccan Chronicle dated 17-10-17).

5. India had a very low rank (136 out of 186 countries in 2013) in UN Human Development Index, which highlights our abysmally low socio-economic level. The situation was actually more alarming because there has been a deterioration from the earlier rank of 122 out of 170 in 2010 (a fall of 14 points). It is ironical that government was smug and exhilarated because GDP growth rate was high during this period!!

6. During 2006 to 2011, about 5.4 lakh persons had complained to National Human Rights Commission (NHRC) that they suffered from human rights violations, at an alarming average of about 90,000 per year (source: NHRC statistics). Shockingly, NHRC had refused to examine about 3.4 lakhs

complaints of which vast majority was likely to be against court judgments (Article 10).

7. World Happiness Report gave India an average low ranking of 118 among 157 countries for 2013-15. What is more alarming, India's rank slipped to 122 out of 155 countries" in 2017 (Deccan Chronicle dated 05.11.17, page 13).

8. Global Human Capital Report published in September 2017 by World Economic Forum ranked India at 103 out of 130 countries, showing its miserable failure to take advantage of having a very large human capital of young population.

9. Business School Insead ranked India 92 out of 118 countries in Global Talent Index which measured ability to grow, attract and retain highly skilled workers (India Today dated 20.11.17, page 12).

10. Economic Survey states that while India emerges as one of the world's largest economies, it is a net consumer of knowledge instead of net producer (India Today dated 26.02.18, page 9).

11. Only 0.7% of India's GDP is spent on research compared to 2% by China, 2.8% by USA and 4.3% by Israel (India Today dated 26.02.18, page 9).

12. India has 156 researchers per 1 million as compared to 1,113 in China, 4,231 in USA and 8,256 in Israel (India Today dated 26.02.18, page 9).

13. India contributed 36,456 research publications compared to 122,672 by China (India Today dated 26.02.18, page 9).

14. India registered 45,658 patents compared to 91,726 by Germany, 213,694 by South Korea, 318,721 by Japan, and 1.1 million by China (India Today dated 26.02.18, page 9).

15. While India gives high priority to FDI to enhance GDP growth, a World Bank report ranked India a lowly 134th out of 183 countries for ease of doing business and world's 2nd worst for enforcing contracts. Though the rank for ease of doing business has improved by 23 points in 2018 it is still at 77th rank. Despite this shameful situation, government is celebrating the improvement in a way that questions whether complacency has set in. Whether rank for enforcing contracts is still world's 2nd worst or has improved has not been reported.

16. India is ranked 71st in the World Economic Forum's annual Global Competitiveness report 2014-15. What is most disturbing is the downward trend since 2007 for the sixth consecutive year resulting in a drop of 11 places this year. India ranks lowest among BRICS countries. The rank differential with China has shot up from 14 in 2007 to 43 today (Deccan Chronicle dated 04-09-14, page11). GDP growth was remarkably high during most of this period!!

17. World Economic Forum report shows that India has plunged 35 places to 62nd rank in terms of effective regulation of stock exchanges. (Deccan Chronicle dated 09-09-14, page 11).

18. The annual "Economic Freedom of the World Report" has ranked India at 111 (Deccan Chronicle dated 02.11.17, page 9).

19. In 2017, India ranked 143 out of 186 countries in Economic Freedom Index by Heritage Foundation (a US Think Tank). What is worse, it was down by 20 places from 2016 (India Today, dated 20.11.17, page 12).

20. A research study on Non-Performing Assets (NPA) by rating agency CARE had grouped countries as very low NPA, low NPA, medium level NPA and high NPA. Among the 16 high

NPA countries, India was ranked fifth and only four nations had higher NPAs (The Times of India dated 28.12.17, page 7).

21. According to Reserve Bank of India NPAs of Indian banks in March 2017 was 7.9 lakh crores of which public sector banks account for 6.8 lakh crores (India Today dated12.03.18, page 12).

22. Global Peace Index 2013 has ranked India at a very low level of 141 among 162 countries because of losing more than two lives a day due to internal conflicts. It is among the 25 least peaceful countries to live in. If the daily reports on rapes are also taken into account, the position may be much worse and India may be having the dubious distinction of topping the list of least peaceful countries. This is despite misleading GDP growth!!

23. A WHO report on suicides states that India ranked the worst with "nearly a third of the global total and more than twice as many as China, which is second in the list" of suicides in 2012. (The Times of India dated 05-09-14, front page). This is despite the misleading GDP growth!!

24. According to a Thomson Reuters Foundation survey last year, India was ranked fourth among the most dangerous countries in the world (The Week, May 20, 2012, page 44). This is despite the misleading GDP growth!!

25. "India stands among the top four countries in the Asia-Pacific regions with the highest number of online fraud incidents according to Asia-Pacific Fraud Insight report" (Deccan Chronicle dated 23-11-17, page 12).

26. In the World Bank Report for 2012, India had an extremely low rank of 133 out of 146 countries in the Gender Inequality Index and even lagged behind Pakistan and war-torn

countries such as Iraq and Sudan. This is despite the misleading GDP growth!!

27. In 2017, "India slipped 21 places on the World Economic Forum's Global Gender Gap index to a lowly 108 out of 144 countries" despite a decade of slow but steady progress on improving parity between the sexes. "At the current rate of progress the gender gap will take 100 years to bridge, compared to 83 last year." (Deccan Chronicle dated 03.11.17, page 11).

28. In the last 50 years of our democracy, the number of women left out from electoral rolls increased fourfold from an already high 15 million to 68 million!! (The Hindu dated 10-02-14, page 8).

29. India ranked 111 out of 189 countries on women in parliament, as reported by the Inter – Parliamentary Union. This makes India one of the worst countries for women in parliament. It is a matter of shame that India is much worse than its neighbours with Nepal 33rd, China 61[st,] Pakistan 72nd and Bangladesh 74th in ranking – all far better than India's 111th. (The Times of India dated 09-03-14). Of the 543 MPs elected in 2014 only (11%) were women. During the period of more than 65 years after the first general election, the proportion of women MPs has only crawled up from 5% to 11%!! (DNA dated 22-05-14, page 8). The proposed Women's Reservation Bill has been pending for many years and shows utter lack of interest in the matter on the part of government, parliament and political leaders.

30. In a report on the "State of World's Mothers" India is 4th worst even among 80 less developed countries. (This is despite the misleading GDP growth!!)

31. "One woman complains of police apathy every 2 hours" (The Times of India dated 02.11.18, page 13).

32. 93% of rape cases are still awaiting trial as trivial matters hold up cases (Deccan Chronicle dated 23.10.17).

33. According to National Crime Records Bureau (NCRB) human trafficking numbers in 2016 rose by 20% against 2015 (The Times of India dated 28.12.17).

34. In connection with a Public Interest Litigation case which alleged that 1,17,480 children had gone missing between January 2008 and January 2010 and of them 41,546 were yet to be traced, SC remarked that "Nobody seems to be concerned about missing children.

35. NCRB data shows that instances of child rape increased by 82% in 2016 compared to the previous year. Overall crime against children has also increased (The Times of India dated 02.12.17, page 16).

36. Recently published National Family Health Survey IV report states that "72% kids don't get timely vaccination" (The Times of India dated 06.02.18, page 1).

37. On infant mortality rate (one of the main indices of health), India is ranked 126 out of 175 countries (Deccan Chronicle dated 22.10.17, page 12). With a rank of 40 among 52 low middle income countries, India has been ranked 12th worst based on IMR (The Times of India dated 20.02.18, page15).

38. Malnutrition is widespread and alarming. According to WHO, 50% of Indian children are either underweight or stunted. This is despite the misleading GDP growth!!

39. In 2015, 10.8 lakhs children under five died – about 2,959 per day (India Today dated 16.09.17, page 10).

40. Global Nutrition Report 2017 placed India at the bottom with maximum number of women with anaemia in the world. More than half of women in reproductive age have anemia (The Times of India dated 07.11.17, page 6). India has these dubious distinctions despite the misleading GDP growth!!

41. Feticide to get rid of girl child is ridiculously high.

42. India retains the dubious distinction of topping the list of nations with most premature births (DNA dated 17-11-13, page 2).

43. With 7.79 lakhs, India also accounts for the highest number of neonatal (new born) deaths in the world. This number is five times higher than that of China (The Hindu dated 22-05-14, page 17), even though it has a smaller population than China. These are despite the misleading GDP growth!!

44. According to UN, diarrhea kills 117,285 children under five in India each year, highest in the world (India Today dated 19.03.18, page 12).

45. About 2.2 million children in Delhi alone are suffering from irreversible lung damage according to Chittaranjan Cancer Institute (India Today dated 23.10.17, page 11).

Items 34 to 45 show beyond any doubt that parliament and government do not care for welfare of children.

46. India had another dubious distinction of topping the list of countries with the most pollution-related deaths in 2015 (The Times of India dated 21.10.17). About 1.2 million people die every year in India because of outdoor pollution (India Today dated 23.10.17, page 11). A study "India: Health of Nation's States 2017" states

that "27% of deaths in India were caused due to pollution, which is the highest for any country." (Deccan Chronicle dated 05.01.18, page 3). This shows that this dubious distinction continued in 2017 also.

47. Yet another dubious distinction is that the WHO global air pollution data base released on 02.05.18 reveals that India has 14 out of 15 most polluted cities in the world (The Times of India dated 02.05.18, front page).

48. According to Wateraid cost of poor sanitation to the Indian economy in 2015 is $106.7 billion compared to $35.9 billion (about one-third) in China and $10.6 billion (about one-tenth) in Brazil (India Today dated 04.12.17, page 11).

49. According to government data, 19% of Indians drink water with lethal levels of arsenic (The Times of India dated 24.12.17, page 6).

50. According to the Global Burden of Disease Study, India has a dismal rank of 154 among 195 countries in the Health Care Index (Deccan Chronicle dated 21.05.17, front page).

51. India ranked 147 out of 184 countries in health care spending in 2014 (India Today, 05.06.17, page 11).

52. India consumed 8 billion antibiotic pills in 2001. This increased by 62% to 12.9 billion by 2010. This is higher than in China (10 billion) and about twice of that in UK (6.8 billion). "Medical experts say it won't be long before treating the simplest of infectious diseases become a nightmare" due to anti-microbial resistance (AMR), "while procedures such as organ transplantation and chemotherapy are rendered risky. India is especially at danger of an explosion of AMR" (The Times of India dated 23.12.17).

53. Use of billions of antibiotic pills every year poses another very serious problem because "64% of antibiotics sold in India are not approved" (The Times of India dated 05.02.18, page 8). This would have caused ineffective treatment to millions of sick people and huge loss of money for many people who cannot afford.

54. Of the world's smokers, 12% live in India says World Health Organisation. Smoking kills about 1 million Indians every year (India Today dated 19.02.18, page 17).

55. Indian Council of Medical Research reported that 42% of male deaths due to cancer was caused by tobacco (India Today dated 19.02.18, page 17).

56. According to WHO, India reported the world's highest number of TB cases (Deccan Chronicle dated 25.03.18, page 4).

57. India spent only 1.4% of GDP on health care in 2014 compared to Cuba 10.6%, Sweden 10%, USA 8.3%, China 3.1% (India Today, 05.06.17, page 11)

58. Central government's contribution to total health spend in 2014 was 30% compared to UK 83.1% and Pakistan 35.2% (India Today, 05.06.17, page 11)

59. 62.4% Indians paid for health care in 2014 compared to Sri Lanka 42.1% and Germany 13.4% (India Today, 05.06.17, page 11)

60. What is most damaging, 50.6 million Indians have been pushed down below poverty line because of health care costs between 2000 and 2014 (India Today, 05.06.17, page 11)

61. World Economic Forum ranked India 62nd among 79 emerging economies in Inclusive Development Index.

India ranked far below China at 26th (Deccan Chronicle dated 23.01.18, page 1). It is shameful that India's 62nd rank was far below that of its close neighbours (Nepal 22nd, Bangladesh 34th, Sri Lanka 40th and Pakistan 47th).

62. "India ranked high among the most unethical of 13 major economies in the 2016 Global Business Ethics Survey." (The Week dated 01.04.18, page 16).

63. Environmental Performance Index ranks India at rock bottom of 177 among 180 countries in 2017. What is worse, it had a steep fall of 36 places from 141 two years ago (The Times of India dated 24.01.18, page 12).

64. National Sample Survey (65th round) showed that only 47% of urban households have individual water connections. Currently, it is estimated that as much as 40 to 50% of water is "lost" in the distribution system even when water shortage is a serious problem!! (The Hindu dated 01-01-14).

65. India has retained another dubious distinction of defecating in the open with more than 620 million people (over half of India's population) being forced to practice open defecation in 2011 ("WHO and UNICEF joint report – The Hindu dated 07-12-13, page 12). A Swachh Bharat programme was started in 2014. Its main focus is on constructing millions of toilets. The tragedy is that most of them are not used because there is no water. India Today dated 04.12.17 reports that Swachh Bharat figures show that 72.03 million households have access to toilets in November 2017. This forms only 28% of about 260 million households in India (calculated on the basis of an average of five persons per household). The report further states that only 7.9 million toilets

in India are actually usable according to an August 2017 report of Centre for Science and Environment. Thus, only about 28% of households have been provided with toilets and of these only about 10% are usable, leading to only 2.8% of households having usable toilets. Consequently, 524 million Indians (about half of India's population) may be still practicing open defecation (India Today dated 19.03.18, page12). Moreover, there are failures in other aspects of having a clean India. These have led to serious consequences. For example, 117,285 children die from diarrhea every year (Item 43). It is shocking and shameful that government claims success despite this miserable picture of failure.

66. In 2009, India had the shameful distinction of having largest backlog of court cases in the world.

67. India has one of the world's lowest ratios of judges to population. There are only 13 judges for every 1 million people compared to 50 in developed nations (Deccan Chronicle dated 23.10.17, page 12).

68. India's conviction rate is 47% compared to more than 85% in developed democracies (The Times of India dated 25.10.17, page 20).

69. One third of MPs has criminal records, involving serious cases such as rape, murder or kidnapping (Deccan Chronicle dated 23.10.17, page 12).

70. World Justice Report puts India at 66th place among 113 countries and exposes its poor status as a lawfully run country (The Times of India dated 21.01.18, page 17). South African countries (South Africa, Ghana & Senegal) have a much better status being ranked 43rd, 44th and 46th respectively.

71. About 65% of government spending does not come under scrutiny of CAG. This is a big gap in the anti-corruption activities of government.

72. Transparency International ranked India at 79 out of 176 countries in Corruption Perception Index 2016 and 1st among 18 Asia-Pacific nations in bribery rate (India Today dated 20.11.17, page 12). What is more damaging, India slipped to rank 81 in 2017 (The Times of India dated 23.02.18, page 1).

73. A survey by corruption watch dog Transparency International reported that in 2017 as many as 45% of respondents claimed they paid a bribe at least once in the past year to get work done. What is worse, this proportion had increased from 43% for the previous year. (The Times of India dated 10.12.17, page 8). Undoubtedly, corruption is widespread now and increasing. It is shocking that government claims that corruption has been eliminated!!

74. "Between 2000 and 2012, jobs grew by a mere 2% per year" "Agricultural employment, the mainstay for over two thirds of the people, has not grown in these thirteen years." (The Times of India dated 09-02-14). The misleading GDP growth rate was remarkably high during most of this period!! Number unemployed is reported to be alarmingly high now.

75. "Over 20% of youth between 15 to 24 years of age were jobless and seeking work according to startling data released" by Census 2011 (The Times of India dated 02-07-14, page 9). Current unemployment situation is even more alarming.

76. According to UNDP, in 2013, India had a very low ranking (136 out of 186 countries) in gross enrolment in

education (both sexes). A survey by the Organization for Economic Cooperation and Development has shown that 15-year old Indian students fared 2nd worst among 73 countries, for reading, mathematics and science.

77. Out of 1.5 crore persons who enter the work force, only 3% undergo vocational training due to limited access to such training institutions. There are major skill gaps across all industries, more so in Information Technology.

78. "Not less than 65 per cent of prisoners in India are under trials making the country one of the world's 10 "worst" in terms of the proportion of under trails languishing in its jails" (The Hindu dated 27-07-14, page 6).

79. Even in information technology, which gives pride of place for India and boosts employment and income, its use for e-governance has fallen from an already dismal rank of 119 to 124 in 2012.

80. "India topped the world with the highest number of internet shutdowns by government authorities…"(The Times of India dated 02.11.18, psage 14).

81. In a recent survey by Open Signal on the state of LTE around the world, out of 77 countries where 4G LTE Internet is present, India has the dubious distinction of ranking the last (Deccan Chronicle dated 23.02.18, page 11).

82. "Six homes were destroyed every hour in 2017 to build a road or community hall, or simply to beautify the city" (The Times of India dated 23.03.18). Thousands of homes were demolished and lakhs evicted without any meaningful rehabilitation or resettlement measures.

83. Instead of helping the poor and down trodden, richer classes have been repeatedly helped to become richer. According to Forbes, there are "55 billionaires in India, making it the fifth biggest country in terms of number of people with at least one billion dollar net-worth." (Deccan Chronicle dated 25-03-13, page 12). Undemocratic and inhuman practices of helping the rich at the cost of the poor have led to the abysmal fall in respectability of parliament and assemblies and their members. This has led to stinking remarks like the following (for example): "……the glaring tale of how a handful of companies are becoming abnormally wealthy by amassing an obscene amount of land and natural resources, that too at throw away prices, thanks to the dacoits running this country in the garb of politicians…" (page 12, Deccan Chronicle, dated 13-04-12). In this context, it is significant that number of crorepatis increased by 23.5% in financial year 2015!! (Deccan Chronicle dated 21.12.17, page11).

84. "According to Credit Suisse Global Wealth data for India, 73 per cent of the increase in wealth in India went to the top one per cent last year" (Deccan Chronicle dated 25.01.18, page 9).

85. According to World Inequality Report, 22% of India's national income went to the top 1% (India Today dated 26.02.18, page 10).

86. India ranked 6th among richest countries with $8,230 billion in total wealth (India Today dated 26.02.18, page 10).

87. India's wealth had the fastest growth rate of 25%. China rose by 22% (India Today dated 26.02.18, page 10).

88. India has 330,400 high net worth individuals worth $1 million (India Today dated 26.02.18, page 10).

89. India with 119 dollar billionaires was only behind USA and China (India Today dated 26.02.18, page 10).

90. India ranks 147th in efforts to cut inequality (Deccan Chronicle dated 12.10.18).

91. According to news paper reports, there are large number of instances in which large private companies seem to have exercised control over government decisions. For Instance, "the government, instead of enforcing the contract given to an oil company and ensuring that it delivers the promised volumes of gas (not to mention penalizing it for causing extensive losses to standard gas consumers) has allowed it to sell the natural gas, a public property extracted by it, at double the price, against public interest." (The Hindu dated 19-02-14). This was allowed even though the company's cost of production was much less and it has already been receiving the highest price that any private company was paid anywhere in the world!! Not only that, according to news paper reports, it seems to have got the minister concerned replaced by a more pliable minister during the discussions for fixing prices. In our sinking democracy voice of people hardly matters but that of the rich does!!

92. Association for Democratic Reforms has observed that 86% of Rajya Sabha members were crorepatis and Lok Sabha 2009 had 58% crorepatis (Article 2). This shows a highly imbalanced and unhealthy representation of people. No wonder, parliament favours the rich and many anomalies like those mentioned above have occurred.

Paragraphs 83 to 92 show how the rich are benefitted while the poor are suffering.

93. "Considering its vast population, India is the worst performing country at the olympics" (The Times of India dated 04.11.18, page18).

94. According to The Melbourne Mercer Global Pension Index "India has emerged as the second lowest among 34 countries providing retirement income systems with good benefits" (Deccan Chronicle dated 23.0.18, page 12).

95. RSF's Press Freedom Index for 2017 has ranked India 136 out of 180 countries. What is worse it has dropped three points after the previous year (India Today dated 29.09.17). In 2016, 47 journalists were attacked in India and government has not been serious to provide security to journalists (The Times of India dated 23.12.17, page 11). These are big blows for democracy.

96. At a recent well attended panel discussion in Delhi Habitat Centre all participants expressed the view that the media scene in India was catastrophic because of the fear among journalists to criticize the present Government. The panel also emphasized that if journalists are so afraid, they will become irrelevant.

97. "It's one of India's greatest shames and it is hidden in plain sight. In absolute terms, India has the largest number of modern day slaves in the world, 18 million and counting. In the Global Slavery Index, compiled by Australia based rights group Walk Free Foundation, India is among the top four offenders in percentage terms... This includes bonded labour, human trafficking, forced marriages, women coerced into prostitution or badly paid menial work. The most vulnerable among these are the children..." (Editorial in India Today dated 13.11.17).

98. What is most damaging, elected parliament and assemblies were void because vast majority of members did not have the

required support of more than 50% of electorate. Shockingly, both Election Commission and Supreme Court ignored this atrocious situation and did not even try to overcome it (Article 2).

99. Breaking of promises given by government during replies to questions in parliament or discussions on bills and motions is alarmingly high. During a 10 year period this immoral action was repeated 1,024 times, as reported by the Ministry of Parliamentary Affairs!! (DNA dated 16-09-13). Over a longer time period many more instances of such disrespect to parliament could have happened. Surprisingly, this shocking situation did not cause even ripples!! Sad to say, parliament has been spinelessly tolerating disrespect more than thousand times, without the dignity expected from the august supreme body and failing to exercise its responsibility of having a check on functioning of government. Besides lack of dignity, parliament also lacked in guts to punish government for breaking promises more than thousand times!!

100. Finally, what is the quality of India's democracy? In the world map prepared by Economic Intelligence Unit for 2017, India is one of the countries with flawed democracy. What is even more shocking and shameful, is that India slipped by 10 points from a rank of 32 in 2016 to 42 in 2017. Their report attributes this to "rise of conservative religious ideologies and increase in vigilantism and violence against minorities as well as other dissenting voices." Moreover, "In the latest rankings of the Varieties of Democracy (V-DEM) Institute, a research project that tries to evolve new measures of democracy, India's rank is seen dropping in the past four years, with a marked concentration of powers in the hands of one individual" (India Today dated 23.07.18, page 28). And most important, the present system of Indian democracy has a fundamental defect (Article 6), has 11 basic

faults in the management infrastructure (Articles 7) and fifteen fundamental weaknesses (Article 14) and is based on nine absurdities (Article 23). If these are also taken into account there is absolutely no doubt that Indian democracy has gone down beyond a completely flawed democracy and has become a pseudo democracy. There is an urgent need to replace this with a true democracy.

All these 100 *shameful and shocking situations covering almost all crucial sectors* happened despite a high growth rate!! Most probably there are many more of such deplorable situations waiting to be highlighted. Government and parliament were so obsessed and boasting about growth rate that they did not have the time and inclination to rectify the shameful and shocking situations pointed out above.

It is also shocking that (a) most of the shameful and shocking situations pointed out above were brought out by investigations by international bodies and (b) neither government nor parliament was keen to carry out systematic and continuous monitoring and evaluation of all progammes to keep a watch and augment these by evaluation studies to get additional information to get in depth knowledge.

Have any of our MPs and political parties bothered to think about these 100 shameful and shocking situations, let alone take any action? Have any questions on these been at least raised in parliament? MPs, being obsessed by party matters and selfish interests, have neither time nor interest in such important national matters. May be, most of them were not even aware of all these shameful and shocking situations because they were preoccupied with their selfish and party interests!!

It is a pity that instead of hanging their heads in shame, government, parliament, MPs, MLAs and political parties assumed airs of superiority and felt smug and exhilarated. No wonder, people have lost respect for government, parliament, MPs, MLAs and political parties who make a mockery of parliament and assemblies!! We ought to be ashamed of having such a parliament even though our government, parliament and MPs have no shame.

It deserves to be reemphasized that parliament brought disgrace on itself due to lack of dignity by spinelessly tolerating disrespect more than thousand times and lack of guts to punish government for breaking promises so often. Moreover, parliament did not even attempt to rectify the large number of shameful and shocking situations faced by the country, pointed out in this article. Significantly, most dismal failures of democracy were contributed by parliament and assemblies which did not exercise the supreme power bestowed on them to ensure checks. They have, suicidingly, lost their right to continue.

Since attempts to stem the suicidal rot in the pillars of democracy are sadly lacking, disillusionments, antagonism, cynicism, intolerance, hostility and violence have already crossed danger levels in many areas (e.g., Maoism, separatism, attempts at disintegration, manipulated violent protests, ethnic violence and disgruntled or intolerant groups resorting even to murders and taking to the streets and burning vehicles). More are likely to follow.

The editorial in The Hindu dated 24.02.14 states: "As the 15th Lok Sabha comes to an ignominious end, it is no longer possible to put off the question: are we a democracy only in name?

Without a proactive course correction, India's robust record of conducting elections could end up being just that – a ritualistic, five yearly obeisance to democracy that hides the appalling state of the country's institutions, in particular parliament which today resembles a wrestling arena. In truth, the comparison would insult the sport of wrestling, which is governed by well laid-out rules and regulations."

These aspects depict the <u>twenty-second</u> and fundamental obstacle which resulted in a distorted and ineffective democracy.

To overcome this fundamental obstacle, we should ask ourselves: why do we spent thousands of crores of public money to maintain a parliament which (a) lacks dignity, guts to punish government for braking promises more than thousand times, accountability and an ethics of care for aam admi and (b) has not shown any interest in rectifying large number of shameful and shocking situations faced by the country? ***Should we not abolish such a parliament?***

The main reason for parliament not punishing government for breaking promises more than thousand times is the basic defect in the system pointed out in Article 6. The political party which forms government also controls parliament because of having majority. This defective system allows a subtle dictatorial attitude in the party and the government towards parliament and defeats the very purpose of having parliament as an independent pillar of democracy. ***This basic defect also justifies abolition of present parliamentary system.***

If a way cannot be found to avoid mostly crorepatis being elected to parliament (paragraph 92 above), abolition of parliament with such distorted and unhealthy representation of people is further justified.

All these emphasize that we should try another system which can uphold the voice of people more efficiently and gracefully and is cheaper. This aspect is discussed in more detail in a later article.

Article 16

Role of Media

Effective functioning of democracy requires an alert media with broad vision which functions as a watch dog of democracy, informs people about the state of affairs and provides a platform for public debate. The media in India needs to improve its functioning in all these aspects.

It has to make more alert checks on functioning of democracy. For example, Articles 1 to 23 had identified thirty-two obstacles which caused a distorted and ineffective democracy. It is shocking that media had covered only some of these aspects (that too only cursorily without required follow up) and many aspects which have led to sinking of democracy did not receive its attention. Sad to say, media was not alert enough to fulfill its responsibility for (1) creating awareness among people about all these obstacles which are ruining democracy and (2) starting meaningful debates to improve democracy. What is worse, media was not alert enough to realize that parliament was void (Article 2).

Article 15 listed 100 deplorable situations which are shocking and shameful for the country. It is shocking that almost all of these were found by other agencies and not by investigations by an active Indian media. Moreover, when the media came to know about some of these, they casually published these but did not adequately question government and MPs/MLAs about these and remedial actions taken. Media also failed to highlight the callous attitude of government towards these shocking and shameful situations to make people aware of all these and to motivate and support people to raise their voice to rectify these matters relating to welfare of people.

Article 15 has also emphasized that government and parliament were so obsessed and boasting about growth rate that they did not have time and inclination to rectify so many shocking and shameful situations pointed out therein. Media failed in its responsibility (as required under a democracy) to (1) exert pressure on government to take proper actions to rectify all shocking and shameful situations and (2) highlight these to make people aware of all these shocking and shameful situations and the callous attitude of government so that they will cease to be misguided by GDP growth and will raise their voice to rectify matters relating to welfare of people.

Moreover, media has not been sufficiently active in provoking and encouraging debates about saving our democracy and arriving at consensus on possible solutions. Editorials did not focus adequately on the decaying democracy and how to save it. Printed media did not adequately encourage journalists and social activists to publish articles discussing need and/or suggestions for improving democracy. Acceptance of articles by media is decided more on the basis of status or influence of the contributor than on quality of the article. This has led to suppression of many pertinent and innovative ideas.

Article 15 has also pointed out that parliament (1) has a highly imbalanced and unhealthy representation of people with a large majority of MPs in both houses being crorepatis and (2) has brought disgrace on itself due to (a) lack of guts to punish government for breaking promises more than thousand times and (b) lack of dignity by spinelessly tolerating such disrespect so often. Media did not emphasize these deficiencies.

Sad to say, media did not start a debate about why we should spend thousands of crores of public money to maintain such an unworthy and void parliament. It ought to do so immediately without further waste of time.

Ministers and important political leaders have not been subjected to periodic media scrutiny to ascertain their assessment of the situation and plans for improving governance and welfare of people. Media did not perform its responsibility to carry out regular checks on fulfillment of accountability by these leaders who have serious responsibilities for governance and ensuring welfare of people. They have not realized that these checks are crucial because there is no system of annual assessment of performance of these leaders who can make serious mistakes because they do not have the qualification and experience required for governance.

Panchayat Raj institutions at different levels play a major role in sustenance of democracy at levels closer to people. But, media did not systematically review their activities (on a sample basis) and inform people about these even though these activities deserved constant scrutiny and praise where due.

There is very little overlapping of readers of different newspapers and journals. How many readers can afford to read all newspapers and journals or have time to do so for getting a fuller picture? To overcome this, newspapers and journals should publish suitable extracts (or summaries) of important articles published in other newspapers and journals (with due acknowledgement). This will benefit their readers and lead to wider awareness and discussion of all aspects. In this manner, media should get rid of the restrictive mind set, which lacks broad vision. Then, people all over the country will get an opportunity to become aware of all important ideas and debate these. Current obstacles in spreading of ideas are antidemocratic and should be removed immediately.

Those who watch panel discussions on TV get the impression that moderators are more interested in hearing their own voice than eliciting views of the panel for benefit of viewers. Their attitude and expressions seem to depict that they are all-knowing "judges" and not investigators of truth. What is worse, these discussions often tend to focus on trivial inter and intra political party matters and not on how to improve democracy.

There is an urgent need to review media's value system. For example, 1.42 lakh people died from accidents in 2011. This was casually reported in bottom corner on page 8 of DNA dated 24 July 2012. Most other newspapers and TV news seem to have even totally ignored this!! Compared to this, when few persons lost life from a terrorist attack, this was splashed in bold headlines in front page of all newspapers and repeatedly splashed on TV as "Big News." It is shocking that media attached more value to few deaths from terror attack than to 1.42 lakh deaths from accidents!! Moreover, media made much larger hue and cry about loss of life due to terrorist attacks than to focusing attention on lapses of government to prevent or reduce grossly bigger losses in lives due to calamities such as collapsing of structures, stampede etc. for which preventive steps could have at least reduced losses. Readers also seem to have accepted this misguided value system instead of protesting against it.

Such mismatch of value of life is grossly illogical and deserves to be condemned outright. Attaching such enormous differences to value of life and splashing these on headlines has only created unnecessary panic among people and did not help to prevent terrorist attacks.

Sad to say, this thoughtless splashing of news has unwittingly helped terrorists in their main aim of creating panic. Media has not realized that terrorists themselves know that they are incapable of doing any large scale harm. They had planned only to create panic and media has helped them exceedingly well to achieve their aim!! Innovative approaches are essential to tackle this delicate situation and ensure that the aim of terrorists to create panic is not realized. One way is to completely suppress news of terrorist attacks in public interest and confidentially exert pressure on government to ensure proper preventive steps. Such a blackout of news will make terrorists frustrated, exasperated and miserable, besides avoiding panic among people which has only a negative consequence. Has there been even one instance in which splashing of such news had helped to prevent terrorist attacks? If not, why not suppress this news to prevent panic and to make terrorists frustrated and miserable? Fighting terrorism needs innovative strategies by media also.

This example also cautions media to always make sure that their unrestricted eagerness to splash news does not help enemies of peace or create problems for the society and country. Eagerness to splash news and right to freedom of expression should not be misused even unwittingly if it creates problems for society. A total review of value system, eagerness to splash news and right to freedom of expression is called for.

Another problem is lopsided priorities. Important aspects of governance and peoples' welfare do not receive adequate attention. Major parts of printing space/TV time are wasted on inter and intra political party disputes and making statements and speculations about these which add fuel to the fire.

Space for news is often displaced by photos of VIPs and their activities like birthday celebrations, weddings etc.; news about their pregnancies, divorces, travels, retirement etc.; and their speeches of doubtful importance. These have no relevance to governance or welfare of people. Gossips about VIPs and politicians are a major weakness of the media. Obsession with celebrities is bad in itself but much worse when it leads to denial of space for problems in development faced by people and activities of their unsung leaders who have contributed to happiness and peace in society.

Semi naked colour pictures of women (not befitting our tradition) have become an essential part of printed media. Is this done for promoting sales of printed media or to provide mini porn? These numerous semi naked female photos give a wrong impression that most women like to be voluptuously dressed!! This also shows disrespect to Indian women because they like to dress with dignity.

Other subjects that fill pages are murders, rapes, molestations of women, extortions, kidnappings, robberies, and other crimes which give a dismal picture every morning. Since giving these news has not motivated concerned authorities to act effectively, the net result has only been creation of helplessness, disgust and cynicism among people.

Media has a short memory even for important matters. It has not realized that government has adopted a strategy of "buying time" based on their correct understanding that media never persists with its "protests" long enough and allows them to die quietly because of loss in news value. Media should develop a system of regular follow up of all serious matters till government action produces desired results. It should think out of the box and adopt innovative methods to have news value for its follow up activities also.

Concentration on news items which give importance to high society gossip or focus on crimes, disasters, failures etc., as mentioned in previous paragraphs reveals a negative mindset which is not conducive to growth of democracy.

On the other hand, number of positive activities which show healthy developments such as individuals or small groups (who may not be VIPs) contributing to welfare of people and/ or peace in different parts of the country hardly find a place because of media's inertia and lack of interest and vision. Very little importance is given to positive consequences of such news to society. Moreover, media does not realize that publicizing positive developments which can motivate more of such events are crucial for development of democracy.

Media has been side tracked by monetary considerations. Nobel Laureate Amartya Sen and Jean Drezse have alleged "Rather than engage with diagnosis of significant injustices and inefficiencies media celebrates only the rich and powerful, perhaps because it is an advertisement driven business." (DNA dated 04-08-13, page 9). Often, in many newspapers front page which should get priority for main news has given way to advertisements, even full page, which fetches large amounts of money. This is in addition to space for advertisements far outstretching space for news. Recent trend is to push main news to the 2nd or 3rd sheet (i.e., 3rd, 4th or 5th page)!! A day may come soon when news papers will be displaced by "advertisement papers" in which a reader has to spend lot of time to hunt here and there for hidden news!!

Paid news is another shameful matter.

Media organizations have become greedy. They forget that their main aim ought to be serving as many people as possible by providing correct information and analyses of situations in the country to make maximum number of people aware of positive developments or lack of these. With increase in cost, newspapers are becoming increasingly out of reach for common people.

Thinking out of the box is a rare phenomenon.

At a recent well attended panel discussion in Delhi Habitat Centre all participants expressed the view that the media scene in India was catastrophic because of the fear among journalists to criticize the present Government. If journalists are so afraid, they will become irrelevant. The only solution they suggested was that journalists should stand up against the undesirable policies and actions of governments. Not doing this immediately will be a death blow to both journalists and democracy.

Even more damaging for democracy is the fact that media owners are unable to criticize government and political parties in power. The Editors' Guild of India condemned "the erosion of right to practice free and independent journalism because of "inability" of media owners to withstand pressures from the political establishment as well as frequent "blocking or interference" in broadcast of content critical of the government" (The Times of India dated 09. 08.18, page 10). Obviously, this curtails employment opportunities for honest journalists. These give another serious death blow to democracy.

All these show lack of vision on the part of media and failures in fulfilling their social responsibilities as a watch dog, information agency and guide for growth of democracy.

These failures of media depict the <u>twenty-third</u> and very serious <u>obstacle</u> which resulted in a distorted and ineffective democracy.

To overcome these drawbacks, media should give immediate attention to the speech by then President Pranab Mukherjee at the Platinum Jubilee Celebrations of the Indian Newspaper Society. Expressing concern over "aberrations" like "paid news" which have crept into the media, he said "Sensationalism should never become a substitute for objective assessment and truthful reporting. Gossip and speculation should not replace hard facts. Every effort should be made to ensure that political or commercial interests are not passed off as legitimate and independent opinion." He also emphasized that the media can undertake its role of cleansing public life only if it's own conduct is above board. He made out a case for not just weeding out "aberrations" but also putting in place self-correcting mechanisms to check such tendencies.

Following his advice, all round introspection on all the aspects mentioned earlier is essential. It should be undertaken by department of journalism in colleges, media establishments and their national organizations like Press Council, Editors' Guild, Indian Newspaper Society etc. and working journalists. After these, a code of ethics to guide their activities should be evolved in a democratic manner. Thinking out of the box needs to be given high priority and widely encouraged by publishing such articles. Lacunae in constructive and positive journalism have to be overcome.

This introspection should be guided by the following exhortations:

1. ***Have vision:*** A blind person asked Swami Vivekananda: Can there be anything worse than losing eye sight?" He replied: "Yes, losing your vision!"

2. ***Overcome defeatist mentality by learning from history:*** "Never forget that a small group of thoughtful committed citizens can change the world; it is the only way that ever does."

– Margarat Mead

3. ***Be bold:*** "Boldness has genius, power and magic in it"

– Goethe

4. ***Conquer silence:*** "Our lives begin to end the day we become silent about things that matter."

– Martin Luther King Jr

5. ***Prevent enemies of democracy to triumph:*** "All that is necessary for the triumph of evil is for good men to do nothing."

– Edmund Burke

Constitution of a national regulatory authority is also needed.

Meanwhile, media ought to immediately start a debate on why we should spend thousands of crores of public money to maintain an unworthy and void parliament, as detailed in Article 15 and mentioned earlier in this article. It should also use this set of articles to create awareness among people about the various obstacles in proper functioning of our democracy so that we can avoid pitfalls while developing a modified system of democracy.

Article 17

Upholders of Democracy

Before independence, the country had leaders who sacrificed a lot to fight for independence. They were supported by freedom fighters who also joined the fight with a spirit of sacrifice. These freedom fighters were from every walk of life such as lawyers, authors, poets, doctors, engineers, actors, cartoonists, farmers, workers, sportsmen etc. After independence, some leaders and freedom fighters became political leaders and adopted a different role viz., governing the country with a commitment to national interests and welfare of people. Unfortunately, over time, there has been steady deterioration in the spirit of sacrifice and commitment to national interests and welfare of people among political leaders. Pranab Mukherjee as President of India expressed concern and disappointment at the "eroding commitment among the legislators who are expected to be custodians of public interests and rights."

On the other hand, remaining leaders and freedom fighters did not take up any role. They became complacent because they felt that the country was safe in the hands of the leaders who fought for freedom. Otherwise they would have sought and found a new role as upholders of democracy. Most of them have realized, as years passed by, that the self-sacrificing political leaders were increasingly replaced by self-serving politicians who were more interested in holding on to power and amassing wealth. They now realize that such leaders not only did not feel the need for support from spirited groups like "freedom fighters" but also feared that such honest and committed people can be a hindrance for their selfish endeavours and avoided or even suppressed them. At present, the survivors among them have become disappointed and cynical and suffer from a defeatist mentality. Younger generations of potential upholders of democracy are either confused without proper leadership or have been cleverly side tracked by misinformation and misdirection.

The above aspects depict the twenty-fourth obstacle which resulted in a distorted and ineffective democracy.

To overcome this obstacle, upholders of democracy (old and potential) should wake up as quickly as possible and organize themselves to save our sinking democracy. Their current cynicism, negative attitude, and defeatist mentality should be replaced with a positive and spirited outlook for fighting for true democracy. They should develop full confidence by following the advice of Margaret Mead: "Never forget that a small group of thoughtful committed citizens can change the world; it is the only way that ever does." They should also patiently persevere by following an anonymous thinker's advice that "There can be efforts that fail but there should not be a failure of efforts" and systematically organize a meaningful and peaceful fight for real democracy. An essential first step is to create wide spread awareness among people about many obstacles which led to the sinking of our democracy. This series of articles can be used to initiate talks and discussions. The ideas which arise from these discussions and the process of creating awareness should be used for wider debates.

Without entering politics, upholders of democracy (old and potential) should peacefully fight for reforming democracy by utilizing their talents and influence as lawyers, authors, poets, doctors, engineers, actors, cartoonists, farmers, workers, sportsmen etc. as their predecessors had done in the fight for independence. For a start, they should create awareness among people, mobilize their support and provide them leadership to fight for a truly vibrant democracy.

Upholders of democracy should also approach celebrities in different fields such as film stars, musicians, authors, doctors, engineers, lawyers, poets, cricketers, cultural and religious groups etc. who have some influence on people. Request them to strengthen awareness among people about the failures which led to sinking of our democracy and possible solutions (detailed in these articles) and thereby help to form a true democracy on sound lines. Some celebrities can also be persuaded to take up non-political leadership of the peaceful movement for true democracy.

Many educated people are members of associations or clubs. They should frequently discuss in their meetings the problems faced by our sinking democracy (detailed in these articles) – firstly to create awareness of these problems and then debate on possible solutions for these problems. These discussions ought to lead to creation of many local leaders all over the country for a peaceful fight for true democracy. They should elect regional and national leaders to strengthen the peaceful movement for true democracy throughout the country. These new leaders should organize public debates to reach a consensus about the reformed system of true democracy. This should be followed by a peaceful agitation to set up a new Constituent Assembly to finalise the reformed system and make suitable changes in the Constitution.

To make meaningful efforts, old and potential upholders of democracy and their new leaders should dare to think and act for developing a reformed system of true democracy for securing welfare of people. They have to awaken and motivate people particularly the youth to act peacefully without fear and with patience to achieve the goal of a truly vibrant democracy. They should be prepared for a long peaceful fight against powerful vested interests who will give threats and play lot of tricks to prevent any meaningful reform of democracy. They should be constantly guided by the fact that India got independence by a peaceful movement against a mighty empire, which had put up a series of obstacles and taken many cruel and violent steps. It is pertinent that these could only prolong attainment of success. With adequate precautions, commitment, determination to fight against all obstacles and patience success can be achieved and will confirm the invincibility of peoples' power. It is encouraging and reassuring that creation of mass awareness will ensure that peoples' power will be forthcoming to take adequate precautions and steps needed from time to time.

Article 18

Responsibilities and Role of People

Democracy has been defined as government of the people by the people for the people. To have a government by the people, we (the people), have to realize our responsibilities and play important roles to ensure that governance is carried out according to true spirit of democracy. Firstly, people have the responsibility to elect representatives who have character and clean image in addition to qualifications and experience needed for governance. We have not only failed to do so in many ways (Articles 1 to 3 and 14) but also have not realized the seriousness of our mistakes and therefore remain callous about these.

People who did not vote have failed in their responsibility. Voting figures show that they form more than 30% of the electorate. This is a matter for serious concern.

Among those who voted, about 90% did not fulfill their responsibility of choosing capable and efficient representatives with character, clean image and required qualifications and thereby caused serious harm (Article 2): large numbers voted in droves and failed in their responsibility to make an independent choice; some others made the serious mistake of selling their vote; some others have allowed themselves to be intimidated even though their vote was secret; some others had preferred persons of their own caste. For example, in a sample survey in 2013 across Karnataka, as many as 41% had stated that caste was very important in deciding who to vote for (Article 1).

These four groups who wrongly voted and those who did not vote have made a mockery of our democracy by failing in their responsibility to elect capable and efficient representatives with character, clean image and required qualifications. Those who sold their vote and those who voted on caste basis together form 70% of the electorate. No estimate is available for the other three groups of irresponsible voters. With their addition, percentage of voters who did not consciously fulfill their responsibility is likely to exceed 90%. Regrettably, these five groups of irresponsible voters, who together constitute more than 90% of voters in most constituencies, did not realize the seriousness of their mistakes. This is a big blow to democracy due to failure of people. Because of this grave failure by people, most of our elected representatives had the support of only a negligible minority (may be less than 10%) of voters who had voted consciously to fulfill their responsibility!! In other words, most of them were elected only because of irresponsible voting by 90% of people. Shockingly, because most elected persons did not get support of more than 50% of the electorate required to become representatives, their ***election was void***. People have not realised that this very serious problem was created by their irresponsible voting.

People have not realized that capacity required for good governance is different from that needed to win an election. Moreover, while winning an election needs capacity for one time hectic effort only, good governance needs capacity for sustained efforts for many years. Another aspect is that politicians often make promises to win elections, without sincerity and ability to meet these. All the above lacunae explain why experts in winning elections have often failed to ensure peoples' welfare. The tragedy is that people have failed to understand the incapacities and failures of politicians explained above. What is worse, they even blindly worship them.

To be efficient voters people should watch out to prevent being duped by experts in winning elections. People should demand proof about their capacity and commitment to ensure peoples' welfare and verify their character and image. People should demand convincing answers about why they (or their party) did not fulfill the promises made earlier. A common practice of merely blaming others without giving positive solutions and resorting to hate speeches should be considered as disqualifications. It is better not to take the risk of supporting candidates with doubtful image.

For this, people should use the NOTA option during elections if they do not "find a right candidate with character and clean image" as exhorted by the anti-corruption crusader Anna Hazare (Article 1). If large number of voters have used NOTA option they should insist on fresh elections after excluding all the candidates who have been rejected by this option. To save our sinking democracy we should not only consciously use NOTA option but also educate and motivate others to do so. This will ensure that political parties will put up only suitable candidates in future elections and also reduce multiplicity of candidates for each constituency.

As responsible voters, we should reject even suitable candidates if they belong to a party which is observed to be "buying votes" or has sponsored candidates with criminal background. This is very important because, after election, even these "honest candidates" will be forced to support party interests at the cost of peoples' interests; for example supporting the party in not punishing those who have amassed wealth or have misused their power to help vested interests.

All these have questioned the appropriateness of continuation of the election system which was designed only for giving voice to people. We (the people), who have not used our voice properly, are responsible for this situation.

Failing in our responsibilities to vote properly as explained earlier is the twenty-fifth and very serious obstacle which resulted in a distorted and ineffective democracy.

A major failure is that after voting once in five years, we close our eyes and allow our representatives and the government they form to govern as they like. We are not alert enough to question when they do not act to ensure our needs and aspirations and repeatedly ignore the principles of democracy and the promises made at election time.

Another major failure is our view that government alone can provide good governance. We have not been sincere enough to cooperate with government efforts and supplement these. Even worse, we often create problems for good governance because of lethargy, narrow selfish interests and intolerance of others.

When faced with problems, we expect government to do everything for us but we do not make any efforts to solve problems or try to reduce them. If we watch carefully with keen intention to reduce problems, we can help a lot. For example, when there is shortage of electricity, we can eliminate avoidable consumption or at least reduce it substantially by always switching off lights and fans when leaving a room. Avoid use of bright lights and too many lights which enhance the problem. If people, particularly owners of large buildings and multistoried flats, install solar power spending affordable funds, shortage will come down drastically.

Similarly, preventing wastage of water will immensely help to reduce shortage of precious water. Leaking taps, leaving taps open for longer time than required, misuses (such as frequent car wash instead of dusting, washing outdoor passages and gate area instead of sweeping etc.) and wasting 90% of full tank for flushing of toilets after urination, add a lot to wastage.

We have no right to complain about any shortage until we prevent wastage.

Where garbage is a serious problem, we expect the authorities to clean up but have no hesitation to throw it anywhere we like. We do not often segregate waste to help garbage disposal.

National integration, which helps to sustain democracy (Article 12), has failed mainly because we have not taken any interest in building up the concept of being Indians. We have also not realized the importance of having a national script for all languages (Article 12). Regrettably, we have nurtured dissipating tendencies instead of building up togetherness with humanitarian approaches.

People have also developed the damaging habit of hero worship which has often resulted in their blindly glorifying some politicians, sometimes even ignoring their criminal past, and their wrong actions which have not only harmed the country (or large sections of population) but also destroyed democracy. People allow themselves to be mesmerized by oratory of politicians or hoodwinked by their clever tactics, even when they did not ensure peoples' welfare with equanimity and killed our system of democracy by becoming enemies of democracy (Article 19). Hero worship is the root cause for anti-democratic dictatorial practices.

Another serious harm resulting from hero worship is that people blindly support and encourage activities performed by such a leader without following democratic procedures and consultations. People wrongly praise such activities as resulting from ability to take quick decisions. This serious mistake allows subtle dictatorship which cuts across the roots of democracy and leads to a climate of fear among people. Gambling with public funds is another causality (for example demonetisation and construction of statues spending enormous funds). Hero worship also leads to slavish mentality. History has number of examples of kings who have done lot of good to people but they had also enforced slavery and gambled with the future of the country. Moreover, they had spread fear among people. These were the main reasons for discarding monarchy in favour of democracy!! People should not allow themselves to be mesmerized and fall into this anti-democratic trap.

People often start fights for trivial or irrelevant matters due to ego, emotional imbalances or selfish interests. People are often carried away by hatred and belief in unverified rumours by trouble makers. These show their inability to discern what is good for welfare of majority of people which is a key principle of democracy.

A fundamental mistake is to consider that democracy is needed only for good governance. People and governments have not realized that many more aspects relating to religion, culture, entertainment, recreation, etc., are creating conflicts and have to be tackled. For example, religion has often led to disturbance of peace, loss of brotherhood, intolerance of other religions, conflicts and even war. Ignoring these is not a solution and shows a defeatist mentality. To avoid such conflicts and to enjoy a peaceful life and be happy organized attention is essential. These cannot and should not be taken up by government. We have to build other organizations to fulfill our responsibility to ensure happy and peaceful environment for all the above aspects, which are not subjected to hatred and fear.

Because our attempts to ensure the noble idea of equality were illogical, impractical and made us hypocrites, people can and should set limits for inequalities in income, expenditure, ownership of land etc. This is another fundamental omission.

These two fundamental aspects are discussed in more detail in another article.

Sad to say, we (the people) have not visualized such important aspects which ought to form the back bone of a democracy which aims at happiness, peace and a good quality of life for people. For this, a new composite approach is essential and new types of organizations have to be set up. This requires a change in mind set. These important aspects are discussed further in later articles.

All these show that we (the people), have some wrong perceptions and inability for intelligent and logical thinking which hindered development and maintenance of a true and vibrant democracy.

This is the <u>twenty-sixth</u> and most serious <u>obstacle</u> which resulted in a distorted and ineffective democracy.

To overcome these obstacles and have a new composite approach we have to introspect and change our mindset. We have to realize and create awareness that all of us have responsibility to ensure that capable and efficient representatives with character and clean image are elected and governance actually reflects the will of the people and effectively functions for the people. We have to be alert to develop and sustain our democracy. We should be watchful to detect signs of deterioration of democracy in any locality or in any manner.

When political leaders speak at public meetings during elections, we should be alert enough to avoid being hoodwinked or mesmerized by their crafty speeches especially when the speaker is cleverly using gift of the gab and dramatic gestures to mislead us. When leaders speak at length criticizing others without giving any positive plans, we should realize that they are doing so because they did not have any positive ideas. They should be interrupted and politely told that we are not interested in fault finding but in what plans they have to improve welfare of people and how they are going to implement these plans. Those who give promises without elaborating their plan to achieve these are not worthy to be elected. Those who make hate speeches should be told that we consider them as enemies of peace.

Some national and regional leaders speak in support of local candidates from their party. We should not trust that what these leaders say fully reflects the views and principles of the candidates and that they are committed to take suitable actions if elected. We should avoid electing persons who are thrust on us by leaders from other areas who cleverly mesmerize us by their oration but choose those local leaders who directly convince us that they can act to solve our problems with vision and compassion, with empathy and empowerment and with qualities of head and heart.

Some leaders cleverly manipulate creation of caste, linguistic, religious and other group conflicts as well as cliques and other favourable conditions to safeguard their interests and to achieve their ignoble ambitions. We should not allow ourselves to become their tools for such anti-social activities which disturb peace in our areas. Some disqualifications for a leader of democracy are explained in Article 20. We should closely watch whether the candidates for election have any of these disqualifications and should not choose them as our representatives.

We have also to be alert to ensure that mischief mongers and selfish groups do not create problems. Constant efforts should be made to identify rumour mongers and to isolate them in the community. Though unintentionally, most newspapers and TV divert our attention from real problems by gossip about celebrities, political parties and politicians. We should not be distracted by such gossip.

We should insist that once in six months the MLA of our area together with our MP should report to us their achievements as well as problems faced and future plans to overcome these, in a meeting of all "groups" of people (without any exceptions). We should insist that during these meetings, they should also advice us about how we can cooperate with them to achieve better results and also help to maintain peace and social harmony in the area, besides striving for national integration. An important result will be that people will become aware of problems faced by government and will not resort to unnecessary agitations.

During these meetings people should give their assessment of the extent to which government has succeeded in meeting their needs and aspirations. We should insist that video recording of these meetings should be immediately sent by the concerned MLA to the State Election Commission so that it can keep a regular watch on the efficiency of these representatives. This method of assessing efficiency of MPs, MLAs and government is a much better way for people to exercise their voice than by voting once in five years to elect representatives, without knowledge and expertise required to elect efficient managers of democracy (Article 14).

Most important, these six-monthly review meetings will ***enable people to exercise their voice directly once in six months*** and there is no need to continue the costly election system which has miserably failed in many ways as highlighted in Articles 1 to 4. This also automatically avoids distraction by extraneous considerations like, caste, party affiliation, monitory incentives etc. discussed in Article 1.

The six-monthly review meetings should be made use of by people to short list efficient local leaders who participated in these meetings, so that they can approach them for help whenever needed, particularly for helping people to bring problems to the notice of the authorities and fight peacefully for solutions.

We have to give full support to social activists who are eager to be upholders of democracy (Article 17) so that they can provide leadership for saving our sinking democracy. We should request them to be our watchful leaders to attend the 6-monthly meetings and help us to bring problems to the notice of the authorities and fight peacefully for solutions.

All the steps mentioned earlier are essential to prevent creation of problems due to our lack of qualifications and expertise to elect efficient managers of democracy and thereby ensure true democracy.

We should develop a sense of discipline to solve problems which come up and to avoid creating other problems. It is important to have a committed approach to fulfill our responsibilities and to making sincere efforts to ourselves solve all social and economic problems to the extent possible. We should be eager to use every opportunity to support helpful government efforts and extend our full cooperation. Where government cannot help we should try to organize ourselves. It is important that we play the dual roles of partners in democracy and watch dogs to detect deficiencies in our democracy.

All this calls for a change in mind set. For this we should be guided by the following exhortations also:

1. ***Have vision:*** A blind person asked Swami Vivekananda: Can there be anything worse than losing eye sight?" He replied: "Yes, losing your vision!"

2. ***Overcome defeatist mentality by learning from history:*** "Never forget that a small group of thoughtful committed citizens can change the world; it is the only way that ever does."

— Margarat Mead

3. ***Be bold:*** "Boldness has genius, power and magic in it"

— Goethe

4. ***Conquer silence:*** "Our lives begin to end the day we become silent about things that matter."

— Martin Luther King Jr

5. ***Prevent enemies of democracy to triumph:*** "All that is necessary for the triumph of evil is for good men to do nothing."

— Edmund Burke

Article 19

Qualifications of Politicians

Dictionary states that politician is a person who is experienced in politics which is the art or science of governance. Often, some persons who have become leaders of some groups of people or joined a political party or formed a political party or organized some protests or did some social service, call themselves politicians. These activities are not enough to claim that they have a recognized qualification in the art or science of governance. Therefore, Indian democracy is managed mostly (if not fully) by persons who are not qualified in the art or science of governance.

Even worse, in addition to lack of qualification in the art or science of governance, many political leaders have at least some of the 14 serious disqualifications mentioned below:

Sworn affidavits of 4,827 MPs and MLAs elected in 2009 showed that as many as 724 (14%) had serious criminal charges against them (Article 2). Shockingly, 30% of ministers in the present central government (more than double the proportion among MPs!!) had filed affidavits that they had criminal cases against them (Deccan Chronicle dated 08-06-15). If confirmed, this is a serious disqualification for a leader of democracy.

Moreover, this raises four important questions. Knowing that Constitution had put a bar on criminals getting registered as voters or becoming MPs/MLAs: (1) why did these suspected criminals stick on to their unlawful positions without taking prior or quick action to clear their innocence? (2) why government, legal experts and hon'ble judges did not fulfill their moral responsibility to the Constitution to quickly clear the doubt and ensure that illegal situations do not continue? (3) why do political parties field suspected criminals for election? and (4) why are people so dumb and callous that they tolerate being governed by suspected criminals, justifying the remark that "A nation of sheep gets a government of wolves"?

Higher their level in the hierarchy the more distant politicians are from people. Moreover, from leaders they transform themselves into bosses and feel smug and exhilarated. They "dictate" to other elected leaders, civil society leaders and professional experts in governance instead of patiently listening to them to ascertain problems and their views, with an open mind. These are serious disqualifications for a leader of democracy.

Some politicians cleverly manipulate creation of caste, linguistic, religious and other group conflicts as well as cliques and other situations to safeguard their selfish interests and to promote dependency on them among people, instead of sincerely helping them to enjoy peace and freedom and have a reasonably good quality of life. Higher their manipulating efficiency the stronger and dictatorial they become. Some of them become faction leaders to increase their bargaining power, ignoring that in this manner they are acting against unity and national integration. These activities are serious disqualifications for a leader of democracy.

Political leaders are openly exhilarated when people go to them with "begging bowl" or at least hang around them (often with garlands or tempting offerings, sometimes immoral) and worship them. Modesty, humility, simplicity, sincerity of purpose and an ethics of care for aam admi steadily decrease with their ascendancy in power. They do not believe in the dictum "serve and deserve respect." These are serious disqualifications for a leader of democracy.

There are many instances of hypocrisy in which their speech and actions are contrary to (1) needs and aspirations of people who elected them, (2) ideology of their party and (3) national interests. Sometimes their actions contradict their own views expressed for public consumption. All such hypocrisy are serious disqualifications for a leader of democracy.

"Deception is a pillar of Indian politics. Election promises are an elaborate exercise in deception." (Deccan Chronicle dated 19.12.13, page 8). Such deceptions are serious disqualifications for a leader of democracy.

Previous President of India expressed concern and disappointment at the "eroding commitment among the legislators." Deterioration in commitment is a serious disqualification for a leader of democracy.

Craving for higher emoluments, entitlements and privileges of political power instead of setting an example of simple life style without greed, is a serious disqualification for a leader of democracy.

According to a TV report on 21.09.12, in the context of allegations against a central minister about immoral activity, an MP said "Where is the question of morality when we have a majority?" What is worse, none of the other political leaders protested. Such devaluation of morality is another serious disqualification for a leader of democracy.

Faced with allegations of financial bungling in a trust formed by him, a central minister told his followers that it was time to "replace the pen with blood" (DNA dated 18.10.12). Shockingly, none of the other political leaders protested against making such threats. Both intolerance of criticism leading to threats to injure or kill others and acceptance of such intolerance of colleagues are serious disqualifications for a leader of democracy.

An MP threatened to unleash rapists on members of another party. He also advised his supporters to slit throats of opposition workers and asked village women to use kitchen vegetable cutters to slit their throats (The Hindu dated 02.07.14, page 10). Such gross intolerance of other political parties and lack of control over emotions are serious disqualifications for a leader of democracy.

MPs and MLAs protest mostly when they (or their parties) are criticized – rarely for issues of importance to the country or people. Being motivated by emotions instead of welfare of the country is a serious disqualification for a leader of democracy.

A politician spends lakhs to get elected. Some of those elected have become much richer quickly. For some politicians election was like a roaring business with chances for making huge "profits." Inability to suppress greed is common among some politicians. Greed and replacing "social service approach" by "a businesslike approach" are serious disqualifications for a leader of democracy.

Abuse of power by politicians for selfish interests is so common that number of pages will be required to discuss these. Abuse of power has also been done to ensure that bills, such as Lok Pal bill and women's quota bill, which ensure ethical practices, were inordinately delayed or blocked in parliament. Abuse of power is a serious disqualification for a leader of democracy.

Many instances of intolerance, double standards and wayward behavior of politicians have been reported from time to time. They have not realized that their uncontrolled attitudes and actions have given repeated death blows to democracy. Editorial of Deccan Chronicle (10.12.12) highlights wayward behavior by politicians and its consequence as follows: "On paper we have the rule of law, but what is visible most to people is the culture of impunity surrounding the political class. Even small fry politicians throw their weight around, routinely break laws, and take pride in doing so. They feel laws and regulations are meant for ordinary mortals, and flouting these is a measure of their own importance. Top leaders of different parties don't crack down hard on criminal behavior by their colleagues......... If a way is not found to rein in such politicians, we simply cannot run a democracy." Ironically, this implies that politicians became enemies of democracy — ***protectors of law themselves becoming destroyers of law!!***

Editorial of another newspaper (DNA dated 13.02.14) has highlighted wayward behavior by politicians as follows: "Politicians, who routinely mourn the fate of parliamentary democracy, when under attack from judicial activism and civil society protests, should spare us the pretence. The worst attack Parliament is facing is from within. Parliamentary democracy — that sacrosanct idea of the people electing their representatives every five years to frame laws on their behalf — is in danger: " This implies for the <u>second time</u> that politicians became enemies of democracy — ***destroying the main pillar of democracy instead of strengthening it!!***

The above aspects, particularly political leaders not having qualifications in the art or science of governance and having serious disqualifications for leader of democracy, depict the <u>twenty-seventh</u> and very serious <u>obstacle</u> which resulted in a distorted and ineffective democracy.

It is universally accepted that professional approach is essential to manage a large organization. This is even more required for efficient governance of a country because of modern day complexities and frequent changes which need skillful attention, besides need to tackle many pulls and pressures, both from within and outside the country. In India also, need for professional approach for efficient governance has been recognized and qualified and specially trained personnel have been functioning for many years in different fields which together ought to have contributed to good governance. But, their efforts have been nullified because of lack of professional approach by politicians with other interests who control all professionals. Even worse, hardly any thought was given to rectify this illogical and topsy-turvy situation. Such continuous diversion of professional activities by politicians implies for the <u>third time</u> that politicians became enemies of democracy – ***hindered professional governance instead of promoting it*** for efficient governance!!

Even though Constitution gives right to any person to occupy any position of governance, qualifications, experience, duties and responsibilities have been prescribed for each position. Most illogically, the only exceptions are for elected representatives even though they are in the highest responsible positions. This impropriety becomes more glaring and risky because many of them have to exercise control over activities carried out by professionals in different fields with prescribed qualifications, experience, duties and responsibilities.

It has not been realized that this damaging omission in prescribing duties and responsibilities to ministers, MPs and MLAs has not led to anarchy only because officers in all other positions have prescribed qualifications, duties and responsibilities!! Moreover, the strong sense of discipline which these officers had developed had prevented them from revolting against illogical supervision by persons (a) without qualifications in the art or science of governance and (b) without prescribed duties and responsibilities.

A historical approach shows how a change in mind set has occurred among politicians and bureaucrats. Soon after independence our leaders, without any facilities or time for acquiring necessary qualifications, had filled the vacuum in top levels of governance by working hard with an open mind, good intentions and determination to build the nation. For this, they wisely made proper use of the qualified and experienced ICS cadre (which the British had built up). To augment such capacities, they created a similarly qualified and trained IAS cadre and involved them also as their partners in governance with mutual understanding and respect. To meet the need for other professional management, other cadres were also built up. They created a chain of scientific institutions to give scientific support to development. In this wise manner, they did not allow their lack of qualifications and experience in governance to ruin the country.

Unfortunately, after majority of wise and committed politicians left the scene, a change in mind set occurred among political leaders. Most of the remaining old leaders were forced to support new leaders who were interested in amassing wealth and were determined to use even foul means to hold on to power and wealth. At present, most political leaders also suffer from at least some serious disqualifications mentioned earlier in this article.

Even worse, instances of ignoring advice of professionally qualified and experienced senior government officers became quite common. To gain their compliance, politicians cleverly adopted two strategies. They enticed some of them to form a politician-cum-bureaucrat nexus to gain benefits for this nexus and their political party. Those who did not fall in line were shunted to less important positions and harassed regularly (Article 7 gives some details). By adopting these two strategies, these politicians destroyed the innate character and strength of our system of governance, without realizing the serious harm they have done to the backbone of our governance system. This serious destruction implies for the <u>fourth time</u> that politicians became enemies of democracy – those ***who were expected to build the system became destroyers of the backbone of the system!!***

Mahatma Gandhi, who led the fight for independence, was keen to have swaraj (self governance) by people. Regrettably, over time, politicians gave less and less attention to his views on self governance by people. They preferred to become masters of people, by cleverly using the pretext of democracy. This implies for the <u>fifth time</u> that politicians became enemies of democracy – ***became masters of people instead of servants of people,*** as required in a democracy!!

The serious damage done by these enemies of democracy is highlighted in an editorial in Deccan Chronicle dated 11.08.17: "It is no secret that......the stumbling block in the nation's progress has been the political class while ordinary Indians – farmers, workers, jawans, teachers, scientists, and industrialists and traders – have made noteworthy contributions to project this country to the rank of leading nations of the world." "As a class, our politicians have engendered both corruption and divisiveness, contrary to the values of the independence movement for which millions of Indians made heroic sacrifices." Instead of working hard for welfare of people and making sacrifices they took credit for what others have done, amassed wealth and enjoyed like kings. This implies for the <u>sixth time</u> that politicians became enemies of democracy – ***taking credit for what others have done instead of working hard for welfare of people.***

Lack of professional approach, non-allotment of duties and responsibilities for top political leaders, destruction of the backbone of our governance system and political leaders becoming enemies of democracy constitute the <u>twenty-eighth</u> and very serious <u>obstacle</u> which resulted in a distorted and ineffective democracy.

It is a matter for serious concern that there are at least six solid reasons for concluding that politicians, by their greed for power and selfish attitudes and actions, gave repeated death blows to democracy and became enemies of democracy. Consequently, parliament, with members who became enemies of democracy, has qualified itself for self destruction. Moreover, as pointed out in Article 6, the system has the basic defect that the political party which forms the government also controls the parliament because of having majority. This defective system allows dictatorial attitude in the party and the government and defeats the very purpose of having parliament as a pillar of democracy. This basic defect itself justifies abolition of the present parliamentary system. It is pertinent that Article 15 also had emphasized the need to abolish parliament because of three more reasons: (a) it lacked dignity and guts to punish government for breaking promises more than thousand times, accountability and an ethics of care for aam admi, (b) has a distorted and unhealthy representation of people with vast majority of its members being crorepatis and (c) the present democracy has deteriorated from a flawed to a pseudo democracy. Other great advantages of this abolition are (1) enormous amounts will be saved which can be used for welfare of people and (2) large areas of prime land and buildings will become available for public use. These strong multiple reasons demand immediate abolition of parliament. An alternative system which is much better and cheaper is discussed in later articles.

Following jokes about politicians are thought provoking:

* I have come to the conclusion that politics is too serious a matter to be left to the politicians.

– Charles de Gaulle

* Politician is a fellow who will lay down your life for his country.

– Texas Guinan

* Politicians are the same all over. They promise to build a bridge even where there is no river.

– Nikita Khrushchev

* Politics is the gentle art of getting votes from the poor and campaign funds from the rich, by promising to protect each from the other.

– Oscar Ameringer

* What do politicians do when faced with a calamity? Make speeches, do aerial surveys and steal credit from those who took risks and worked hard to solve problems.

– Anonymous

* Politicians are like mosquitoes – they not only suck our blood but also help disease agents (mafia) to ruin our health (life)

– Anonymous

* What happens if a politician drowns in a river? That is pollution.

What happens if all of them drown? That is solution!!

– Anonymous

* We hang the petty thieves and appoint the great ones to public office.

– Aesop

Article 20

Representation through Political Parties

When a political party manages to form a government its total share of votes may at best be 35% of adult population, often much less (Article 2). This falls much short of the target of more than 50% to make them representative of total adult population. For example, even after spectacular success in 2014 elections, the main ruling party has support of only 31% of electorate!! What makes such non-representation worse and questionable is that vast majority of these 31% supporters consisted of irresponsible voters who: (a) voted in droves and shirked their individual responsibility, (b) sold their vote, (c) allowed themselves to be intimidated, and (d) preferred persons of their own caste and included only a negligible minority who voted responsibly (Articles 1 and 2). If political parties can have support of only a minority of the electorate, of which responsible voters form only a negligible proportion, how can a party system for governance be justified?

Hardly any political party has effective internal democracy. How can parties which do not have respect for internal democracy safeguard democracy in the country?

Further, even the elected persons are not free to express their opinions frankly to support needs and aspirations of people because of being subservient to their party and use of whip while voting. If there is no party system, elected persons can act with freedom to ensure peoples' welfare.

There are talented persons in political parties. If only they were encouraged (or at least allowed) to think and act giving more priority to national interest than to party interest, the 100 shocking and shameful situations pointed out in Article 15 could have been avoided. A pertinent example is that Dr. Manmohan Singh saved the country from financial collapse when he was allowed to act. But, later on, he lost freedom to act and earned the unsavory reputation of being a man without his own ideas!! Elected leaders (even if talented) can be either puppets in the hands of a coterie within the party or victims of coalition politics. If there is no party system, talented representatives will be able to act keeping benefit for the country in mind.

Another serious drawback of party system is that the large gold mines of talents outside the party in power have seldom been made use of!! These can be used for benefit of the country if there is no party system.

Important legislations are manipulated by the party in power with an eye on votes. In this dismal situation which shows lack of ethics of care for people, how can political parties justify their existence as makers of law for people? If there is no party system, legislations with an eye on votes will not occur.

Party interests get much higher priority than country's interests. This diversion of interest led to 100 shocking and shameful situations for the country (Article 15). But political parties did not bother to take any action – did not even question about these in parliament. If there is no party system, such callous neglect of country's interest will not arise.

Most parties have large army of grass root level workers. The main (or only) interest of these workers is safeguarding party interests even by illegal actions. They often start inter party disputes and quarrels. Resort to violence is quite common and even murders have occurred. Now the country has the burden of tackling problems created by these workers with conflicting ideologies and without any vision about national interests. At present, some fringe elements of a party have taken the law into their hands and committed lynching and even murders because of intolerance. Government seems to have lost control. It is possible that political parties may have created Frankensteins over which they will have no control in future. All these can be prevented if there is no party system.

A similar situation prevails among college students who are carried away by party interests and create campus problems. Attention of these young minds is diverted from their studies and a positive attitude to peoples' problems to a negative one of raving and fighting for party interests. If there is no party system, diversion of interest from studies and fights among college students can be avoided.

These young minds are thrilled to copy some undesirable behaviour and attitudes of present day politicians (listed in Article 19). When these fertile minds grow up in this background they will imbibe undesirable traits. They will become faction leaders, manipulators and traders of hatred. This explosive situation can lead to many undesirable outcomes in future. These undesirable developments can be avoided if there is no party system.

Political parties use their large army of grass root level workers to cleverly manipulate creation of caste, linguistic, religious and other group conflicts as well as cliques, crimes and other situations to safeguard their selfish interests.

They are also used for spreading rumours. Top leaders of parties do not curb criminal behaviour of members and workers. Thus, political parties are responsible for crimes and creation of hatred and violence in many parts of the country. Crime, hatred and violence will be reduced to a large extent and peace will prevail if there is no party system.

Another problem is that their hero worship has led to many unfortunate situations such as blindly supporting undesirable or ill planned or criminal activities of their heroes and side tracking of honest persons who could have helped the country. These can be prevented if there is no party system.

While people are suffering from hunger and poverty, some political parties spend huge amounts to celebrate party events. If in power, they manipulate to use tax payers' money for these celebrations. For example, UPA-2 government spent about Rs. 30 lakhs for hosting a dinner for their third anniversary bash. Atrociously, this single meal cost Rs. 7,700 per head as compared Rs. 22.42 and Rs. 28.6 considered sufficient by Planning Commission for total daily expenses of the poor in rural and urban areas respectively!! "Taxpayers' money was treated as if it was the party's to burn" (Deccan Chronicle dated 01.10.12). If there is no party system, all these (and some more hidden misuses of money) can be avoided.

As stated by Chief Information Commission, six major political parties are "substantially financed" by central government (DNA dated 04.06.13, front page). Large amounts are also spent on providing security to top political leaders, besides deputing many police officials. If there is no party system, public funds spent to support political parties can be used for benefit of people and diversion of police from their normal duties can be avoided.

"Illegal money circulates at every level in every party." (Deccan Chronicle dated 25.01.12) Political parties, being beneficiaries of black money, are a root cause for its creation and sustenance. Abolition of party system will lead to substantial reduction in black money.

Another serious problem is creation of duel power centres (multiple in case of coalition governments) which lead to obstacles and delays in decision making. These can be avoided if there is no party system.

An editorial in Deccan Chronicle dated 04.12.12 also highlights harm done by party system: "The trouble with us is we have become too politicized a society and cannot look beyond our nose. The culprits are political parties, not the people." If there is no party system, distracting politicization of society will not happen.

In a TV discussion, a former police commissioner stated that police have now become an "armed militia of the politicians in power." (Deccan Chronicle dated 06.02.13, page 8). "Today, our political leaders not only want the police to do their dirty work but also to collect money for them." Abolition of party system will free police from malignant and suffocating political control and improve law and order situation in the country by leaps and bounds.

Political parties have to amass huge amounts of money to fight elections. For this, illegal activities and generation of black money which harm the country are resorted to. Use of money also leads to dishonest voting in elections. This dismal situation can be avoided if there is no party system.

These important aspects constitute the <u>twenty-ninth</u> and most serious <u>obstacle</u> which resulted in a distorted and ineffective democracy.

To overcome this serious obstacle, we have to seriously and objectively ask ourselves whether having party system helps or hinders democracy.

It may be argued that having political parties helps in two ways: (a) they can serve as peoples' voice as their representatives and (b) provide a check on misgovernance. But, both can be done effectively (unlike at present) by efficient elected representatives without forming political parties (for example paragraph 4 of this article).

Moreover, these claims have not been realized. With regard to (a), representativeness has been denied because a party can at best get only less than 35% of votes, often much less (Article 2). With regard to having a check on misgovernance, these articles show that they have instead become a root cause of misgovernance!! As many as 100 instances of unquestioned shameful and shocking situations showing callousness for peoples' welfare (Article 15) confirm that political parties have not only failed miserably in exercising this check but by their connivance encouraged and is encouraging continuation of many shameful situations: e.g., helping the rich and not the poor and reduction in press freedom.

Even if party system can succeed in providing proper checks on governance, another basic question is: how can political parties justify their position under a democracy when (a) they failed to become representatives because they got only less than 35% of votes cast, despite getting about 90% of votes by using caste manipulations, money, threats etc., and (b) they do not have internal democracy?

Evidently, there is no real advantage in having party system. On the other hand, it can be reemphasized that abolishing it has the following 17 advantages discussed in this article.

If political parties are abolished:

1. Elected persons can act with freedom to ensure peoples' welfare.

2. Talented elected representatives will be allowed to act keeping benefit for the country in mind.

3. Large gold mines of talents outside political parties can be used for benefit of the country.

4. Legislations with an eye on votes will not occur.

5. Callousness in preventing at least 100 shocking and shameful situations for the country due to diversion to party interest will not arise.

6. Creation of large army of grass root level workers by political parties has led to massive diversion from peoples' interest to party interests and has resulted in conflicts and crime. Political parties may have created Frankensteins over which they will not have control in future? These can be prevented.

7. Hero worship of party leaders has led to many unfortunate situations such as blindly supporting undesirable or ill planned or criminal activities of their heroes and side tracking of honest and efficient leaders. These can be avoided.

8. Diversion of interest from studies and peoples' interests to party interests among college students and resulting campus violence can be avoided.

9. When youngsters with party interests and hero worship of political leaders grow up they are likely to imbibe some undesirable traits and become faction leaders, manipulators and traders of hatred. These undesirable developments can be avoided.

10. Because political parties manipulate creation of caste, linguistic, religious and other group conflicts as well as cliques, they are often responsible for crimes, hatred and violence in many parts of the country. These can be avoided.

11. Wasting huge amounts of money on party celebrations can be avoided.

12. Public funds need not be wasted for funding political parties and security of politicians. Diversion of police for political activities can be stopped.

13. Will lead to substantial reduction in black money because political parties are beneficiaries of black money and a root cause for its creation and sustenance.

14. Creation of duel power centres (multiple in case of coalition governments) which lead to problems, obstacles and delays in decision making can be avoided.

15. Because of political parties, society has become too politicized and cannot look beyond their nose. Such distracting politicization of society can be avoided.

16. Will free police from malignant and suffocating political control and improve law and order situation in the country by leaps and bounds.

17. Political parties have to amass huge amounts of money to fight elections. For this, illegal activities and generation of black money are resorted to. Use of money also leads to dishonesty in voting. These can be avoided.

This objective analysis clearly shows that advantages of not having party system far outweigh advantages of having it, even if they can provide an effective check on government (which has not happened). Party system becomes even alarming and harmful when members of political parties suffer from many disqualifications and have become enemies of democracy (Article 19).

If parliament is abolished as strongly urged at the end of Articles 15 and 19, there is no need for political parties.

All these demand abolition of party system.

A better alternative system with more effective checks on governance is discussed in later articles.

Article 21

Antidemocratic Approach and Disrespect to Parliament

After 2014, many reforms were started in quick succession. Prior approval of parliament or subsequent ratification by it was not obtained for these important reforms with serious national implications. Repeated disrespect of parliament became a practice. These are death blows to democracy.

Speed thrills but kills. This is a caution for drivers of vehicles. It applies to drivers of governance also. Reforms planned and implemented in a hurry can result in damaging failures and/or setting the clock back. What is worse for our democracy is that this speed has resulted in many antidemocratic practices and decisions which have not been questioned.

First of these hurried reforms was abolition of Planning Commission. This decision was taken without adequate discussion among experts or any public debate or debate in parliament. Besides being antidemocratic, this decision questions whether government has lost interest in planning systematically.

Within a short period, this was followed by a spate of reforms such as Swatch Bharat Mission, Make in India, Skill Development, Smart Cities and Digital India without adequate discussion among experts or any public debate or debate in parliament as required in a democracy. Yet another antidemocratic feature is that no systematic attempts have been made to inform the public about the progress of these schemes.

Successful completion of these reforms requires sustained commitment till their completion. Absence of periodic progress reports on each reform indicates reluctance to keep people informed. This is antidemocratic.

Neglecting the sustained attention required for these important schemes in progress (as pointed out earlier), demonetization of currency notes for Rs. 500 and Rs. 1,000, which rocked the country, was resorted to in a hurry. While this also was in progress it was followed by inconsistent and confusing announcements almost every day about "cash less India" and "less cash India" schemes and repetition of Digital India. These indicate that democratic approaches were not followed.

Jumping from one scheme to another within a short period without adequate discussions and approval of parliament and absence of proper planning, implementation and concurrent evaluation of schemes highlighted failure of democracy.

It was well known that government machinery is quite sluggish in implementing projects. Thrusting of so many additional schemes on it in a hurry, that too without adequate discussions with those who have to execute these, highlights that democratic approaches were not followed. Lack of preparation of the management infrastructure made matters worse. This tantamounts to putting the cart before the horse and experimenting with public money in an antidemocratic manner.

Whether demonetization of currency has achieved its aims or not has not been properly evaluated even after two years. What is evident is that the manner in which it was thrust overnight on people illustrates antidemocratic planning and disrespect to parliament as illustrated below:

It was well known that three attempts had been made earlier for demonetization of currency. First mistake vis-a-vis democratic planning was ignoring, without any discussions, the lessons from the attempts which did not succeed. While the first two attempts had failed, the third was abandoned because a high power committee set up by government in 2013 recommended against it. If the government felt that the situation has changed, it should have set up another high power committee to make a deep study and make confidential recommendations to ensure the required secrecy. But, it seems, government did not follow any democratic procedure because it felt (without any discussion) that secrecy could not be assured. For the same reason, the government did not obtain prior approval of parliament. For an undisclosed reason its ratification by parliament later on was not done even though secrecy was no longer required. Ignoring the earlier recommendation against demonetization by a high power committee, preferring to bypass the democratic approach and disrespecting parliament are serious death blows to democracy.

Moreover, it was known that only about 6% of black money was stocked in cash and demonetization can at best get rid of only this negligible part of black money. The government ought to have discussed this aspect and abandoned the scheme which can have only a negligible impact on black money even after causing immense hardship to people. This was the second mistake for a democracy.

Spreading misinformation that the government had planned demonetization of currency to get rid of all black money while it was only attempting to get rid of 6% of black money was the third mistake which was antidemocratic (misleading people).

About 86% of currency in the country was in denominations of Rs. 500 and Rs. 1000. Withdrawing these will create a huge cash vacuum and create chaos in the economy as well as prolonged hardship for people unless adequate number of new notes are printed and supplied before withdrawing old notes. No questions would have been asked because Reserve Bank of India has the right to introduce new notes at any time. Ignoring this need to prevent cash vacuum was the fourth mistake which caused enormous misery for people and was, therefore, antidemocratic. This defective approach is another blow to democracy which has welfare of people as its main aim.

For some unexplained reasons a new currency of Rs. 2000 was introduced. This posed problems for vast majority of people who need smaller denominations for daily use and for making needed purchases. This currency is not appropriate for paying daily wages to lakhs of workers. Moreover, this high denomination is likely to act against the aim of monetization because it made it easier for those who want to stock money secretly. Government did not use all this information to decide on the type and number of currency notes to be printed. This is the fifth mistake in planning which failed to meet the needs of people which is paramount in a democracy.

Unsystematic, defective and antidemocratic approach was all too common. This can be illustrated by other examples also. Skill Development project was started because corporate establishments faced shortage of skilled staff. In other words, this was planned to help these rich establishments. A democratic approach should have given highest priority to projects which will immediately meet the felt needs of people e.g., help millions of unskilled and semi skilled persons who were suffering due to unemployment.

Smart Cities and Digital India also were not felt needs of people most of whom live in rural areas. Under democracy, Smart Villages deserved higher priority.

There are number of examples of damaging production in India despite tom toming about the new "Make in India" project. For example, "India's state-owned aerospace giant is facing a crisis: it doesn't have enough fighter jet orders to sustain the massive production facilities." "Between 2004 and 2014 HAL received orders of Rs. 1.06 lakh crore…" But "between 2014 and 2018, it received orders of just Rs. 26,570 crores (India Today dated 29.10.18, pages 44-45). This huge reduction in orders is despite acute shortage of jet aircraft for defence of the country. What is worse, HAL was denied a chance to produce Rafale aircraft in India by giving this opportunity to a new firm which has no experience in producing aircrafts!! Questions of possible long delay in production in India and risk in quality of aircraft produced by inexperienced organistons have not received any attention of government and even of SC which studied the problem. Another example is: India's beef producers who are the biggest beef exporters in the world and major employers of workers in India suddenly faced many risks and may become extinct in some states because of insecurity (more details in Article 22).

There are four glaring defects common to all these reforms. (1) These were not discussed adequately with Niti Ayog which was set up to perform some of the functions of the dissolved Planning Commission. (2) The management infrastructure was not briefed and trained if necessary to implement the schemes, (3) Concurrent evaluation which could have helped to make midterm correction was not even planned (4) None of these schemes had prior approval of parliament or subsequent ratification by it.

There are many more instances of bypassing parliament in an autocratic manner. The following examples illustrate this:

During the last two years, many bills were introduced in parliament as money bills to bypass Rajya Sabha in which the ruling party did not have a majority (Deccan Chronicle dated 24.07.17).

Instead of passing bills in parliament, ordinances were issued number of times. President of India cautioned the government against using the ordinance route to bring in laws, saying it should be used only in a compelling situation (Deccan Chronicle dated 24.07.17).

An ordinance amending the Enemy Property Act was sent to the President four times without clearance from the Cabinet. (The Times of India dated 24.07.17, page 8). May be there are more instances of bypassing the Cabinet. For instance, some of the decisions regarding demonetization appear to have been taken without Cabinet clearance. Bypassing Cabinet is anti-democratic.

These are triple blows to democracy viz., repeated attempts to bypass parliament by taking the ordinance route, misuse of money bill provision to bypass the upper house and bypassing the Cabinet.

All these aspects discussed earlier illustrate an unsystematic and antidemocratic tendency to attempt a spate of reforms (a) ignoring whether these are justified by a democratic approach, (b) without proper planning and (c) without preparing the management infrastructure to implement and evaluate these concurrently. Ignoring the checks provided under democracy such as discussions with experts and within the management machinery and debates in both houses of parliament shows a serious weakness in the functioning of the democratic system. This also confirms the remarks in Articles 5 and 6 that the systems of government formation and government functioning show only lip sympathy to democracy but actually result in a type of subtle and concealed dictatorship.

During a 10 year period government had broken promises given by it during replies to questions in parliament or discussions on bills and motions 1,024 times (Article 6). Over a longer time period such disrespect to parliament could have happened many more times. Bypassing parliament while implementing each of the new multiple reforms is another example in the series of disrespects to parliament. Disrespect to parliament more than thousand times and in a number of ways shows that disrespect to parliament was obviously intentional. These are severe blows to democracy.

All this has also raised the question of abolishing a parliament which has tolerated disrespect more than thousand times.

The short cut manner in which views and support of people are obtained through social media is defective. The well recognized systems of discussions and evaluation which can study matters in depth and evaluate achievements respectively have been replaced by exchange of superficial tit bits through social media like twitter, face book etc. Thus important decisions are justified by superficial tit bits and not by in depth studies and discussions by experts and parliament. The flimsy views superficially expressed by casual participants in social media are given much more importance than that of parliament and experts – a mockery of democracy and big blows to parliament and experts.

What is worse, this social media system can be cleverly misused by some leaders to get wide popular support from millions of people who, guided by their emotional admiration for these leaders, will casually and effortlessly express their views without an in depth study of the issue and without explaining the reasons for these views. If this is not curbed immediately by parliament and ignored completely by government for serious discussions and debates, it can result in a big blow to efficiency of democracy. Persons indulging in making superficial and irresponsible remarks in social media about governance have to be warned that they should confine their remarks to light social issues only (as intended by that media) and that viewing governance in a casual and superficial manner will lead to serious consequences for the country for which they will be responsible.

The social media has also created many serious problems by spreading hatred among people and poisoning young minds. Sad to say, emotional problems are spreading like wild fire and anger, fear, suspicion, resentment, frustration, prejudice and malice are all too common. A thoughtless or misleading or saucy or mischievous message through social media can provide the trigger which suddenly blows things out of control. Often posts in social media go viral and spread rumours leading to violence and loss of peace. For instance, "An objectionable Face book post by a Class IX student in Baduria, a neighbouring town, was said to have sparked off the violence that continued unabated for a week from July 3 night, resulting in one death." (India Today dated 24.07.17). Another example of social media going viral to spread hate was followed by the murder of a labourer. It was "filmed and the video was uploaded on social media. His crime was a supposed act of "love jihad" of which the man, who is a grandfather, had no inkling!!" The video of the supposed gruesome incident "went viral on social media with those originally posting it doing so perhaps to pass on a chilling message of communal hate" (Deccan Chronicle dated 11.12.17, page 8).

Social media across all platforms is being used to undermine transparency, accountability and trust in our democracy (The Times of India dated 18.10.17). The newspaper reports that "one study has identified the following six key areas where social media has become a direct threat to our democratic ideals: (1) Creates bubbles of one-sided information and opinions, perpetuating biased views and diminishing opportunities for healthy discourses. (2) Spreads false or misleading information. (3) The idea that likes or retweets can be used to measure support of a person, message or organization creates a distorted system of evaluating information and provides a false pulse on the popularity of certain views or persons. This is compounded by how challenging it is to distinguish legitimately expressed opinions from those generated by trolls and bots. (4) Such trolls and bots, disguised as ordinary citizens, have become a weapon of choice for governments and political leaders to shape online conversations. (5) Manipulation, micro-targeting and behavioral change through disguised advertising. (6) These platforms can amplify hate speech, terrorist appeals, and racial and sexual harassment. The study calls upon social media companies to help navigate the serious threats posed by their platforms." In an interview, Obama (former president of USA) "opined that the way people communicate via social media risked splintering society." (Deccan Chronicle dated 28.12.17, page10).

A thorough review of the social media system, including the issues pointed out above, has to be conducted and acted upon to come out of the rut and ensure a peaceful and efficient democracy.

These important aspects constitute the <u>thirtieth</u> and most serious <u>obstacle</u> which resulted in a distorted and ineffective democracy.

To overcome these antidemocratic aspects, steps should be taken to ensure that (a) no one can ignore the checks under the democratic system and act according to his/her whims in an autocratic manner, (b) parliament invariably exerts its authority to curb actions which cause disrespect to it and (c) social media does not lead to an inefficient democracy with violence and loss of peace. It is pertinent that checks can be effective only if majority of MPs who have to ensure compliance of these checks, are committed to these. As a safeguard against possible lack of commitment (as has happened now), an eminent independent authority other than politicians and government with adequate staff and other facilities should be entrusted with monitoring of these checks.

An alternative system which can overcome these problems is discussed in a later article.

Article 22

Stem the Rot Quickly to Prevent Chaos and Anarchy

This series of articles have emphasized that neglect of problems other than economic growth has led not only to worsening of peoples' problems but also to at least 100 shameful and shocking situations for the country (Article 15). Hundreds of farmers have committed suicide and lack of adequate remedial measures by government have created other humanitarian problems also. What are worse, violent attacks and even murders due to intolerance, curbs on freedom of expression, interference in the private domain of people, denouncement of core values of Indian civilization and dictatorial tendencies (illustrated below) are death blows to democracy and are leading to chaos and anarchy in the country.

When writer Nayantara Sehgal returned her Sahitya Akademi award in protest, in a statement titled "The Unmaking of India" she stated: "In memory of the Indians who have been murdered, in support of all Indians who uphold the right to dissent, and of all the dissenters who live in fear and uncertainty, I am returning my Sahitya Akademi Award." (The Times of India dated 07.10.15).

Citing the killing of some writers and rationalists, she said that India is going backwards by rejecting our great idea of cultural diversity and debate. (Deccan Chronicle dated 07.10.15).

Writers Shashi Deshpande, Ashok Vajpeyi, Sara Joseph and Rahman Abbas joined the protest. Protests increased day by day.

Sara Joseph stated: "An alarming situation is being created in the country in all spheres of life" (Deccan Chronicle dated 11.10.15).

Anand Patwardhan was disappointed that about 31% of Indians "brought to power an extremely narrow-minded ideology that contradicted the ethos of those who had fought for India's freedom." "The rapid rise of an armed lunatic fringe in our society is a real danger." He added that many ways are adopted to crush dissent – censorship, attacking and killing social activists and appointments of heads of key institutions on extraneous considerations ignoring merit. Fr. Prakash was upset that there is interference in the private domain of what people should eat and wear, what films they should see and whether or not an Indian girl can even be out late at night. (The Week dated 04.10.15, page 47).

Intolerance in some peaceful fields of entertainment which many people enjoy is becoming shamefully common. For example, ghazal (music) maestro Ghulam Ali was not allowed to perform in Mumbai; Sudheendra Kulkarni was smeared with black paint for organizing a book launch; Dr. Suma Sudhindra said: "it is time people opened their eyes. Music, books, art – these are the things that bring people together. We should be encouraging these activities, not hindering these." (Deccan Chronicle dated 13.10.15)

Film director Govind Nihalani said: "These are worrying times. There is a tremendous unease in general over the recent incidents. One feels that very dark clouds are gathering over the cultural horizon of this country. We can see communal divide and polarization becoming more and more acute." (The Times of India dated 11.10.15)

Swaminathan Ankalesaria Aiyer has exposed some crucial aspects of the Dadri murder on mere suspicion: "The clincher is the refusal of BJP leaders to condemn the lynching by a Hindu mob of a Muslim in Dadri for supposedly eating beef – which is entirely legal. BJP apologists have performed verbal acrobatics to somehow avoid condemning this murder." (The Times of India dated 11.10.15)

He further cautioned: "The Dadri murder is not just a moral but economic issue. Fear of RSS goons has forced many shop keepers to stop selling even buffalo meat. Transporters of cattle are fearful of arrest and worse. India has a large leather and footwear industry employing millions of workers (including many dalits). All these face shortages of hides and rising prices that make them uncompetitive in exports. Farmers have always sold aged cows, oxen and buffaloes in abattoirs. Indeed, this has enabled India to become the biggest beef exporter in the world. Suddenly this large industry, a major employer, has become very risky and may become extinct in some states. The price of aged cattle has crashed or gone to zero, diminishing the wealth of millions of cattle owners." Firstly, this shows indifference to welfare of millions of rural people who form the vast majority. This indifference is confirmed by lack of effective measures to prevent farmer suicides and non allocation of funds to create smart villages while spending huge amounts to develop 100 smart cities. Secondly, this is an instance of a huge "make in India" industry employing millions of workers and a major exporter being forced to wither away and questions the government's commitment to even its loudly proclaimed "make in India" project. These are other serious consequences of not taking proper action after the Dadri murder.

Editorial of India Today (19.10.15) supports these views: "The narrow politics propelling the cow agenda and ethnic vigilantism puts road blocks on Prime Minister Modi's drive on development. The mandate given to government by 2014 election was for development and not for reviving a brand of Hinduism adopted by some groups. The government will do well to remember that. Also, it should know that once you uncork the gene of religious tensions in a multicultural society like India, it is difficult to put it back. It will only hurtle India towards anarchy and chaos." Being confident that the government will remain silent, Hindutva groups like RSS, VHP, Shiv Sena and Rama Sene have thoughtlessly uncorked the gene and contributed to creeping in of anarchy. If all of them do not use their ingenuity to re-cork the gene matters will go beyond their control.

In the context of all such interferences and curbs on freedom, L.K. Advani, a top visionary leader who had built up BJP, cautioned that an emergency like situation seems to be coming up.

There are violent acts of intolerance by people taking law into their hands. President of India cautioned: "the core values of India's civilization that celebrate diversity, plurality and tolerance should not be allowed to wither away." (The Times of India dated 08.10.15). But, effective deterrent action to punish the criminals and hate mongers has not been taken to ensure that respect for law is re-established and the core values of India's civilization do not wither away.

What is worse, instead of punishing the criminals, the victims of these criminals are punished. For example, a Regional Inspector in Regional Transport Office, Meerut was "physically assaulted by at least 50 BJP men after he refused to give in to "political pressure" from one of the agents" (The Times of India dated 02.01.17, page 11). Instead of praising the honest officer for doing his duty even after political pressure and punishing these men for taking law into their hands, the government suspended the honest officer three days later for "continuous complaints coming in against him and behavioural issues with the public due to which official work was being hampered."

All these show that government is unable to control criminal intolerance and anarchy that are creeping in due to allowing some extremists to take law into their hands and even glorify commitment of murders.

Are these not signs of anarchy coming up?

The worst damage is development of autocracy. "In the latest rankings of the Varieties of Democracy (V-DEM) Institute a research project that tries to evolve new measures of democracy, ***India's rank is seen dropping in the past four years,*** with a marked concentration of powers in the hands of one individual" (India Today dated 23.07.18, page 28).

In order to prevent publicity to its failures, government has resorted to muzzling the media. At a recent well attended panel discussion in Delhi Habitat Centre all participants expressed the view that the media scene in India was catastrophic because of the fear among journalists to criticize the present government. If journalists are so afraid, they will become irrelevant. The only solution they suggested was that journalists should stand up against the undesirable policies and actions of governments. This need was emphasized by President of India also. He said that the press will be failing in its duty if it does not ask questions to those in power. (The Times of India dated 26.05.17)

Fortunately for India, contrary to the widespread fear among journalists to criticize the present government there are some who are bold enough to question government. For example, Shobha De (a journalist and author) in an article in Deccan Chronicle dated 15.07.17 presented some illustrations which confirm the anti-democratic and intolerant situation which needs urgent correction. Referring to the denial of certificate to a documentary by Central Board of Film Certification, she stated that we are now living in a "world in which words like "Hindu," "cow," "Gujarat," "Hindu India" and "Hindutva" are considered potentially dangerous and incendiary." She further stated that when she asked a bureaucrat, whose father also was a bureaucrat, whether his experiences with minister log were qualitatively different from his father's, he laughed and said "My dad followed Indira G's diktats, and my batch follows Modi's. You cannot win against the system." Articles 5 and 6 have stressed that the systems of government formation and government functioning show only lip sympathy to democracy but actually result in a type of subtle and concealed dictatorship. This is confirmed by the above reply.

Another example of forthright exposure of the pitiable situation in India is an article by Antara Dev Sen, Editor of "The Little Magazine," in Deccan Chronicle dated 29.12.17, page 9. She wrote: A bunch of people sat exchanging sighs when Santa came up to them. "Why are you sad? he asked. "We don't have jobs," said one. We don't have food," said another. "We don't have a future for our children," "We don't have hospitals," "We toil in the fields all day, yet we don't get our dues." "The complaints went on." Santa smiled and consoled "… You will be safe. All of you will get jobs. Farmers will get their dues, and make big profits… Corruption will be finished off. You will have a good life – happy days are here." In anticipation of these good days promised, the bunch of people "…threw themselves into abject misery by following every word of their new leader." They did not complain that "they had even fewer jobs than before, farmers made bigger losses every day…their sick continued to die without health care and the future of their children remained bleak." They told Santa "softly after some years, it's so much worse than before. And we haven't got the Rs. 15 lakhs that you promised either." … Santa laughed. "…you still believe in Santa?" (*The moral from this story: It is important to realize that all political Santas are laughing like this at our blind belief in them.*)

Sen aptly added "We are a nation of the gullible. We want to believe, too lazy to use logic, too exhausted to think, we choose blind belief instead. We go with the flow, powered by mob mentality and guided by our biases." This seriously damaging gullibility of people is discussed further in Article 23 titled "Some unquestioned absurdities – Can the gift of the gab lead to mental slavery?"

A third example is an editorial in Deccan Chronicle dated 29.12.17 which boldly cautioned: "Meddling with people's lives must stop. Reactionary forces are seemingly trying to have a say in everything that people do – what they eat, how they dress, fall in love, worship or celebrate festivals."

A fourth example of boldly fulfilling the responsibility of exposing government to sustain democracy is a column in The Times of India dated 30.12.17, page 14 by Kanti Bajpai: "Prime Minister Narendra Modi promised he would promote a "Make in India" revolution. Nearly four years later, a manufacturing revolution is nowhere in sight. Make in India was supposed to not just boost manufacturing, it was also supposed to generate employment. Estimates show there has been virtually no jobs growth."

If more and more journalists and writers do not feel encouraged by such bold examples and come forward to fulfill their responsibility to question government, our already sinking democracy (Article 15) will be doomed.

It has to be re-emphasized that all the unchecked incidents of intolerance and disrespect for law as well as muzzling of the media, films and authors will lead to complete chaos and anarchy. The editorial of India Today mentioned earlier also cautioned that the present situation if not "corked" will ***only hurtle India towards anarchy and chaos.***

Moreover, Article 21 has pointed out that ignoring the checks provided under the democratic system is a serious weakness. Drastic changes are needed for this also.

All these exhortations give added justification and urgency to expedite drastic changes needed in our sinking democracy.

These important aspects constitute the <u>thirty-first</u> and most serious <u>obstacle</u> which resulted in a distorted and ineffective democracy.

Immediate action has to be taken to stem the rot before it results in chaos, anarchy and violent revolution.

Article 23

Some Unquestioned Absurdities – Can the Gift of the Gab Lead to Mental Slavery?

Professionally qualified, trained and experienced persons in different disciplines at different levels are essential to successfully manage any large complex organization. Governments also had recognized this need. For example, Union Public Service Commission (UPSC) in India selects officers who have the required basic qualifications and intellectual capacity to develop the functioning efficiency required. They are then given special training wherever necessary. During the process of selection, UPSC takes advice of professional experts in pertinent fields to ensure that selected persons have the best professional competence and intellectual capacity to develop the required functioning efficiency. The selected persons reach top levels after gaining working experience for many years.

Shockingly, these professionally qualified, trained and experienced officers at top levels are supervised and controlled by persons who have not been assessed to have (1) pertinent professional qualifications, (2) intellectual capacity to develop the required functioning efficiency, (3) special training and (4) long working experience!! Though this practice is obviously illogical and against principles of management, it has continued for years **because no one has questioned this** (first) **absurdity.**

A related paradox is that for higher education bright students prefer fields such as engineering, medicine, management, commerce etc. The duller students who cannot get admission for these preferred courses often become politicians and later on supervise and control the more intelligent persons and have the last laugh!! As a result, the bewildered former tend to fear the latter (politicians) and develop an inferiority complex and type of mental slavery (to the latter) despite superior intelligence. ***This second absurdity also has not been questioned.*** Psychological research (covering students, parents and teachers) is needed to understand this paradox. A possible reason may be that the former restricts himself/herself to a close circle and hardly engages in social work among people in general and, therefore, does not develop a wider vision which also helps to improve confidence.

Albert Einstein, one of the greatest thinkers and scientists had cautioned: "The important thing is not to stop questioning." But, the irony is that we have not even started questioning absurdities. Why? The next four paragraphs explain how politicians cleverly fooled both professionals and people to ensure that they are in a situation which does not allow questioning of absurdities.

Parliamentary democracy was started to save people from slavery to autocratic monarchs. With passage of time it deteriorated into a pseudo democracy in which a clique of power hungry political leaders replaced monarch and cleverly developed a slavish mentality among people, using the gift of the gab.

When political leaders observed the tremendous powers they have acquired, they started to fight among themselves for power. To survive in these fights they had to become cunning and clever strategists. They first utilized these two qualities to develop strength for fighting by joining together and forming political parties and gaining from group might and solidarity.

Political leaders who had become cunning and clever then used two strategies to remain in power: (1) they isolated professionals from the power structure at the highest level so that they do not have strength to fight or question absurdities, (2) using the gift of the gab, they mesmerized people to start hero worship and to get deeply involved in their political fights. This way they succeeded in diverting peoples' attention away from absurd situations.

By adopting these two clever strategies, they fooled both professionals and people to ensure that they ***do not question absurdities.***

Under the present system, brilliant top level officers had spent enormous amounts of time, efforts and money for acquiring basic qualifications, faced competitive selection, underwent special training and worked for many years to gain experience. But they were not allowed to use their expertise freely for efficient functioning because of being controlled by unqualified politicians. Ironically, they were not even given a chance to prove their worth to make sure that they do not pose a threat to politicians by more efficient performance. Allowing this cunning strategy which prevented more efficient performance by expert professionals is the ***third absurdity.*** This deliberate wastage of highly qualified and experienced professional expertise is a mockery of the system. This is the ***fourth absurdity.*** Shockingly, these two absurdities also have been accepted without questioning, Why?

Root cause for not questioning these contemptible situations is that political leaders, by becoming heroes using the gift of the gab, fooled people to believe the ***fifth absurdity*** that they had the super human capacity to effectively supervise and control professionally qualified, specially trained and experienced persons, that too in a variety of disciplines in which the political leaders had no knowledge!!

Political leaders also claimed that this supervision and control was necessary to ensure that professional managers listen to peoples' voice. The most obvious and effective method to ensure this was to give these brilliant professional managers the necessary additional training to listen to peoples' voice. Ignoring this solution is the *sixth absurdity.*

Instead, politicians diverted attention to the election system which they had cleverly created so that they can claim that they represent people. But, this has turned out to be a contemptible hollow claim as explained in Articles 1 and 2. Even in the highly praised Lok Sabha election in 2014, the ruling party got support of only a minority (31%) of the electorate and clearly showed that they were far away from representing majority of people. What is worse, even this minority support is of questionable quality because most of these voters had voted in an irresponsible manner (for example selling their votes), as explained in Article 1. Why was this obviously startling revelation of contemptible hollow claim ignored? Because, blind hero worship of politicians prevented people from opening their eyes to this obvious *seventh absurdity* of hollow claim also.

An *eighth absurdity* is the wrong belief that voters, among whom large proportions are illiterate or inadequately educated, have the capacity to judge and elect persons who can perform functions of governance efficiently!!

In the absence of this judging capacity, blind hero worship influenced election and political leaders with the gift of the gab gained. This has continued for years *because no one has questioned this ninth absurdity.*

These unquestioned contemptible absurdities favouring political leaders have led to prolonged mis-governance with lop sided priorities which made the rich richer. India has the dubious distinction of being the second most unequal economy in the world with 57 billionaires controlling 70% of the country's wealth (The Times of India dated 27.01.17, page 8). Number of rich persons (millionaires and even billionaires) has increased rapidly during 2015 to 2017. Crorepatis (owning more than 10 millions) increased by 23.5% in one year (2015) (Deccan Chronicle dated 21.12.17, page11) and the number of super rich grew by 12% in 2017 (The Times of India dated 14.02.18, page 21). In 2017, while India has 101 dollar billionaires, 96% adults have wealth below $10,000 (India Today dated 29-09-17). In contrast, vast majority of people has to struggle for basic necessities of life and have been forced to live without dignity, as second or third class citizens. Millions are suffering from poverty, hunger and lack of shelter at night while the rich live in palatial bungalows/flats, squander money and waste food. According to Global Hunger Index 2016, India was ranked a lowly 97 out of 118 developing countries. Even worse, its rank slipped from 83 to 97 in 16 years (The Times of India dated 13.10.16). Neighbours Sri Lanka, Bangladesh, Nepal and China are all ranked above India. Children suffering from malnutrition get low priority, if at all!! Highest priority is given for growth rate at the expense of important social priorities like education and health which are essential for good quality of life with dignity. All these are matters for serious concern.

Blind acceptance of the nine absurdities discussed above depicts a type of mental slavery to politicians which has continued for many years. Sadly, hardly anyone woke up from this stupor. What is worse, even the wish to come out of this mental slavery seems to be absent!!

Being accustomed to mental slavery, we have closed our eyes to another type of slavery also: "It's one of India's greatest shames and it is hidden in plain sight. In absolute terms, India has the largest number of modern-day slaves in the world, 18 million and counting. This includes bonded labour, human trafficking, forced marriages, women coerced into prostitution or badly paid menial work. The most vulnerable among these are the children." (Editorial in India Today dated 13.11.17).In the Global Slavery Index, compiled by Australia-based rights group Walk Free Foundation, India is among the top four offenders in percentage terms...... If mental slavery to politicians also is taken into account, India will most probably get the dubious distinction of topping the Global Slavery Index.

All these important aspects constitute the <u>thirty-second</u> (may be the most serious) <u>obstacle</u> which resulted in a distorted and ineffective democracy.

If you agree that a change in our sinking democracy which is based on the nine absurdities explained above is overdue, let us strive to make people aware of the need to join together to overcome hero worship and mental slavery to political leaders. Then set the ball rolling towards a peaceful revolution to free ourselves from mental slavery to politicians and achieve true democracy. A system of democracy which avoids mental slavery to politicians is discussed in Article 27.

To demonstrate that they have succeeded in getting rid of mental slavery to politicians people should demand setting up of a new Constituent Assembly to discuss and finalize all details of the comprehensive democracy without politicians outlined in Article 27 and appoint interim governments at the centre and in all states comprising of qualified and honest experts selected by it to govern the country after expiry of the current parliament till the comprehensive democracy is set up. ***Another step which can be taken effortlessly is to click NOTA option in coming elections.***

A caution: If we hesitate to put all our efforts on this peaceful revolution, a violent bloody revolution which is already looming in the horizon will engulf us soon!!

Let us be encouraged by the fact that Mahatma Gandhi (who got us independence from the mightiest empire by leading a non-violent movement) has shown us how even unbelievable changes can be achieved when ordinary people come together and use their hidden power to do extraordinary things.

Organizers of the peaceful revolution can learn the following lessons from the recent Jallikuttu protest: (a) Victory of the Jallikattu agitation within a few days shows that it is still possible for hundreds of thousands of people to rise unitedly and become a force so powerful and so swift that no power on earth can resist such peaceful agitations. (b) Eruption of violence after few days cautions that rowdy elements and/or vested interests can infiltrate to spoil a peaceful movement. Steps should be taken to guard against this and continue the peaceful revolution.

Note:

The gift of the gab: Ability to speak easily and confidently in a way that makes people want to listen to you and believe you.

This mesmerizing ability has often been misused to develop blind hero worship resulting in mind slavery and mockery of independent thinking resulting in sinking of our democracy.

Article 24

Summing Up

The main points brought out by the preceding articles are summed up in this article to provide a quick review which will provide a background for the remaining articles.

Article 1

Even after 70 years, most voters do not have the proper attitude of mind and capacity to use their right to vote independently and effectively to develop a sound democracy. It is better to confine voting to only voters who are interested in safeguarding democracy and make them vote.

Confining eligibility to adults only, as at present, will exclude large number of younger persons who are capable of balanced thinking and energetic action to safeguard democracy because of modern (technological) advances in education and knowledge environment.

NOTA option, which should have been respected as peoples' voice, has become meaningless. Only a guarantee from EC that such a clear expression of rejection of all candidates when none are suitable by majority of voters will lead to fresh election, in which the rejected candidates cannot take part, will help to get over the feeling of meaninglessness of NOTA option.

Article 2

Large proportions of voters make mockery of democracy by either not making independent choice or by "selling" votes. Voters who did not consciously fulfill their responsibility is likely to exceed 90%. Therefore, elected persons were supported only by a negligible minority who had honestly voted. Another mockery is that during last 50 years, number of women left out from electoral roll increased fourfold from the already large 15 millions to 68 millions, showing gross and increasing undervaluation of right of women to vote.

To really represent people an MP or MLA has to be elected by more than 50% of the electorate. ***Claim of most MPs and MLAs that they are representatives of people is void*** because they had support of much less than 50% of the electorate only. Consequently the ***parliament and assemblies they formed were void.*** Shockingly, EC and SC overlooked this fact despite having the relevant data to judge which elected persons represented more than 50% of the electorate.

Out of 543 MPs elected in 2009, majority of 78% had even mocked approval of only less than half of the electorate and did not qualify to be representatives. In 2014 elections, BJP had even mocked approval of only 31% of electorate!! Thus, its claim of being representatives of people is outright hollow.

It is likely that most candidates failed to satisfy this requirement because votes were shared by large number of candidates in each constituency. To overcome this problem, EC ought to have introduced a two stage voting system. The two candidates who secure first and second positions at the first stage only will become eligible for the second stage. Winner of second stage will then have valid majority support.

Constitution had put a bar on criminals getting registered as voters or becoming MPs/MLAs. Shockingly, 162 Lok Sabha members and 1,268 MLAs, with declared criminal records seem to have violated this bar in 2009. Most probably, present parliament also has this defect. This large scale suspected violation of the Constitution casts doubt on legitimacy of these parliaments. Moreover, 30% of ministers in present central government had filed affidavits that they had criminal cases against them. This casts doubt about legality of this government.

All these raise three important questions: (1) Why have governments, hon'ble judges and legal experts not fulfilled their moral responsibility to ensure that there is no illegal parliament and government? (2) Why were these suspected criminals not keen to prove that they are innocent by taking prior/quick action? (3) Why are people so dumb and callous to tolerate being governed by suspected criminals, justifying the remark that "A nation of sheep gets a government of wolves."

An MP or MLA has to perform important functions of governance. The expectation that voters have knowledge and expertise to select persons who can perform these functions efficiently is a fundamental fault of the election system. Most elected persons not only did not have even mocked majority approval but also may not have the required capacity because of being selected by laymen, that too mainly on extraneous considerations.

86% of Rajya Sabha members were crorepatis and Lok Sabha 2009 had 58% crorepatis. This shows a highly imbalanced and unhealthy representation of people in parliament.

All these prove the utter inefficiency of the election system to elect representatives of people of good quality. Should we continue to be hoodwinked by this system or should we seriously consider an alternative system for giving voice to people?

Article 3

When elections are carried out once in five years (or even earlier), some efficient representatives, who are governing admirably with efficiency and accountability, are unnecessarily weeded out along with the inefficient and tainted ones, unlike the management infrastructure which has continuity because it is not broken up completely and reassembled. This lack of continuity in top levels of governance leads to avoidable distortions and distractions in governance and in functioning of democratic and other institutions.

Moreover, a fixed five year period is likely to allow inefficiency and lack of transparency to continue for five years. Instead of allowing these to continue, we should replace the ministers and other representatives responsible for these failures on the basis of yearly assessment. This will also serve as a warning to representatives who are inefficient or tainted. Another definite advantage of the flexible system of elections is that the management infrastructure, which has adjusted to a political power system, will not have to waste time and energy to readjust to another political power system once in five years or even less.

A system of flexible elections based on yearly assessment will, besides ensuring continuity and efficiency of governance, reduce expenditure on elections to a much smaller number of seats every year. This flexible election system should be guided solely by the need to weed out only inefficient and tainted representatives to improve governance.

Article 4

Candidates for election and political parties who sponsor them need enormous amounts for election. This attracts criminal mafia also to get elected, or get their stooges elected, by using money power and/or intimidation. Thus, the election system not only failed to elect valid representatives having support of majority of people, despite wasting huge amounts of public money, but also is the root cause of unlimited corruption and control by mafia. EC did not even try to remove these anomalies.

Sole purpose of election is to give voice to people. Even after the election system failed miserably to elect true representatives of people with majority support for many elections, EC continued to focus on this faulty system. It did not apply its mind to develop a better method for giving voice to people, that too not just once in five years as an ineffective ritual as at present, but more frequently and effectively. EC did not also apply its mind to the fact that it is empowered to adopt any better method for giving voice to people, despite a SC judgment stating that, where the enacted laws are silent or make insufficient provision to deal with a given situation, EC has the residuary powers under the Constitution to act in an appropriate manner.

Because of this inaction, the election system failed miserably to elect true representatives of people (Article 2). Moreover, it threw up some challenging situations which it did not tackle. Three examples are given below:

1. Number of times a political party which had higher share of votes (showing higher peoples' support) had a lower share of elected representatives as happened in the recent assembly elections in Karnataka in which a party which had a 2% higher vote share

(peoples' support) got 26 representatives less than the party with lower vote share. This is a mockery of the higher support given by people which ought to be a backbone of democracy. Repeatedly overlooking this important fact exposes a major defect of the system.

2. Another example relates to complaints about "horse trading" to secure majority in assembly. Recently, opposition parties claimed that the party in power at the centre paid enormous amounts to those who agreed to defect. EC failed to verify the facts and take action, if necessary. It did not also try to remove loopholes in the system if any to stop such corrupt practices.

3. Recently, Central Bureau of Investigation (CBI) became unusually super active and filed large number of cases, mostly against political opponents of government. The opposition parties claimed that the government is misusing CBI for a political witch hunt to spoil their image and have focused on the selection of the state, victim and time chosen for these attacks to give credence to their claim. EC failed to verify the facts and take action, if necessary. It did not also try to remove loopholes in the system if any to stop such antidemocratic practices.

The manner of functioning of parliament and assemblies has clearly shown that political party system may be more a hindrance than help to democracy. Sad to say EC, the statutory custodian of democracy (<u>not</u> for conducting elections alone), had closed its eyes to the fact that political parties had repeatedly stalled functioning of parliament or distorted it to serve their interests. It has not cared to apply its mind to retrieve the situation e.g., by warning political parties about disqualifying them for undemocratic and undisciplined behaviour.

Only after repeated criticism, EC expressed concern about criminalization of politics instead of acting to prevent it by using its constitutional powers. It is not clear what prevented EC from being more assertive in taking suitable actions against criminalization of politics by exercising its wide powers instead of only expressing concern or making recommendations.

All these show that EC has violated the Constitution by acting like a modest advisor to government instead of a statutory authority with wide powers given by the Constitution and despite the strong support from SC judgments. Governments also have violated the Constitution by not recognizing EC as a statutory authority.

Article 5

Selection of Prime Minister (PM)/Chief Minister of a state (CM) is often done by a coterie of powerful leaders based not on capacity for governance but on extent of hero worship and other extraneous considerations like caste. PM/CM does not often have the capacity and power to manage a heterogeneous team. Moreover, the method of selection does not have even a semblance of democracy. All these actually result in a type of subtle and concealed dictatorship rather than a democracy.

To overcome this PM/CM should be directly elected by parliament/assembly, preferably through secret ballot. PM/CM can then select the team of ministers from MPs/MLAs. Efficiency assessments of MPs/MLAs suggested in Articles 3 and 4 will immensely help to form an efficient team without extraneous considerations.

Another defect is that a government can function only for a maximum period of five years even if its performance has immensely benefited the country. Why dismiss an efficient government just because a new parliament/assembly has to be constituted? Will a corporate body or private enterprise change an efficient CEO merely to have a change at regular intervals? Will it wait for years to dismiss an inefficient CEO? Why are we not applying such thoughts to decide on change of government?

This undesirable convention is mainly due to linking government formation with parliament/assembly formation. Why dismiss an efficient government just because a new parliament/assembly has to be constituted? Need for change of government should be based only on a regular system of assessment of efficiency of governance and follow up actions.

All that is necessary is that the efficient government team should automatically continue as MPs/MLAs and should continue to be efficient and answerable to the new parliament/assembly.

Overcoming this situation requires flexibility in choosing periodicity of elections (as suggested in Article 3) and de-linking parliament/assembly formation from government formation. These will help in two ways: (1) either continue an efficient government even after five years or dismiss an inefficient government whenever required and (2) save huge election expenses. What is urgently required is to start a regular system of assessment of efficiency of government to decide on change of government. This ought to be organized and conducted by a statutory body like EC as suggested in Article 4.

Article 6

In a democracy, government has to function by giving utmost attention to feeling the pulse of people. But, government does not have a systematic proactive approach to make use of all multiple agencies to feel the pulse of people. What is worse, it is not inclined to set up an organization to do this. This also resulted in a dictatorial attitude that listening to others is a weakness. It has not been realized that real strength of democracy lies in its ability to (1) listen to people, (2) accept useful ideas and (3) act on these with vision and commitment.

An organization has to be set up to (1) encourage people to freely express their views (particularly innovative ideas), (2) analyze these and (3) sort out and accept important/useful ones for implementation with commitment by concerned ministries. If any important idea selected by that organization or any recommendation of an expert group or constitutional authority is rejected by government, it should approach parliament/assembly for ratification. The latter should either ratify the rejection if there are valid reasons for it or disallow the rejection.

Faced with problems of faulty governance, a strategy of escapism and/or buying time is chosen by referring these matters to Commissions, Standing Committees of Parliament etc. The findings of these top expert bodies are more often put in cold storage than acted upon.

The government has scant respect for parliament. During a period of 10 years, promises given during replies to questions in parliament or discussions on bills and motions were broken 1,024 times. This speaks volumes about (1) government's gross lack of credibility and disrespect for parliament, (2) the latter spinelessly tolerating disrespect more than thousand times, without the dignity expected from the august supreme body of democracy and (3) failure of parliament to exercise the responsibility of having a check on functioning of government.

A main reason for disrespect to parliament is a basic defect in the system. The political party which forms government also controls parliament because of having majority. This defective system allows dictatorial attitude in the party and the government and defeats the very purpose of having parliament as a pillar of democracy.

Successful governance requires qualified professionals to be completely in charge of activities which can be properly handled by them only. But most technical departments are headed by IAS officers. This illogical positioning allows professionals to be supervised by administrators and leads to disputes and lack of cohesion and efficiency.

All departments carrying out professional services should be headed by professionals who should be given training in management to organize effective professional services. In addition, they should be assisted by qualified administrators for tackling problems in administration within the department.

Almost every year audit reports caution about large scale wastages and surrendering of budgeted amounts because of lack of commitment. But, these reports gather dust and hardly result in suitable action.

Government is obsessed with GDP growth and revenue collection. It becomes upset if GDP growth falls but is not bothered if people suffer. The fact that higher GDP has only resulted in widening gap between the rich and the poor is not its concern.

Article 7

Management infrastructure (MI), consisting of ministers and government officials at all levels, has <u>eleven</u> basic faults as mentioned below:

To sustain a vibrant democracy, ministers and all officials at all levels of MI should have a mind set to comply with democratic principles and proper perceptions about (a) democracy and (b) different aspects of management of democracy. But, there is no uniformity in mind set and perceptions within the management infrastructure and it cannot function as a well-knit unit with full focus on democracy.

The indisputable fact that most efficient governance can be provided only by professionally qualified and experienced persons, without hindrance from persons without required qualifications has been ignored.

Dictatorial decision making practice by ministers without required qualifications makes a mockery of the "officer selection system" in which some of the best and energetic minds in the country are selected through competitive examinations and interviews and given special training. This practice also allows extraneous factors like party interests to score over merit and honesty.

MI is not people friendly and has developed arrogance and a negative approach in using their powers. This has put spokes in almost all activities for welfare of people. The resultant red tape has given a bad name for bureaucracy in the country. Even worse, when tackling any problem faced by people, an arrogant and negative attitude of denial of help to people has been all pervasive in a government for the people!! People, whose welfare is of utmost importance in a democracy, have been ironically made to run from pillar to post with anxiety for months.

Lack of transparency has increased. Due to a protective approach by government many officers continue to misuse their powers and indulge in undemocratic and non-transparent activities, besides amassing wealth.

Curbs on positive actions to safeguard democracy are quite common in the guise of enforcing discipline, leading to harassment of honest officers who are either sidelined or transferred frequently with some officers being transferred 40 times or more. Even more shocking, some dishonest officers have been given promotions or choice postings!! Both create distractions and emotional problems which affect proper functioning of MI. In the process, development and needs of people get sidelined or even ignored.

Interests of political parties are given more importance and national interests are sidetracked or abandoned. Because of this also development and needs of people get sidelined or even ignored.

Inter-service rivalries hinder progress as well as accountability.

Some archaic acts, rules and procedures and undemocratic attitudes of officials are not conducive for healthy development and attending to welfare of people.

Successful governance requires qualified professionals to be in charge of various activities which can be properly handled by them only. But most technical departments are headed by IAS officers. This illogical positioning allows professionals to be supervised by non-professionals and thereby hinders progress and accountability.

When faced with problems of faulty governance, strategy of escapism and buying time is chosen by referring to Commissions, Standing Committees of Parliament etc. Findings of these top bodies are seldom acted upon.

When senior officers, after thorough study based on their long experience, submit "proposals" to the minster, quite often these are modified or rejected by the minster in a dictatorial manner to serve party interests or selfish interests or vested interests. These obviously dishonest and dictatorial practices not only score over merit of proposals but also destroy belief of officers in honest functioning, in addition to belittling their expertise and longer experience compared to those of the minister. Therefore, many of them lose their sense of commitment and/or become cynical – both detrimental to efficient functioning. Even worse, some of them are tempted or forced to form a nexus with minster for undemocratic and non-transparent activities. These result in misgovernance and scams. This dictatorial decision making practice also makes a mockery of the "officer selection system" in which some of the brilliant and energetic minds in the country are selected through competitive examinations and interviews and given long training.

A thorough study has to be undertaken to ascertain what stands in the way of (1) MI functioning as a well-knit unit with proper mindset, perceptions about democracy and different aspects of management of democracy, (2) compliance with democratic principles and (3) developing an attitude of helping people instead of denying services on some pretext or the other. This should be followed by specially conducted courses about democracy for all officials and other actions to remove the bottlenecks and enable them to function effectively as a part of a well-knit organization with full focus on democracy.

Article 8

Rape and violence against women have rocked the whole country. Robberies also are daily features. Murders are quite common, that too of senior citizens. Police are not only ineffective but also callous.

Police have earned a reputation of being corrupt in dealing with problems faced by people. Most people are afraid to complain to police. Filing of cases is subject to whims of police or pressures they face. Burking of crime is so common that every year about 60 lakh cases are not registered.

In connection with a Public Interest Litigation case which alleged that 1,17,480 children had gone missing between January 2008 and January 2010 and of them 41,546 were yet to be traced, SC remarked that "Nobody seems to be concerned about missing children."

In a TV discussion, a former police commissioner stated that police have now become an "armed militia of politicians in power."

There are only 106 policemen for one lakh people, which is less than half of the recommended 222. Even worse, available policemen are frequently misused or deputed for non-governmental activities. Consequently, there are at least three policemen for every VIP and just one for every 8,000 people!!

Democracy also requires equality in application of laws. Violations of this requirement are far too common. Poor people hardly benefit from the law and order machinery. In fact, they are even afraid of the protectors of law. No committed efforts have been made to rectify matters. Peoples' representatives (MPs and MLAs) often close their eyes to such dreadful realities and allow matters to drift. All these have made people unhappy, frustrated and cynical.

Faced with decay in functioning of police, a National Police Commission was set up to recommend reforms. This Commission made many important recommendations. But, these were put in cold storage despite directions issued by SC.

Like any democracy, we have all the laws. But we don't have the courage, the competence or the candour to implement them. There are many instances of lawmakers taking law into their hands and demonstrating their contempt for law. Apathy and callous attitude of government continue, even after multiple failures in law and order are highlighted by media every day.

Most people are unhappy with police who are "criminals in uniform" and "armed militia of politicians," as stated by a former police commissioner. "We not only need to free police from malignant and suffocating political control but also streamline its organization to ensure a people friendly and highly efficient police force."

It is also necessary to build up a good relationship between police and people. For example, the entire area of a police station should be divided into as many sub areas as number of constables in the police station. Each constable should have frequent interaction with the people living in the sub area allotted to him/her by forming a "Police People Interaction Club." All such interactions by police will lead to mutual understanding of the problems faced by both groups and also make police "friends of people" instead of "criminals in uniform" and "armed militia of politicians" as at present. (For details see Article 8.)

An expert body should make a thorough study of all existing laws to weed out those which are obsolete and to modify the remaining laws to reduce differing interpretations by judges and lawyers and to make these understandable to people.

Article 9

The Constitution opted for a corruption free government. It was envisaged that the institutions set up to ensure checks and balances will help to control corruption. But, all these have failed miserably mainly due to callous (or may be even hostile) attitude of government to enable them to work independently, as explained below:

Besides corruption being rampant in every sphere of activity, mega scams have been exposed with alarming frequency. Punishment to persons involved in these is dragging on indefinitely and causing concern and increasing cynicism among people. This lack of interest in pursuing cases shows that these scams were exposed only to gain political advantage and not to end corruption!! This is _one instance_ which exposes hypocrisy about zero tolerance to corruption. This view is supported by the following additional 26 instances of hypocrisy about highest priority to getting rid of corruption.

The long delay of 53 years in conferring statutory status to CVC (an anticorruption organization) speaks volumes about the lack of interest of government and parliament to control corruption. This is _the second instance_ of hypocrisy about highest priority to getting rid of corruption.

CVC has grossly inadequate staff and resources to investigate corruption in more than 1500 central government ministries and departments. CVC can investigate corruption against government officials only after government permits it, though CVC is now a statutory body. Government is not confident that there is nothing to hide and prefers a toothless CVC.

Delays and denials of permission were quite common and show government's reluctance to allow proper checks. This check has been deliberately watered down in this manner. This is a third instance of hypocrisy about highest priority to getting rid of corruption.

Annual reports of CVC gave not only details of work done by it but also brought out the system failures which led to corruption in various Departments/Organizations and suggested improvements in the system and various preventive measures needed. Hardly any action was taken on any of the important recommendations. This is a fourth instance of hypocrisy about highest priority to getting rid of corruption.

CVC has neither resources nor powers to inquire and take action on complaints of corruption that may act as an effective deterrence against corruption. Government has not taken any action to rectify the situation. This is a fifth instance of hypocrisy about highest priority to getting rid of corruption.

Control on appointments of staff of CBI is a sixth instance of hypocrisy about highest priority to getting rid of corruption.

To begin any corruption investigation, CBI needs approval of Ministry of Personnel. Further these are monitored by CVC. It must also have permission from chief minister of the state where it wants to conduct an investigation. Restrictions on CBI to start work are a seventh instance which exposes hypocrisy about zero tolerance to corruption.

CBI is dependent on Home Ministry for staffing. It depends on law ministry for lawyers. Allowing these suffocating dependencies is an <u>eighth instance</u> which exposes hypocrisy about zero tolerance to corruption.

Despite repeated recommendations and court orders, CBI continues to be hampered and cannot play an independent role. This shows a <u>ninth (and most serious) instance</u> which exposes hypocrisy about zero tolerance to corruption.

CBI has been dragging its feet while investigating prominent politicians, leading to their acquittal or non-prosecution. CBI has not been allowed to make a dent on the rampant corruption in the country. This is a <u>tenth (and most serious) instance</u> which exposes hypocrisy about zero tolerance to corruption.

Joginder Singh and B. R. Lall (former director and joint director respectively of CBI) have exposed government for engaging in nepotism, wrongful prosecution and corruption. In Lall's book, "Who Owns CBI," he details how investigations are manipulated and derailed by government. Government resorting to manipulations and derailments is a <u>eleventh (and most serious) instance</u> which exposes hypocrisy about zero tolerance to corruption.

Information obtained under RTI has revealed corruption within CBI. Instead of setting matters right, in 2011, government exempted CBI from the provisions of <u>RTI Act</u> on the pretext of national security!! This has been criticized by CIC and RTI activists because this blanket exemption violated the letter and intent of RTI Act. These form a <u>twelfth instance</u> which exposes hypocrisy about zero tolerance to corruption.

CBI became the subject of ridicule because it allowed a minister and government officials to modify its report on allocation of coal mining licenses. SC then criticized CBI for making changes in its report at the request of a minister and two bureaucrats and remarked that CBI is "like a caged parrot" of government. Because of this and particular mention of manipulation in Lall's book it is reasonably to conclude that government has been making changes in CBI report. Making such manipulations is a <u>thirteenth (and most serious) instance</u> which exposes hypocrisy about zero tolerance to corruption

The court gave government time till July 3, 2013 to lay out steps to make CBI independent. It is shocking that no steps have been taken to make CBI independent even by 2018 (i.e., more than four years after the time limit set by SC) though this is a contempt of the highest court. This is a <u>fourteenth (and most serious) instance</u> which exposes hypocrisy about zero tolerance to corruption.

Recently, CBI became unusually super active and filed large number of cases mostly against political opponents of government. The opposition parties claimed that government is misusing CBI for political witch hunts to spoil their image and have focused on the selection of the state, victim and time chosen for these attacks to give credence to their claim. If true, CBI now deserves to be called a "caged ferocious dog" of government.

The series of raids by Income Tax department (IT) and Enforcement Directorate (ED) during the same time period has led to doubts about political control on functioning of these three state investigative agencies. Government should ensure that, besides CBI, these agencies also are insulated from political control. Else, IT and ED also will deserve to be called "caged ferocious dog" of government.

A disturbing fact, which confirms political control, is that these simultaneous raids were not only carried out on premises of number of political opponents of government but IT and ED also resorted to a highly objectionable act to spoil the image of these persons viz., giving wide publicity to what they found during the raids, even before establishing that they are guilty.

All these depict a <u>fifteenth (and most serious) instance</u> which exposes hypocrisy about zero tolerance to corruption.

Following criticisms by SC to ensure "functional autonomy," CBI asked for sufficient financial and administrative powers and a minimum three-year tenure for its director who should be vested with ex-officio powers of Secretary to Government of India, reporting directly to the minister, without having to go through the DoPT. Decisions on these are still pending. This is a <u>sixteenth</u> instance which exposes hypocrisy about zero tolerance to corruption.

Creation of Lokpal to probe complaints against public functionaries in high positions was pending for more than 44 years!! Though a bill for this was passed in Lok Sabha in 1969, Rajya Sabha rejected it as many as nine times up to 2008!! The bill was revived several times in subsequent years. Each time, after the bill was introduced in parliament, it was stalled using devious methods. These repeated impediments extending over many years show lack of interest in passing such an important bill to provide a check on corruption. This is a <u>seventeenth (and most serious) instance</u> which exposes hypocrisy about zero tolerance to corruption.

The Lokpal and Lokayuktas Act, 2013 was passed and approved by President. But, Lok Pal has not been appointed even in 2018 (after more than four years). This inordinate delay is an <u>eighteenth (and most serious) instance</u> which exposes hypocrisy about zero tolerance to corruption.

Considering the prolonged series of obstacles in passing this important anti-corruption bill which covers persons in high positions, it is reasonable to believe that implementation of the bill also will have to face lot of obstacles which will cause long delay. This long delay of more than four years in implementation and possibility of further delay are a <u>nineteenth (and most serious) instance</u> which exposes hypocrisy about zero tolerance to corruption.

In 1966, Administrative Reforms Commission recommended setting up of 'Lok Ayukta' for redressal of citizens' grievances. Despite a long interval of 52 years, 10 states do not have Lok Ayuktas. Even in states with Lok Ayukta, proper action was not taken against persons charged with corruption by it. It has no power to take independent action to penalize those found guilty. Its capacity has been further downgraded by not providing it with adequate staff and other facilities. Evidently, state governments want to avoid such checks on criminal activities by their staff. Central government has not taken any action to rectify this atrocious situation. This is a <u>twentieth instance</u> which exposes hypocrisy about zero tolerance to corruption.

RTI Act provides to citizens the right to access information under the control of public authorities, in order to promote transparency and accountability in the working of every public authority. But, many government departments either employ delaying tactics or refuse to give information. Moreover, some departments have started feeling uncomfortable about the disclosures, leading to government thinking of how to curtail use of the Act and expressing the need to make changes in the Act. This is a <u>twenty-first instance</u> which exposes hypocrisy about zero tolerance to corruption.

Many RTI activists have been harassed and even murdered for seeking information to promote transparency and accountability in the working of public authorities. Many face assaults regularly. A few activists who sought information related to MGNREGA scams were killed. Government has not taken any worthwhile action to protect RTI activists. This callous approach of government towards this important check by people which can expose corruption is a matter for serious concern in a democracy. This is a twenty-second (and most serious) instance which exposes hypocrisy about zero tolerance to corruption.

When CIC ruled that political parties are answerable under the Act about funds given to them, it was reported that government hurriedly planned to introduce an amendment to the Act to nullify this. It will not be surprising if political parties use their combined strength to safe guard their secrecy, although transparency in political funding should be a vital necessity for democracy. They may be afraid that right to information will, in due course, force them to be accountable for the funds they collect. This is a twenty-third instance which exposes hypocrisy about zero tolerance to corruption.

CAG regularly reports deficiencies observed and system failures and suggests improvements. But hardly any worthwhile action is taken even on serious matters involving corruption. This is a twenty-fourth instance which exposes hypocrisy about zero tolerance to corruption.

In 2009, CAG requested government to amend Audit Act 1971 to bring all private-public partnerships (PPP), Panchayti Raj Institutions and societies getting government funds within the ambit of CAG and to enhance CAG's powers to access information because almost 30% of documents demanded by CAG were denied. Though projects worth millions of rupees are executed under PPP model, these projects are not audited by CAG. About 65% of government spending does not come under scrutiny of CAG!! But government has not cared to amend the Act even after eight years. Thus, the very purpose of having this authority to provide checks has been callously defeated. This is a <u>twenty-fifth instance</u> which exposes hypocrisy about zero tolerance to corruption.

Whistleblowers (persons who expose misconduct, alleged dishonesty or illegal activity occurring in an organization) play an important part in control of corruption. Unfortunately, they face many reprisals and devastating situations. There have been multiple instances of threatening, harassment and even murder of whistleblowers. The harsh reality is that vested interests usually triumph because laws are inadequate, media are ineffective and citizens are silent. Peoples' representatives do not care to set things right. Consequently, culprits in influential positions manage to suppress embarrassing facts, discredit whistleblowers and subject them to demoralizing situations. Long delays in disposing of such cases also help them to get away without punishment. Under these circumstances, only a few whistleblowers can succeed or lead a stress free life. Many are subject to debilitating anxiety or depression forever. Lack of action to improve the situation is a <u>twenty-sixth instance</u> which exposes hypocrisy about zero tolerance to corruption.

Judiciary has repeatedly directed government to formulate suitable guidelines/regulations to protect whistleblowers. In 2001, Law Commission of India recommended a specific legislation to encourage disclosure of information regarding corruption or maladministration by public servants and to provide protection to informers. Only after ten years, the Whistleblowers' Protection Bill, 2011 was passed by the Lok Sabha. But, sad to say, the Bill is pending in Rajya Sabha for more than six years!! Moreover, the proposed law has no provision to encourage whistle blowing (e.g., financial incentives). Nor does it provide a penalty for those attacking a whistle blower. Its jurisdiction is restricted to those who are working for central government or its agencies and does not cover state government employees. Corporate and private sectors also are not within its jurisdiction.

Moreover, ministries proposing draft legislation usually involve a process of public consultation but such an opportunity has been denied to the public for this bill. It is shocking that even after a gap of more than 16 years after the Law Commission recommendation, a full-fledged law to protect whistleblowers, drafted with public consultation, is still a long way off. This is a twenty-seventh instance which exposes hypocrisy about zero tolerance to corruption. In the absence of such a law, people have a low level of confidence in fighting corruption because they fear retaliation and intimidation against those who file complaints.

It is shocking that there are at least twenty-seven instances which expose hypocrisy about zero tolerance to corruption. May be there are some more instances of not taking suitable actins to remove corruption, which have not been reported so far. This convincingly proves that government is only fooling people by bluffing that it has zero tolerance to corruption.

Despite strictures from SC, it did not take any action to rectify the atrocious situations and ensure that the anti-corruption agencies have been provided with adequate power and facilities to function smoothly and effectively with full independence without interference from government. What is worse, government put spokes in their functioning. This deliberate misuse of power resulted in wide spread corruption as confirmed by the following studies.

Transparency International ranked India at 79 out of 176 countries in Corruption Perception Index 2016 and 1st among 18 Asia – Pacific nations in bribery rate (India Today dated 20.11.17, page 12). What is more damaging, India slipped to rank 81 in 2017 (The Times of India dated 23.02.18, page 1).

This organisation reported that in 2017 as many as 45% of respondents claimed they paid a bribe at least once in the past year to get work done. What is worse, this proportion had increased from 43% for the previous year (The Times of India dated 10.12.17, page 8).

A survey by Centre for Study of Developing Societies, India in May 2018 found that two-thirds of people surveyed were of the view that government is corrupt and that demonetization to end corruption has boomeranged (Deccan Chronicle dated 24.08.18, page 8). "People also think that instead of curbing corruption, DeMo was a reckless move and dealt a telling blow to small businesses, especially in the informal sector."

All these data for three consecutive years undoubtedly show that corruption is widespread now and increasing. But, government claims that corruption has been eliminated!!

Article 10

During 2006 to 2011, about 5.4 lakh persons had complained to NHRC that they suffered from human rights violations, at an alarming average of about 90,000 per year. Among these, about 1.1 lakhs *(about one fifth)* only were "disposed with directions." NHRC had no qualms in refusing to examine about 3.4 lakhs *(about two-thirds of the violation complaints)* and "dismissing these in limini" – a deeply disgusting picture of inaction to remove human rights violations. Thus, even the last channel of hope has been cruelly cut off for lakhs of possible sufferers from human rights violations. This is a matter for serious concern in a democracy. But, parliament and government did not take any action to rectify the atrocious situation of lakhs of complaints against human rights violations being dismissed without examination.

This atrocious situation arose on account of NHRC (procedure) Regulations 1997 which did not give powers to NHRC to review judgments by courts and commissions.

NHRC statistics did not give the important information about how many of the 3.4 lakh cases not examined were complaints against court judgments. It is reasonable to presume that vast majority of this huge number of violation complaints arose from peoples' perceived denial of justice by courts and did not arise from recommendations of commissions. NHRC did not give serious thought as to why lakhs of people were complaining to it against court judgments. NHRC was so callous that it did not take suitable remedial actions which were in its power!!

NHRC is an autonomous body with operational and financial authority and had powers to regulate its own procedure for disposal of complaints. Yet, it did not act to remove the regulation which stood in its way to overcome the shameful and dismal picture of refusing to examine lakhs of complaints. An obvious reason why NHRC did not use its statutory powers to delete the obsolete regulation may be that it was headed by retired judges who did not want to open a Pandora's box of injustices to which they and their colleagues might have contributed. May be, many of these complaints to HRCs were deliberately ignored because these were against political leaders who are known to take the law into their hands (Article 8).

A new set of top officers of NHRC should be appointed to exercise its statutory power to regulate its own procedure for disposal of complaints by removing all obsolete procedural regulations. No judges should be appointed in NHRC for the reason explained earlier.

Moreover, central and state governments have not cared to ensure that Human Rights Commissions are well equipped to carry out their functions properly.

All these show a grossly dismal picture of human rights violations which is an utter shame for the Indian democracy.

As stated earlier, neither parliament nor government cared to take any action to rectify the atrocious situation of lakhs of complaints against human rights violations being dismissed without examination. Probably, they did not even care to keep a watch on the human rights situation and were, therefore, not even aware of what was happening!!

Article 11

The present judicial system has failed in many aspects. Lakhs of cases have been pending in courts for many years and denying justice to lakhs of people. One of the main reasons for piling up of cases is shortage of judges. There are only 13 judges for every 1 million people compared to 50 (i.e., four times) in developed nations. Parliament and government have not been sincere enough to tackle this serious problem. The meager allocations made are due to low priority and not lack of resources. Many fast–track courts set up in 2000 to speed up justice are not functioning now because of lack of funds. This shows lack of priority for speeding up justice. Administrative Reforms Commission and the Committee that reviewed the Constitution had stressed on setting up special benches in High Courts for disposing of poll suits within six months. But, about 13,500 cases are pending judicial scrutiny after more than seven years. All these have to be condemned outright as a blot on our democracy.

It is universally accepted that justice delayed is justice denied. SC is partly responsible for this dismal situation. As the Statutory Authority responsible for providing justice, it should have warned government that the low priority given to providing funds and its unhelpful attitude to ensure quick justice are violating the spirit of the Constitution. It should have demanded appointment of more judges and staff by avoiding wrong priorities and reducing wastages repeatedly pointed out by auditors. When lakhs of cases are pending for years and millions of people are suffering from delay of justice, the courts enjoy vacations regularly unlike other functionaries!!

Because of a laissez faire attitude, judges have not applied their mind to identify and remove archaic procedures followed for many years. "A study of over 8,000 orders in Delhi high court cases filed between 2011 and 2015 revealed runaway 'inefficiency' that clogs the justice delivery mechanism. An in-depth study of all procedures followed by different courts and making necessary innovative changes to quicken justice are long overdue. But the real problem is that neither parliament nor government nor judges are committed to make innovative changes.

Bulk of the people cannot afford to fight for justice even at one level. Allowing repeated appeals is made use of by rich people or organizations. The prohibitive costs makes it almost impossible for most people to get justice. Because of this, costs incurred should be subsidized to help poor people to get justice.

Another matter of serious concern is that transparency of courts is being increasingly questioned by people. Moreover, Article 10 has highlighted that, on an average, about 90,000 persons had complained to NHRC every year for violation of human rights. Many more would have complained to SHRCs. Majority of these appear to be against denial of justice by courts. It is highly significant and shocking that lakhs of people did not have faith in judgments by courts and appealed to HRCs.

Providing quick and affordable justice to all people is so fundamental in a democracy that other budgets should be pruned by parliament/government, if necessary, to ensure adequate funds. People want a democratic government to spend their money to meet their essential needs (e.g., justice) and not according to its whims or to help the rich!!

The increasing number of reported allegations of judicial misconduct emphasizes the need for investigation. There is a general impression that judges are inclined to "listening" to senior advocates while passing judgments. Can it be that there is a nexus between these advocates and judges? Quite often, behavior of Indian courts tend to show a feeling of superiority and contempt for people. Letters to SC from ordinary people are ignored, forgetting that this is antidemocratic and feedback information from them could have helped to improve delivery of justice.

Recommendations made by judicial commission were not implemented and gather dust. Ignoring these and other suggestions questions the sincerity of parliament and government in providing justice.

The dismal functioning of our justice system is also due to basic defects in the system. A basic defect is that there are number of instances where judgments of courts were ignored without being punished. For example, SC gave government time till July 3, 2013 to lay out steps to make CBI independent. But, no steps have been taken to make CBI independent even by 2018 (i.e., more than five years after the time limit set by SC) though this is a contempt of the highest court. In the case of a hung assembly, SC had ordered that if a group of parties had agreed to join together and form a government they should be allowed to do so. But, after the recent assembly elections in Karnataka the Governor ignored this and invited the largest single party to form government instead of a combined group of two parties who had more members. Is this not a contempt of SC? Or, is the governor exempted from the law of the land? What is more shocking SC itself ignored its previous order when the aggrieved parties approached it for relief.

Another basic defect was pointed out by a highly respected and experienced retired judge of SC who stated: "A radical transformation of the robed brethren has become necessary." "…the law of interpretation that the judiciary adopts tends to favour the haves, not the have-nots. The social structure and the fundamental character of the instruments of the Executive, the Legislature and the Judiciary have political character."

Top priority for radical transformation of the judicial system should be given to abolition of the age old conservative court system in which lawyers tell judges about legal aspects, when judges have the special knowledge, ability and experience to take a fair decision themselves, without help from lawyers. Abolition of the conservative system will remove a blur on judges that they do not have the knowledge and ability to take fair decisions without help from lawyers. And equally important, this abolition will not only make justice affordable to most people who cannot afford to engage lawyers, particularly poor people, but also expedite justice. Thus, the change to court-less system will overcome at least some of the most serious defects in the present judicial system which are major blots in our democracy.

Most important, another major defect of the court system is that lawyers are constantly engaged in fighting for their clients (even criminal) and not for justice. This damaging situation is encouraged inadvertently by judges "listening" to senior advocates while passing judgments and a possible nexus between these advocates and judges leading to an increasing number of reported allegations of judicial misconduct discussed in an earlier paragraph. This may be a reason for lakhs of people not having faith in judgments by courts and appealing to HRCs (Article 10). A method for utilizing the services of lawyers to fight for justice instead of for injustice as at present is discussed later on. All these aspects justify beyond any doubt that abolition of court system is essential to improve the justice system and remove injustice.

In addition to this, it is essential to think out of the box and ask many basic questions to reform the judicial system and make it simple, quick, faultless and people-friendly. For example, when a person wants to seek justice why can't he/she file a petition in writing on ordinary paper (with or without help from a lawyer) and send it through post to a judge and save money and time? To file a petition why is it necessary for the petitioner to pay fees when provision of justice is an essential function of democracy which has to serve the peoples' needs? Why is it necessary to argue civil cases in a court of law instead of the judge, who is well versed in laws of the country, disposing it off himself/herself, after discussing/seeking clarifications from both parties to clarify matters? Why ask both parties to a case to engage lawyers (who charge huge fees) to argue before a court of law when a qualified judge is capable of considering all legal aspects of the case and can provide justice without being side tracked or biased or mesmerized by clever lawyers? When appeals are made against a judgment, can't these be disposed of by senior judges without constituting a bench and bringing in lawyers who charge exorbitant fees? Will not abolition of the court system reduce the cost incurred by both people and government for providing justice? Why is it that there is wide disparity in interpretation of laws among judges and lawyers? Why even experienced judges and legal experts did not think out of the box and ask lot of questions to simplify the system? If the system is simplified based on answers to many relevant questions including those given above it will speed up justice and immensely reduce the cost of providing justice.

A thorough review of the working of the judicial system should also be carried out by an independent body with adequate expertise and its recommendations should be immediately implemented in full. Any rejection should be confirmed by both houses of parliament.

Article 12

India should have a democracy which attends to the needs and aspirations of people all over the country. But the situation is very complex and intricate because of wide spread diversities in needs and aspirations of people. A well planned and actively implemented national integration programme which will reduce disparities is essential for developing a democracy which satisfies the needs and aspirations of maximum number of people to the extent possible. Thinking out of the box and implementing innovative ideas are absolutely necessary.

Attempts at national integration have not succeeded even after 70 years because of a bureaucratic approach with least priority and commitment. Attempts made have been sporadic, patchy and ineffective due to lack of vision and commitment. A positive approach is to encourage interstate migration in larger numbers by giving financial and other incentives to settle down after migration. Inter-caste, interreligious and interstate marriages should also be encouraged by giving grants to such couples. Award for panchayats and wards or residential associations in towns and cities with maximum number of such inter marriages should be instituted. People should also be educated about the genetic advantages of such inter marriages. School children and college students should be regularly taken on "know your country" education trips to areas with a different culture and provided opportunities to understand and appreciate different cultural practices. Multiple languages in the country with their own scripts complicate the problem. A national script to be used by all languages should be developed to mitigate this problem.

An additional approach is to identify institutions which have been struggling to reduce alienations and support these and identify and motivate some more institutions to do so. Attempts should be systematically made to have dialogues with political and social leaders to motivate them to enthuse a national identity among their followers.

It is important to have a change in mind set to provide adequate funds for all national integration schemes on top priority basis in order to achieve the worthy aim of national integration, which is essential to have a successful democracy.

Article 13

Many aspects of good governance will suffer in many parts of a large state in the absence of frequent intensive supervision which is essential for efficient administration. Moreover, people in many parts of a large state are unhappy that they have to waste more time and money to visit the capital of the state to sort out their problems with government. As a result of such inadequate interaction between government and people, large states are less efficient in satisfying the needs and aspirations of people which is crucial for success of democracy. Intra state rivalries between different identity groups have made functioning of democracy more difficult and ineffective in large states. These have also led to increasing demands and even violent protests for dividing large states to create more states. Other law and order problems also become more difficult to handle in large states. Large states have more MPs and are able to put more pressure to derive additional benefits for their states and/ or to block developments in other states to spite their neighbours and to show off their superiority. This makes people in smaller states unhappy.

Thus, having large states causes dissatisfaction among people in both large and small states and results in a discordant democracy which can explode into violent revolution.

Despite facing many problems and even violent protests, government does not have the vision to apply its mind to carry out studies to ascertain optimum size for states to mitigate problems. Because of a laissez-faire attitude, parliament and government have not given thought to improving democracy by having optimal small states.

There is an urgent need to set up another States Reorganization Commission with instructions to ascertain optimum size of state to have successful democracy in different demographic situations and carve out small compact states which can satisfy needs and aspirations of different identity groups to maximum extent possible.

Article 14

The present system of democracy has fifteen fundamental weaknesses.

A <u>fundamental weakness</u> of parliamentary system of democracy is that parliament cannot be an independent pillar of democracy (as it ought to be) because the political party which controls government also controls parliament, having majority of MPs (Article 6). This basically defective system results in a servile parliament which allows dictatorial attitude in the party and the government and defeats the very purpose of having parliament as a pillar of democracy. There are more than thousand instances of government continuously ignoring parliament (Articles 6 and 23).

In addition, parliament totally failed to represent people because (a) large majority of MPs have support of only less than 35% of electorate (often much less) and shockingly resulted in a void parliament (Article 2) and (b) majority of MPs are rich crorepatis (Article 2). Because majority of MPs are very rich parliament's ability to speak for the poor is seriously curtailed.

Shockingly, everyone including EC and SC have accepted these atrocious situations. Moreover, propriety and efficiency of parliament are doubtful when MPs are elected by people who do not have the knowledge and expertise needed to select efficient persons with specialized qualifications and experience to enact laws, make policies and govern the country. These situations form a second fundamental weakness of the present system of democracy.

People who elected MPs did not have the knowledge and expertise needed to select efficient persons with specialized qualifications and experience to enact laws, make policies and govern the country. This lack of knowledge and expertise among people (the selectors) becomes deplorable when large numbers of them (often the majority) are illiterate or do not have even a moderate level of general education. Just imagine what will happen to patients if surgeons are selected by such people; or to dams, bridges and houses if engineers are selected by such people; or to delivery of justice if judges are selected by such people; or to students if the teachers/professors are selected such people; and so on!! Selecting top managers of government by such people is bound to have similar atrocious consequences. It is significant that such calamities have not occurred only because multiple professionals responsible for governance have been selected by specialized institutions manned by highly qualified selectors with many years of experience. In sharp contrast, political leaders who have to supervise these expert professionals are selected by people without requisite knowledge and expertise!! This ridiculous mockery is the third fundamental weakness of present system of democracy.

Successful governance of a country requires multiple professionals with specialized qualifications and experience working at the top levels without hindrance. But, functions of policy making, enactment of laws, planning and implementation of projects and overall governance have been usurped from qualified professionals by politicians without the required qualifications and experience who also became enemies of democracy and could take risky decisions (Article 19). This topsy-turvy and dangerous situation is a <u>fourth fundamental weakness</u> of the present system of democracy.

While people are not competent to select efficient governments they throw out inefficient governments after they caused them prolonged pain and suffering. Inability to get rid of bad governments before such long gaps is a <u>fifth fundamental weakness</u> of the present system of democracy.

A spate of political defections in number of states has led to confusion and disruptions in functioning of democracy. There were allegations that large amounts of money have been paid by the party in power at the centre to manipulate these defections. Election Commission shirked its responsibility to verify the facts and take further action. It did not also try to remove loopholes in the system, if any, which stood in its way to verify and stop such corrupt practices. These constitute a <u>sixth fundamental weakness</u> of the present system of democracy.

A <u>seventh fundamental weakness</u> of the present system of democracy is that there is no system to assess efficiency of performance of political leaders in highly responsible positions every year as is regularly done for the qualified professionals involved in governance. Lack of such crucial assessment is obviously illogical and risky when these leaders did not have the required qualifications and experience and can make serious mistakes. The risk can be very high because they have become enemies of democracy (Article 19).

Moreover, by contrast, it makes a mockery of the education and training given to qualified professionals and the assessment of efficiency of their performance. This is an <u>eighth fundamental weakness</u> of the present system of democracy.

It is also not realized that the illogical situations explained above are actually proclaiming loudly that politics is a strange profession which can be practiced by anyone, even without basic education or qualification or popular support or facing assessment of work. Yet, shockingly, politicians have been given the responsibility of managing government, even when their claim that they represent people was hollow also (Article 2). Thus political leaders need neither education, nor qualification nor true popular support to hold high positions without assessment of their work – a completely farcical situation!! Acceptance of this highly illogical and absurd situation about this profession is a <u>ninth fundamental weakness of the present system of democracy</u>.

Even more damaging, people have even welcomed politicians (often gladly) to occupy any position (including highly responsible positions) without having requisite qualifications or true popular support and without being assessed for efficiency in performance. Why is it that people are so gullible and do not ask any questions? People behaved like slaves when under British rule for about 200 years and, sadly, are not able (or not even inclined) to come out of the slavish mentality to rulers even after 70 years of independence!! This is a <u>tenth fundamental weakness</u> of the present system of democracy.

Political leaders, instead of helping people to come out of this slavish situation, took advantage of it and, by becoming heroes using the gift of the gab, fooled people to believe in number of absurdities about the system without questioning these

(Article 23). For instance, they fooled people to believe that they (even without requisite qualifications) had the super human capacity to effectively supervise and control professionally qualified, specially trained and experienced persons, that too in a variety of disciplines!! Absence of efforts to get rid of absurdities is a <u>eleventh fundamental weakness</u> of the present system of democracy.

By their callousness and repeated, uncontrolled and selfish activities, politicians also became enemies of democracy (Articles 19 and 20) – Article 19 has given five solid reasons). This is a <u>twelfth fundamental weakness</u> of present system of democracy.

The parliament they formed did nothing to overcome at least 100 shameful and shocking situations faced by the country (Article 15). This is a <u>thirteenth fundamental weakness</u> of present system of democracy.

To complete the shock, parliament also brought disgrace on itself because of lack of guts to punish government for breaking promises to it and lack of dignity by spinelessly tolerating such disrespect by government (Article 6 pointed out more than thousand instances of lack of guts and lack of dignity of parliament). This is a <u>fourteenth fundamental weakness</u> of present system of democracy.

Lastly, because of mental slavery to politicians (Article 23) people were so dumb and callous that they tolerated being governed by suspected criminals (Article 2), justifying the remark that "A nation of sheep gets a government of wolves." This is a <u>fifteenth fundamental weakness</u> of present system of democracy.

To overcome these, this article stresses the need to abolish election system and parliament. Meanwhile (a) train elected representatives before they start functioning, (b) assess efficiency of elected representatives every year and (c) thoroughly overhaul the system using a professional approach which is badly needed.

Article 15

Disruptions and walk outs in parliament are so common that lot of time and public money are wasted. Shameful "photographic" exposures of MPs and MLAs sleeping or watching porn during sessions speak volumes about their lack of desirable character, dignity and sense of responsibility.

The callous and interrupted manner in which parliament (an important pillar of democracy) works is notorious and has resulted in loss of respect for this institution, besides huge wastage of public money. Attitude of MPs and their actions show that they are always guided by their party's interest or selfish interests only and peoples' needs and aspirations are often ignored. Moreover, they became enemies of democracy (Article 19).

Neglect of peoples' interests has led to at least 100 shocking and shameful consequences which showed that India had a very poor rank in many social and economic indicators (Article 15). It is likely that there are many more of such deplorable situations waiting to be highlighted. Though MPs have become enemies of democracy, they quite often greedily and shamelessly vote without conscience to increase their remuneration and perquisites (which are already very high), forgetting that they have neither fulfilled their responsibilities to ensure development and peace in the country nor acted sincerely to reduce sufferings of lakhs of people!!

All these shocking and shameful situations covering almost all crucial sectors happened despite a high growth rate!! Government and parliament were so obsessed and boasting about growth rate that they did not have the time and inclination to rectify these shocking and shameful situations.

Sad to say, (a) most of the shameful and shocking situations pointed out in article 15 were exposed by investigations by international bodies and (b) neither government nor parliament was keen to carry out systematic continuous monitoring and evaluation of all programmes to keep a watch and augment these by special studies to get additional information to get in depth knowledge.

All these show absence of both accountability and commitment of parliament to the work for which they have been elected by people.

According to the 2017 report of Economic Intelligence Unit for 2017, India is one of the countries with flawed democracy. What is even more shocking and shameful, is that India slipped by 10 points from a rank of 32 in 2016 to 42 in 2017. Their report attributes this to "rise of conservative religious ideologies and increase in vigilantism and violence against minorities as well as other dissenting voices." "In the latest rankings of the Varieties of Democracy (V-DEM) Institute a research project that tries to evolve new measures of democracy, India's rank is seen dropping in the past four years, with a marked concentration of powers in the hands of one individual."

The present system of Indian democracy also has 11 basic faults in the management infrastucraure (Articles 7) and fifteen fundamental weaknesses (Article 14) and is based on nine absurdities (Article 23). If these are also taken into account there is absolutely no doubt that *Indian democracy* has gone down beyond a completely flawed democracy and ***has become a***

pseudo democracy. There is an urgent need to replace this by a true democracy.

To overcome this atrocious situation, we should ask ourselves: why do we spent thousands of crores of public money to maintain a parliament which (a) lacks dignity, guts to punish government for braking promises more than thousand times, accountability and an ethics of care for aam admi and (b) has not shown any interest in rectifying large number of shameful and shocking situations faced by the country? ***Should we not abolish such a parliament?***

The main reason for parliament not punishing government for breaking promises more than thousand times is the basic defect in the system pointed out in Article 6. The political party which forms government also controls parliament because of having majority. This defective system allows a subtle dictatorial attitude in the party and the government towards parliament and defeats the very purpose of having parliament as an independent pillar of democracy. ***This basic defect also justifies abolition of present parliamentary system.***

If a way cannot be found to avoid mostly crorepatis being elected to parliament, abolition of parliament with such distorted and unhealthy representation of people is further justified.

It is a pity that instead of hanging their heads in shame, government, parliament, MPs, MLAs and political parties assume airs of superiority and feel smug and exhilarated. No wonder, people have lost respect for government, parliament, MPs, MLAs and political parties who make a mockery of parliament and assemblies!! We ought to be ashamed of having such a parliament even though our government, parliament and MPs seem to have no shame.

Since attempts to stem the suicidal rot in the pillars of democracy are sadly lacking, disillusionments, antagonism, cynicism, intolerance, hostility and violence have already crossed danger levels in many areas. More are likely to follow.

As pointed out twice earlier, parliament brought disgrace on itself due to lack of dignity by spinelessly tolerating disrespect more than thousand times and lack of guts to punish government for breaking promises so often. Moreover, parliament did not even attempt to rectify the large number of shameful and shocking situations faced by the country, pointed out in this article. Significantly, most dismal failures of democracy were contributed by parliament and assemblies which did not exercise the supreme power bestowed on them to ensure checks. They have, suicidingly, lost their right to continue.

All these emphasize that we should try another system which can uphold the voice of people more efficiently and gracefully and is cheaper. This aspect is discussed in more detail in a later article.

Article 16

Effective functioning of democracy requires an alert media with broad vision which functions as a watch dog of democracy, informs people about the state of affairs and provides a platform for public debate. Media in India needs to improve its functioning in all these aspects.

Article 15 listed 100 deplorable situations which are shocking and shameful for the country. Sad to say, almost all of these were found by other agencies and not by investigations by an active Indian media. Moreover, even when media came to know about some of these, they casually published these but did not adequately question government and MPs/MLAs about these and remedial actions taken. Media also failed to highlight the callous attitude of government towards these shocking and shameful situations to make people aware of all these and to motivate and support people to raise their voice to rectify these matters relating to welfare of people.

Moreover, media has not been sufficiently active in provoking and encouraging debates about saving our democracy and arriving at consensus on possible solutions. Media did not start a debate on why we should spend thousands of crores of public money to maintain an unworthy parliament. Editorials did not focus adequately on the decaying democracy and how to save it. Printed media did not adequately encourage journalists and social activists to publish articles discussing need and/or suggestions for improving democracy.

What is worse, media was not alert enough to realize that parliament was void (Article 2).

Media did nothing to ensure welfare of people. It did not perform its responsibility to carry out regular checks on fulfillment of accountability by political leaders who have serious responsibilities for governance.

There is very little overlapping of readers of different newspapers and journals. Yet, newspapers and journals did not have the broad vision to publish even important articles published in other newspapers and journals (or their brief extracts) (with due acknowledgement), which would have benefited their readers and led to wider awareness and discussion of all aspects. Because of this restrictive mind set, which lacks broad vision, people all over the country do not get an opportunity to become aware of all important ideas and debate these. Media failed in this important responsibility. Obstacles in spreading of ideas openly are antidemocratic and should be removed immediately.

Panel discussions on TV mostly focus on trivial inter and intra political party matters and not on the condition of democracy and how to improve it.

There is an urgent need to review media's value system. It is shocking that media attached more value to one death from terror attack than to about 10,000 deaths from accidents which was only casually reported by few newspapers only!! Moreover, loss of even less than 10 lives due to terrorist attacks has been followed by much larger hue and cry than for even grossly bigger losses in lives due to preventable calamities such as collapsing of structures, stampede etc. Such mismatch of value of life is grossly illogical and has only created unnecessary panic among people and did not help to prevent terrorist attacks.

What is worse, this thoughtless splashing of news has unwittingly helped terrorists in their main aim of creating panic. Media has not realized that terrorists themselves know that they are incapable of doing any large scale harm. They had planned only to create panic and media has helped them exceedingly well to achieve their aim!! Innovative approaches are essential to tackle this delicate situation and spoil the aim of terrorists to create panic. One way is to completely suppress news of terrorist attacks in public interest and confidentially take up with government the need to ensure proper preventive steps. Such a blackout of news will make terrorists frustrated, exasperated and miserable. It will also prevent scare among the public. A total review of value system and right to freedom of expression is called for, particularly for splashing news.

Another problem is lopsided priorities. Important aspects of governance and peoples' welfare do not receive adequate attention. Major parts of printing space/TV time are wasted on inter and intra political party disputes and making statements and speculations about these to add fuel to the fire. Space for proper news is often thoughtlessly displaced by photos of VIPs and their activities like celebration of birthdays, weddings and other events; news about their pregnancies, divorces, travels, retirement etc.; and their speeches of doubtful importance. These have absolutely no relevance to governance or welfare of people. Gossips about VIPs and politicians are a major weakness of the media. Besides irrelevance, these also lead to denial of space for problems in development faced by people and activities of their unsung leaders who have contributed to happiness and peace in society.

Semi naked colour pictures of women (not befitting our culture) have become an essential part of printed media. These numerous semi naked female photos give a wrong impression that most women like to be voluptuously dressed!! This also shows disrespect to Indian women because they like to dress with dignity.

Media has a short memory even for important matters. It has not realized that government has adopted a strategy of "buying time" on their correct understanding that media never persists with its "protests" long enough and allows them to die quietly because of loss in news value. Media has the responsibility to develop a system of regular follow up of all serious matters till government action produces desired results. It should think out of the box and adopt innovative methods to have news value for its follow up activities also.

Concentration on news items which give importance to gossip about politicians and high society or focus on crimes, disasters, failures etc., reveals a negative mind set which is not conducive to growth of democracy. Positive news which show healthy developments such as individuals or small groups (who are not VIPs) contributing to welfare of people and/or peace in different parts of the country hardly find a place because of media's inertia and lack of interest and vision. Very little importance is given to the positive consequences of such news to the society. Moreover, media does not realize that publicizing positive developments which can set healthy examples are crucial.

Media has been side tracked by monetary considerations. Often, in many newspapers front page which should get priority for main news has given way to advertisements, even full page, which fetches large amounts of money. This is in addition to space for advertisements far outstretching space for news. Paid news is another shameful matter.

Thinking out of the box is a rare phenomenon.

At a recent well attended panel discussion in Delhi Habitat Centre all participants expressed the view that the media scene in India was catastrophic because of the fear among journalists to criticize the present government. If journalists are so afraid, they will become irrelevant. The only solution they suggested was that journalists should stand up against the undesirable policies and actions of governments. Not doing this immediately will be a death blow to both journalists and democracy.

All these show lack of vision on the part of media and failures in fulfilling their social responsibilities as a watch dog, information agency and guide for growth of democracy.

To overcome these drawbacks, media should give immediate attention to a speech by President Pranab Mukherjee. expressing concern over "aberrations" like "paid news" which have crept into the media. He said "Sensationalism should never become a substitute for objective assessment and truthful reporting. Gossip and speculation should not replace hard facts. Every effort should be made to ensure that political or commercial interests are not passed off as legitimate and independent opinion." He also emphasized that the media can undertake its role of cleansing public life only if it's own conduct is above board. He made out a case for not just weeding out "aberrations" but also putting in place self-correcting mechanisms to check such tendencies.

Introspection on all the aspects mentioned in Article 16 is essential. This should be undertaken by colleges teaching journalism, media establishments, working journalists and organizations like Press Council, Editors' Guild, newspaper associations etc. After that a code of ethics to guide their activities should be evolved in a democratic manner. Thinking out of the box needs to be given high priority and widely encouraged by publishing such articles. Constitution of a national regulatory authority is also needed.

Meanwhile, media ought to immediately start a debate on why we should spend thousands of crores of public money to maintain an unworthy parliament, as detailed in Article 15. It should also use this set of articles to create awareness among people about the various obstacles in proper functioning of our democracy so that pitfalls while developing a modified system of democracy can be avoided.

Article 17

Before independence, the country had leaders who sacrificed a lot to fight for independence. After independence, some of the freedom fighters became politicians and adopted a different role viz., governing the country with a commitment to national interests and welfare of people. Unfortunately, over time, there has been steady deterioration in the spirit of sacrifice and commitment to national interests and welfare of people among political leaders. President Pranab Mukherjee expressed concern and disappointment at the "eroding commitment among the legislators who are expected to be custodians of public interests and rights."

On the other hand, most of the freedom fighters did not take up any new role. They were complacent because they felt that the country was safe in the hands of the leaders who fought for freedom. They now realize that political leaders not only do not feel the need for support from spirited groups like "freedom fighters" but also feared that such people can be a hindrance for their selfish endeavours and avoided or even suppressed them. Most of them have become disappointed and cynical and suffer from a defeatist mentality. Younger generations of potential upholders of democracy are either confused without proper leadership or have been cleverly side tracked by misinformation and misdirection.

To overcome this situation, upholders of democracy (old and potential) should wake up as quickly as possible and organize themselves to save the sinking democracy. To make meaningful efforts, they and their new leaders should dare to think and act for securing welfare of the people. An essential first step is to create wide spread awareness among people about many obstacles which led to the sinking of our democracy. Then they have to awaken and motivate people, particularly the youth, to act peacefully without fear and with patience to achieve the goal of a truly vibrant democracy. They should be prepared for a long peaceful fight against powerful vested interests who will give threats and play lot of tricks to prevent any meaningful reform of democracy.

It is pertinent, encouraging and reassuring that creation of mass awareness will ensure that peoples' power will be forthcoming to take adequate precautions needed from time to time. With adequate precautions, commitment, determination to fight against all obstacles and patience success can be achieved and will confirm the invincibility of peoples' power.

Article 18

To sustain democracy, we (the people), have to realize our responsibilities and play important roles to ensure that governance is carried out according to the true spirit of democracy. For this, we have the responsibility to elect representatives who have character, clean image and the qualifications and experience needed for governance. We have not only miserably failed to do so but also have not realized the seriousness of our mistakes and therefore remain callous about these.

About 30% who did not vote totally failed in their responsibility. Among those who voted, 90% did not fulfill their responsibility of choosing capable and efficient representatives with character and clean image (Articles 1 and 2). Shockingly, because most elected persons did not get support of more than 50% of the electorate required to become representatives their ***election was void.*** People have not realised that this very serious problem was created by their irresponsible voting.

While electing representatives, we have not realized that capacity required for good governance is different from that needed to win an election and that while winning an election needs capacity for one time hectic effort only, good governance needs capacity for sustained efforts for many years. We also forget that politicians often make promises only to win elections. We do not realize that all these explain why experts in winning elections have often failed to ensure good governance and peoples' welfare. The tragedy is that people have failed to understand the incapacities and failures of politicians explained above. What is worse, we even blindly worship them.

To be efficient voters people should watch out to prevent being duped by experts in winning elections. The common practices of merely blaming others without giving positive solutions and resorting to hate speeches should be considered as disqualifications. People should demand proof about their capacity and commitment to ensure peoples' welfare and verify their character and image. Most important, people should demand convincing answers about why they (or their party) did not fulfill the promises made earlier.

As responsible voters, we should reject even suitable candidates if they belong to a party which is observed to be "buying votes" or has sponsored candidates with criminal background. This is very important because, after election, even these "honest candidates" will be forced to support party interests at the cost of peoples' interests; for example supporting the party in not punishing those who have amassed wealth or have misused their power to help vested interests.

All these question the appropriateness of continuation of the election system which was designed for giving voice to people. We (the people), who have not used our voice properly, are responsible for this suicidal situation.

Another major failure is that after voting once in five years, we close our eyes and allow our representatives and the government they form to govern as they like. We are not alert enough to question when they do not act to ensure our needs and aspirations and repeatedly ignore the principles of democracy and the promises made at election time.

A third major failure is the misconception that government alone can provide good governance. This has led to a totally negative and callous attitude about cooperating with government efforts and supplementing these. Even worse, we often create problems for good governance because of lethargy, narrow selfish interests and intolerance of others.

When faced with problems, we expect government to do everything for us but we do not make any efforts to cooperate with government to solve problems or try to reduce them. If we watch carefully with the keen intention to reduce problems, we can help a lot.

We have also developed the damaging habit of hero worship which has often resulted in our blindly glorifying some politicians – sometimes even ignoring their criminal past and their wrong actions which have not only harmed the country (or large sections of population) but also destroyed democracy. We allow ourselves to be mesmerized by their oratory or hoodwinked by clever tactics, even when they did not ensure peoples' welfare with equanimity and killed our democracy by becoming enemies of democracy (Article 19).

A fundamental mistake is to consider that democracy is needed only for good governance. We have not realized that many more aspects (e.g., those relating to religion, culture, entertainment, recreation, sports etc.) require organized attention to avoid conflicts and to enjoy a peaceful life and be happy. These cannot and should not be taken up by government. We have to build other organizations to fulfill our responsibility to ensure happy and peaceful environment for all the above aspects, which are not subjected to hatred and fear.

National integration, which helps to sustain democracy (Article 12), has failed mainly because we have not taken any interest in building up the concept of being Indians. We have not realized the importance of having a national script for all languages (Article 12). Regrettably, we have nurtured dissipating tendencies instead of building up togetherness with humanitarian approaches.

Because our attempts to ensure the noble idea of equality were illogical, impractical and made us hypocrites, we can and should set limits for inequalities in income, expenditure, ownership of land etc. (for more details see the article). This is another fundamental omission.

We should insist that once in six months the MLA of our area together with our MP should report to us their achievements as well as problems faced and future plans to overcome these in a meeting of all "groups" of people (without any exceptions). During these meetings, they should also advice us about how we can cooperate with them to achieve better results and also help to maintain peace and social harmony in the area, besides striving for national integration. An important result will be that people will become aware of problems faced by government and will not resort to unnecessary agitations.

During these meetings people should also give their assessment of the extent to which government has succeeded in meeting their needs and aspirations. This method of assessing efficiency of MPs, MLAs and government is a much better way for people to exercise their voice than by voting once in five years to elect representatives without (a) knowledge and expertise required to elect efficient managers of democracy (Article 14) and (b) being misguided by other considerations like, caste, party affiliation, monitory incentives etc.

These aspects are discussed in more detail in a later article.

Some cunning leaders cleverly manipulate creation of caste, linguistic, religious and other group conflicts as well as cliques and other favourable conditions to safeguard their interests and to achieve their ignoble ambitions. We should not allow ourselves to become their tools for such anti-social activities which disturb peace in our areas.

Some disqualifications for a leader of democracy are explained in Article 19. We should closely watch whether our leaders have any of these disqualifications and, if so, should not choose them as our representatives.

We have also to be alert to ensure that mischief mongers and selfish groups do not create problems. Constant efforts should be made to identify rumour mongers and to isolate them in the community.

We have to give full support to social activists who are eager to be upholders of democracy so that they can provide leadership for saving our sinking democracy. We should request them to be our watchful leaders to attend the 6-monthly meetings suggested earlier and to bring problems to the notice of the authorities and fight peacefully for solutions.

We should develop a sense of discipline to solve problems which come up and to avoid creating other problems. We have to play the dual roles of partners in democracy and watch dogs to detect deficiencies in our democracy.

All these show that we, the people, have some wrong perceptions which hinder development and maintenance of vibrant democracy leading to a happy life. To overcome these we have to ***change our mindset.***

Article 19

Indian democracy is managed by politicians who are not qualified in the art or science of governance. In addition to lack of such qualification, many political leaders have acquired at least some of the <u>fourteen serious disqualifications</u> mentioned in this article (for details see full article).

Even small fry politicians throw their weight around, routinely break laws, and take pride in doing so. They feel laws and regulations are meant for ordinary mortals, and flouting these as a measure of their own importance. Top leaders of different parties don't crack down hard on criminal behaviour by their colleagues. All these imply that politicians became enemies of democracy – ***protectors of law themselves becoming violators of law.***

The worst attack parliament is facing is from within, by numerous instances of undisciplined behaviour of MPs which do not allow parliament to function properly. This implies for the <u>second time</u> that politicians became enemies of democracy – ***destroying the main pillar of democracy instead of strengthening it.***

Continuous control of activities of professionally qualified and experienced officers at top level by politicians without relevant qualifications implies for the <u>third time</u> that politicians became enemies of democracy – ***hindered professional governance instead of promoting it.***

Some political leaders enticed top level officers to form a politician-cum-bureaucrat nexus to gain benefits for this nexus and their political party. Those who did not fall in line were shunted to less important positions and harassed regularly. Officers who were honest and sincere were either sidelined or transferred frequently with some officers being transferred 40 times or more (Article 7). By adopting these two strategies, politicians destroyed the innate character and strength of our system of governance, without realizing the serious harm they have done to the backbone of our governance system. This serious destruction implies for <u>the fourth time</u> that politicians became enemies of democracy – ***those who were expected to build the system became destroyers of the backbone of the system.***

Mahatma Gandhi, who led the fight for independence, was keen to have swaraj (self governance) by people. Regrettably, over time, politicians gave less and less attention to his views on self governance by people. They preferred to become masters of people, by cleverly using the pretext of democracy. This implies for <u>the fifth time</u> that politicians became enemies of democracy – ***became masters of people instead of servants of people.***

The serious damage done by these enemies of democracy is highlighted in an editorial in Deccan Chronicle dated 11.08.17: "It is no secret that......the stumbling block in the nation's progress has been the political class while ordinary Indians – farmers, workers, jawans, teachers, scientists, and industrialists and traders – have made noteworthy contributions to project this country to the rank of leading nations of the world." "As a class, our politicians have engendered both corruption and divisiveness, contrary to the values of the independence movement for which millions of Indians made heroic sacrifices." Instead of working hard for welfare of people and making sacrifices they took credit for what others have done, amassed wealth and enjoyed like kings. This implies for <u>the sixth time</u> that politicians became enemies of democracy – ***taking credit for what others have done instead of working hard for welfare of people.***

Shockingly, qualifications, experience, duties and responsibilities have <u>not</u> been prescribed only for political leaders who have to exercise control over activities carried out by professionals in different fields with prescribed qualifications, experience, duties and responsibilities. It has not been realized that this damaging omission in prescribing duties and responsibilities to MPs and MLAs (particularly ministers) has not led to anarchy only because persons in all other positions have prescribed qualifications, duties and responsibilities!! Moreover, fortunately for the country, the strong sense of discipline, which these officers had, has prevented them from revolting against illogical and absurd supervision by persons (a) without relevant qualifications and (b) without prescribed duties and responsibilities, even though both are sure signs of anarchy.

It is a matter for serious concern that there are ***at least six solid reasons*** for concluding that politicians gave repeated death blows to democracy and became enemies of democracy. Consequently, parliament, with members who became enemies of democracy, has qualified itself for self destruction. Moreover, as pointed out in Article 6, the system has the basic defect that the political party which forms the government also controls the parliament because of having majority. This defective system allows dictatorial attitude in the party and the government and defeats the very purpose of having parliament as an independent pillar of democracy. This basic defect itself is sufficient justification for abolition of the present parliamentary system. It is pertinent that Article 15 also had emphasized the need to abolish parliament because (a) it lacked dignity, guts to punish government for breaking promises more than thousand times, accountability and an ethics of care for aam admi and (b) has a distorted and unhealthy representation of people with vast majority of its members being crorepatis. Most important, our democracy has deteriorated from a flawed democracy to a pseudo democracy (Article 15, item 95). Thus, there are *five strong justifications for abolishing parliament.* Other great advantages of this abolition are (1) enormous amounts will be saved which can be used for welfare of people and (2) large areas of prime land and buildings will be available for public use. An alternative system which is much cheaper and better is discussed in a later article.

For some thought provoking jokes about politicians see full article.

Article 20

How can a party system for governance be justified if political parties can have support of only a minority of the electorate, of which responsible voters form only a small proportion? (Article 2).

Hardly any political party has effective internal democracy. How can parties which do not have respect for internal democracy safeguard democracy in the country?

If there is no party system, elected persons can act with freedom to ensure peoples' welfare and support their needs and aspirations without being subservient to their party's interest and curbed by use of whip while voting.

The large gold mines of talents outside the party in power can be used for benefit of the country if there is no party system.

If there is no party system, legislations with an eye on votes will not occur.

Focus on party's interest led to at least 100 shocking and shameful situations (Article 15). If there is no party system, such callous neglect of peoples' interest will not arise.

Most parties have large army of grass root level workers whose main (or only) interest is safeguarding party interests. They often start inter party disputes and quarrels. Resort to violence is quite common and even murders have occurred. All these can be prevented if there is no party system.

Hero worship has led to many unfortunate situations such as blindly supporting undesirable or ill planned or criminal activities of their heroes and side tracking of honest persons who could have helped the country. These can be prevented if there is no party system.

Attention of the young minds of college students is diverted from their studies and a positive attitude to peoples' problems to a negative one of raving and fighting for party interests. If there is no party system, diversion of interest from studies and fights among college students can be avoided.

These young unbridled minds are thrilled to copy some undesirable behavior and attitudes of present day politicians (Article 19). When these fertile minds grow up in this background they will imbibe undesirable traits. They will become faction leaders, manipulators and traders of hatred. This explosive situation can lead to many undesirable outcomes in future. These undesirable developments can be avoided if there is no party system.

Political parties are responsible for crimes and creation of hatred and violence in many parts of the country. These will be reduced to a large extent and peace will prevail if there is no party system.

While people are suffering from hunger and poverty, most political parties spend huge amounts to celebrate party events. If there is no party system, all these (and some other hidden misuses of money) can be avoided.

If there is no party system, public funds spent to support political parties and their security can be used for benefit of people and diversion of police from their normal duties to protect politicians can be avoided.

Political parties, being beneficiaries of black money, are a root cause for its creation and sustenance. Abolition of party system will lead to substantial reduction in black money.

Another serious problem is creation of duel power centres (multiple in case of coalition governments) which lead to obstacles and delays in decision making. These can be avoided if there is no party system.

The trouble with us is: we have become too politicized a society and cannot look beyond our nose. The culprits are political parties, not the people. If there is no party system, distracting politicization of society will not happen.

Abolition of party system will free police from malignant and suffocating political control and improve law and order situation in the country by leaps and bounds.

Political parties have to amass huge amounts of money to fight elections. For this, illegal activities and generation of black money which harm the country are resorted to. Use of money also leads to dishonest voting in elections. This dismal situation can be avoided if there is no party system.

It may be argued that having political parties helps in two ways: (a) they can serve as peoples' voice as their representatives and (b) provide a check on misgovernance. But, both can be done effectively (unlike at present) by efficient elected representatives without any restriction by their parties. Article 19 shows that politicians became enemies of democracy. Party system is the main cause for this. Therefore, while there is no real advantage in having party system it is harmful. On the other hand, abolishing it has the 17 advantages listed in this article.

If parliament is abolished as strongly urged at the end of Article 19, the need for political parties becomes further questionable. All these demand abolition of party system. Evidently, there is absolutely no doubt that political party system should be abolished.

Article 21

After 2014, many reforms were started in such quick succession that it resulted in a mad rush for reforms. Prior approval of parliament or subsequent ratification by it was not specifically obtained for these important reforms with serious national implications. These are severe death blows to democracy.

This jumping from one scheme to another within a short period without adequate discussions, proper planning, implementation and concurrent evaluation of these schemes has highlighted the unsystematic methods of government and failure of democracy. Successful completion of these reforms requires sustained commitment till their completion. Sad to say, this commitment seems doubtful (for details see full article).

There are four glaring defects common to all these reforms. (1) These were not discussed adequately with Niti Ayog which was set up to perform some of the functions of the dissolved Planning Commission. (2) MI was not adequately briefed and trained (if necessary) to implement the schemes, (3) Concurrent evaluation which could have helped to make midterm correction was not even planned (4) None of these schemes had prior approval of parliament or subsequent ratification by it.

What is worse, all these illustrate a tendency among politicians to attempt a spate of reforms in a hurry ignoring whether these are justified and without proper planning and development of the required infrastructure to implement these. Government has also given triple blows to democracy by (a) repeated attempts to bypass parliament by taking the ordinance route, (b) misuse of money bill provision to bypass the upper house and (c) bypassing the Cabinet.

The fact that these could be done ignoring the checks provided under democracy shows a serious weakness in the functioning of the democratic system. This also confirms the remarks in Articles 5 and 6 that the systems of government formation and government functioning show only lip sympathy to democracy but actually result in a type of subtle and concealed dictatorship.

During a 10 year period, government had broken promises given by it to parliament <u>1,024 times</u> (Article 6). Bypassing parliament while implementing each of the new multiple reforms are other examples in the series of disrespects to parliament. Disrespect to parliament more than thousand times and in number of ways shows that disrespect to parliament was obviously intentional. These are severe death blows to democracy.

All this is possible because of the basic defect in the system that the political party which forms the government also controls the parliament because of having majority (Article 6). Should we not abolish such a fundamentally defective parliament?.

The short cut manner in which views and support of people are obtained through social media is also fundamentally defective. The flimsy views superficially expressed by casual participants in social media are given much more importance than that of parliament and experts – a mockery of democracy and big blows to parliament and experts.

What is worse, social media can be cleverly misused by some leaders to get wide popular support from millions of people who will casually support their views. If this is not curbed immediately by parliament or ignored completely for serious discussions and decisions, it can result in a big blow to efficiency of democracy. Persons indulging in making superficial and irresponsible remarks about governance in social media have to be warned that expressing views on governance (or serious social problems) in a casual and superficial manner will lead to serious consequences for the country for which they will be held responsible.

Social media has also created many serious problems by spreading hatred among people and poisoning young minds. Emotional problems are spread virally, with serious consequences. A thoughtless, misleading and saucy message spread virally through social media can provide the trigger which suddenly blows things out of control.

One study has identified six key areas where social media has become a direct threat to our democratic ideals: (1) Creates bubbles of one-sided information and opinions, perpetuating biased views and diminishing opportunities for healthy discourses. (2) Spreads false or misleading information. (3) The idea that likes or retweets can be used to measure support of a person, message or organization creates a distorted system of evaluating information and provides a false pulse on the popularity of certain views or persons. This is compounded by how challenging it is to distinguish legitimately expressed opinions from those generated by trolls and bots. (4) Such trolls and bots, disguised as ordinary citizens, have become a weapon of choice for governments and political leaders to shape online conversations. (5) Leads to manipulation, micro-targeting and behavioral change through disguised advertising. (6) These platforms can amplify hate speech, terrorist appeals, and racial and sexual harassment. The study calls upon social media companies to help navigate the serious threats posed by their platforms. In an interview, Obama (former president of USA) "opined that the way people communicate via social media risked splintering society."

A thorough review of social media, including the issues pointed out above, has to be conducted and acted upon to ensure a peaceful and efficient democracy.

Article 22

Neglect of problems other than economic growth has led not only to worsening of peoples' problems but also to at least 100 shocking and shameful situations for the country (Article 15). Even recently, hundreds of farmers have committed suicide and lack of adequate remedial measures by government has created other humanitarian problems also. What are worse, violent attacks and even murders due to intolerance of dissent, curbs on freedom of expression, interference in the private domain of people, denouncement of core values of civilization and dictatorial tendencies (see full article for details) are serious death blows to democracy and are ***leading to chaos and anarchy in the country.***

Media has reported many instances of criticism of the present situation. Some of these are briefly pointed out below:

Intolerance in some peaceful fields of entertainment, which many people enjoy, is becoming shamefully common. The narrow politics propelling the cow agenda and ethnic vigilantism puts road blocks on the drive for development. The mandate given to government by 2014 election was for development and not for reviving a brand of Hinduism adopted by some groups.

There are violent acts of intolerance by people taking law into their hands. Reactionary forces are trying to have a say in everything that people do – what they eat, how they dress, fall in love, worship or celebrate festivals. What is alarming is that these atrocities appear to be state sponsored/sanctioned violence rather than a result of lawlessness. Meddling with people's lives by state must stop.

Evidently, government is not serious about controlling criminal intolerance and anarchy is creeping in due to allowing some extremists to take law into their hands and even glorify commitment of murders.

The worst damage is development of autocracy, "In the latest rankings of the Varieties of Democracy (V-DEM) Institute a research project that tries to evolve new measures of democracy, ***India's rank is seen dropping in the past four years,*** with a marked concentration of powers in the hands of one individual."

In order to prevent publicity to this failure of democracy, government has resorted to muzzling the media. At a recent well attended panel discussion in Delhi Habitat Centre all participants expressed the view that the media scene in India was catastrophic because of the fear among journalists to criticize the present Government. If journalists are so afraid, they will become irrelevant. The only solution they suggested was that journalists should stand up against the undesirable policies and actions of governments. This need was emphasized by President Pranab Mukherjee also. He said that the press will be failing in its duty if it does not ask questions to those in power.

President Pranab Mukherjee also exhorted that withering away of the core values of our civilization should not be allowed. L.K. Advani, an erstwhile top visionary BJP leader, also cautioned some months back that an emergency like situation seems to be coming up.

All these give added justification and urgency to expedite drastic changes needed in our democracy. Since this will take some time to materialize even after taking it up with vision and commitment, immediate action has to be taken *to stem the rot before it results in chaos, anarchy and violent revolution.*

Steps should be taken to ensure that (a) no one can ignore the checks under the democratic system and act according to his/her whims in an autocratic manner, (b) parliament invariably exerts its authority to curb actions which cause disrespect to it and (c) social media does not lead to false support to political leaders and a distorted democracy with violence and loss of peace. It is pertinent that checks can be effective only if majority of MPs who have to ensure compliance of these checks, are committed to these. As a safeguard against possible lack of commitment (as has happened now), eminent independent authorities (other than politicians and government) with adequate staff and other facilities should be entrusted with monitoring these checks.

Article 23

This article highlights *nine absurdities* which have not been questioned.

Shockingly, professionally qualified, trained and experienced officers at top levels are supervised and controlled by persons who have not been assessed to have (1) pertinent professional qualifications, (2) intellectual capacity to develop the required functioning efficiency, (3) special training and (4) adequate working experience!! Though this practice is obviously illogical and against the principles of management, it has continued for years *because no one has questioned this absurdity.*

For higher education, bright students prefer fields such as engineering, medicine, management, commerce etc. The duller students who cannot get admission for these preferred courses often become politicians and later on supervise and control the more intelligent persons and have the last laugh!! As a result, the bewildered former tend to fear the latter (politicians) and develop an inferiority complex and type of mental slavery (to the latter) despite topping in intelligence. *This second absurdity also has not been questioned.* Why?

Political leaders used two clever strategies: (1) They cleverly isolated professionals from the power structure at the highest level so that they do not have strength to fight or question absurdities. (2) Using the gift of the gab, they mesmerized people to start hero worship and to get deeply involved in their political fights. This way they cleverly succeeded in diverting peoples' attention away from absurdities.

Top level officers had spent enormous amounts of time, efforts and money for acquiring the basic qualifications, faced competitive selection, underwent special training and worked for many years to gain experience. But they were not allowed to use their expertise freely for efficient functioning because of being controlled by unqualified politicians. Ironically, they were not even given a chance to prove their worth. Allowing this cunning strategy is the ***third absurdity.*** This deliberate wastage of professional training and expertise is a mockery of the system of selection and training of professionals. This is the ***fourth absurdity.***

Root cause for not questioning these contemptible absurdities is that political leaders, by becoming heroes using the gift of the gab, fooled people to believe the ***fifth absurdity*** that they had the super human capacity to effectively supervise and control professionally qualified, specially trained and experienced persons, that too in a variety of disciplines!!

Political leaders also claimed that their supervision and control was necessary to ensure that professional managers listen to peoples' voice. The obvious and effective method to overcome this was to give these brilliant professional managers the necessary additional training. Ignoring this is the ***sixth absurdity.***

Instead, politicians diverted attention to the election system which they had cleverly created so that they can claim that they represent people. But, this turned out to be a contemptible hollow claim because most of them did not get support of more than 50% of the electorate which was required to become valid representatives, even after managing mocked support through irresponsible voting (Article 2). Why was this obviously startling revelation of contemptible hollow claim ignored? Because, blind hero worship of politicians prevented people from opening their eyes to this ***seventh absurdity*** of hollow claim also.

The ***eighth absurdity*** is the belief that voters, among whom large proportions are illiterate or inadequately educated, have the capacity to judge and elect persons who can perform functions of governance efficiently!!

In the absence of this judging capacity, blind hero worship influenced election and political leaders with the gift of the gab gained. This has continued for years ***because no one questioned this ninth absurdity.***

These unquestioned contemptible absurdities favouring political leaders have led to prolonged mis-governance with lop sided priorities which not only did not benefit vast majority of people but also made the rich richer. India has the dubious distinction of being the second most unequal. Number of rich persons (millionaires and even billionaires) has increased rapidly during 2015 to 2017. Crorepatis (owning more than 10 millions) increased by 23.5% in 2015 and the number of super rich grew by 12% in 2017. In 2017, while India had 101 dollar billionaires, 96% adults had wealth below $10,000. Vast majority of people has to struggle for basic necessities of life and has been forced to live without dignity, as second or even third class citizens. Millions are suffering from poverty, hunger and lack of shelter at night while the rich live in palatial bunglows/flats, squander money and waste food (for some more details see full article). Such gross inequalities are severe death blows to democracy. Highest priority given for growth rate at the expense of important social priorities like education and health which are essential for good quality of life with dignity, is a matter for serious concern.

Blind acceptance of the nine absurdities discussed above depicts a type of mental slavery to politicians which has continued for many years. Sad to say, hardly anyone woke up from this stupor. What is worse, ***even the wish to come out of this mental slavery seems to be absent!!*** Does anyone really want independence?

Being accustomed to mental slavery, people have closed their eyes to another type of slavery also: India has the dubious distinction of having the largest number of modern-day slaves in the world, 18 million and counting. This includes bonded labour, human trafficking, forced marriages, women coerced into prostitution or badly paid menial work. The most vulnerable among these are the children.

In the Global Slavery Index, compiled by Walk Free Foundation, India is among the top four offenders in percentage terms. If mental slavery to politicians also is taken into account, India will most probably get another dubious distinction of topping the Global Slavery Index.

If you agree that a change in our democracy which is wrongly based on the nine absurdities explained above, is overdue, let us strive to make people aware of the need to (1) wake up and join together to overcome hero worship and mental slavery to political leaders and (2) set the ball rolling towards a peaceful revolution to free ourselves from mental slavery to politicians and to achieve true democracy.

To demonstrate that they have succeeded in getting rid of mental slavery to politicians people should demand setting up of a new Constituent Assembly to (1) discuss and finalize all details of the comprehensive democracy outlined in Article 27 in which political leaders have no part and (2) appoint interim governments at the centre and in all states comprising of qualified and honest experts selected by it to govern the country after expiry of the current parliament till the comprehensive democracy is set up. ***Another step which can be taken effortlessly is to click NOTA option in coming elections.***

If we hesitate to put all our efforts on such a peaceful revolution, a violent bloody revolution which is already looming in the horizon will engulf us soon.

Let us be encouraged by the fact that Mahatma Gandhi (who got us independence from the mightiest empire by leading a non-violent movement) has shown us how even unbelievable changes can be achieved when ordinary people come together and use their hidden power to do extraordinary things.

Organizers of the peaceful revolution can learn the following lessons from the recent Jalikattu protest: (a) Victory of the Jallikattu agitation within a few days shows that it is still possible for hundreds of thousands of people to rise unitedly and become a force so powerful and so swift that no power on earth can resist such peaceful agitations and (b) Eruption of violence after few days shows that rowdy elements and/or vested interests can infiltrate to spoil a peaceful movement. Steps should be taken to continue the peaceful revolution.

Note:

The gift of the gab: Ability to speak easily and confidently in a way that makes people want to listen to you and believe you.

This mesmerizing ability has often been misused to develop blind hero worship resulting in mind slavery and mockery of independent thinking.

Article 25

Basic Principles

Articles 1 to 23 of this series have described thirty-two obstacles which resulted in a distorted and ineffective democracy. These articles also gave some suggestions to overcome these. The summing up (Article 24) reiterated some important aspects in earlier articles to reemphasize the back ground and to focus on necessary changes required to revive our sinking democracy.

It is crystal clear from these that tinkering with individual aspects of present system of democracy, with naïve and unrealistic expectations, is thoroughly inadequate because there are too many serious faults in the functioning of democracy (32 have been identified in these articles – there may be more). Of these, the following defects deserve recapitulation:

The present system of democracy has many basic faults (Articles 6&7) and fifteen fundamental weaknesses (Article 14) and is based on nine absurdities (Article 23). Moreover, elections have resulted in void parliament (Article 2) which also had faulty representation because majority of members were crorepatis. MPs and ministers not only did not have required qualifications but also have many disqualifications. What is worse, they became enemies of democracy (Article 19). Parliament tolerated disrespect from government more than thousand times and failed to control government (Articles 6 and 22). The political party system has no real advantages but many disadvantages and is more a hindrance than help to democracy (Article 20). Judicial system has basic defects (Article 11). Moreover, lakhs of complaints about human rights violations were dismissed by NHRC without examination because of a faulty regulation (Article 10). Management infrastructure comprising of ministers and officials has 11 basic faults (Article 7). Government formation and its working have resulted in a pseudo democracy (Article 5). Journalists and media owners are afraid to criticize government. Both have resulted in serious death blows to democracy (Article 16). There are at least 27 instances of hypocrisy of government about zero tolerance to corruption and undoubtedly corruption is widespread now and increasing (Article 9). The system has deteriorated from flawed democracy to pseudo democracy and the rank of Indian democracy has consistently "dropped in the past four years, with marked concentration of powers in the hands of one individual" (Items 95 and 96 of Article 15, Articles 21 and 22). Intolerance and people taking law into their hands are leading to anarchy and chaos (Article 21). Antidemocratic approach by government has become quite common and social media has displaced in depth study, discussions and debates and spread hate and violence (Article 22). Present democracy is restricted to governance only and does not focus on many other aspects which have influence on having a happy life with peace and dignity (Article 18). This has to be replaced with a comprehensive democracy to fully meet needs and aspirations of people. The new system cannot be built correctly without discarding the old system which has many basic faults and fundamental weaknesses and is based on nine absurdities.

To tackle all these issues bravely it is essential to think out of the box and replace present democracy by a comprehensive democracy as suggested above.

Concept of comprehensive democracy: As explained in Article 18, a fundamental mistake in present concept of democracy is to consider that democracy is needed only for good governance. Many more aspects e.g., religion, culture, entertainment, recreation etc., have influence on quality of life – may be even more than governance. To live happily with good quality of life and dignity under peaceful environments and carry on activities without hindrance all these aspects require careful attention and proper direction, which are lacking at present. Present democracy has ignored the fact that conflicts in some of these activities have been responsible for many unhappy situations and disturbance of peace and harmony. For example, all religions have laudable principles which, if channeled properly without interfering with their freedom, can lead to peace and harmony. If not, it can lead to disharmony and even fights, riots and wars as had happened number of times in the past all over the world. Evidently, a more comprehensive concept of democracy, that takes into account all aspects which have influence on living happily with good quality of life with dignity under peaceful environment and carrying on activities without hindrance, is essential. Keeping these in view the following aim and definition of comprehensive democracy are suggested:

Aim of comprehensive democracy: Ensure that people can live happily with good quality of life and dignity under peaceful environment and carry on their activities without hindrance.

Definition of comprehensive democracy: A system which ensures that people can live happily with good quality of life and dignity under peaceful environments and carry on their activities without hindrance.

The above aim and definition does not specifically mention about need for governance, health, education, employment or enterprise, prosperity, etc. because these are essential to live happily with good quality of life and dignity under peaceful environments and carry on activities without hindrance.

Government cannot and should not be involved in all the aspects mentioned earlier. To ensure proper development of economic, social, religious, cultural, entertainment and other activities to serve the aim of comprehensive democracy, it is important to establish some more authorities under the system, in addition to governance authority (government). Details of setting up these authorities and allocation of responsibilities between them have to be formulated by expert groups in various fields and debated to arrive at a consensus. This consensus should not be rigid and should be reviewed at suitable intervals to adapt to changes in socio-economic, religious, cultural, entertainment and other environments.

As pointed out in earlier articles, highest priority should be given to various professional activities which are essential for welfare of people. For this, each Authority should be managed by professionally qualified and experienced staff of the required disciplines and should be allowed to function without any hindrance from non-professionals and with full accountability. To ensure that these independent authorities continue to perform properly, a system of checks and balances should be created.

Comprehensive democracy should continuously ascertain needs and aspirations of people and carry out activities to fulfill these as best as possible. Mechanisms should also be created to (a) involve people in planning and implementation of all types of activities, (b) assess performance of the system (e.g., through the six-monthly meetings suggested in Article 18) and (c) ensure proper functioning of all checks and balances. We (the people) also have the responsibility to ensure happy and peaceful environments which are not subjected to jealousy, hatred, vengeance and fear. ***This is the way to have a true and vibrant comprehensive democracy.***

We have to visualize some other important basic principles also which ought to form the back bone of a true and vibrant comprehensive democracy. For example, because ensuring the noble idea of equality is impractical, comprehensive democracy can and should set limits for inequalities in income and expenditure, ownership of land etc.

These important aspects are discussed further in a later article.

Some realities:

Mahatma Gandhi, who had fought for freedom, dignity and swaraj throughout his life, would be most unhappy if he were alive today. For example, how many present leaders, who habitually pay tributes to him on his birth and death anniversaries, really care to reach the goals set by him? For reaching these goals, utmost care has to be taken to avoid discontinuities in purposeful activities.

Government has been sitting for more than ten years on poll reforms suggested by Election Commission. Moreover, the new type of comprehensive democracy will bring in more authorities and weaken its superiority. Therefore, it is naïve to depend on government to develop comprehensive democracy.

This series of articles emphasize that development, sustenance and growth of democracy are the responsibility of all citizens, organized groups and statutory institutions, besides government.

All of them have to wake up and act peacefully if they sincerely want a true and vibrant comprehensive democracy.

The real problem is that because of mental slavery to politicians we allow them to govern even when they do not have any specific qualifications to govern, as explained in Article 23. Howard Zinn calls it "silent obedience of people to the dictates of their leaders who are running the country." He says: "Our problem is the numbers of people all over the world who have obeyed the dictates of the leaders of their government and have gone to war, and millions have been killed because of this obedience." "Our problem is that people are obedient all over the world, in the face of poverty and starvation and stupidity, and war and cruelty." "Our problem is that people are obedient while the jails are full of petty thieves, and all the while the grand thieves are running the country." "That's our problem."

Another serious problem: Most democracies are predominantly influenced by the rich and the powerful and have become pseudo democracies. According to Henry Montzberg, celebrated academician, author and faculty of McCall University, Canada "governments all over the world have reached a point where they can do nothing at all for the society" (Deccan Chronicle dated 06-02-13, page 6).

Moreover, the fundamental misconception that democracy is needed only for good governance is a global phenomenon. This will be a main hindrance for comprehensive democracy besides the opposition by politicians and the rich and the powerful, who are hoodwinking people in different ways.

To overcome this difficult situation, we have to free ourselves from mental slavery to politicians and dominance of the rich and the powerful, break our silence and take meaningful actions in a peaceful manner. An inspiring fact is that when hundreds of thousands of people rise unitedly for a peaceful movement it can become a force so powerful and so swift that no power on earth can resist it.

However, because absence of comprehensive democracy is a global reality we have to act without looking for guidance or models from other countries. It has to be built up in stages. When we develop comprehensive democracy people from many more countries will welcome our efforts with admiration.

To strengthen our resolve it is high time we ask ourselves:

Why should we not abolish the present system of democracy which has many basic faults (Articles 6 & 7) and fifteen fundamental weaknesses (Article 14) and is based on nine absurdities (Article 23)?

Are we happy with the present distorted and ineffective democracy which is actually a subtle invisible dictatorship (Article 5)?

Is the present pseudo democracy not against the spirit of our Constitution?

Why should we spend huge amounts on elections which is not able to elect true representatives of people (Article 2) particularly when, globally, "more and more younger people are believing that voting is not essential to the effective functioning of democracy"? (The Week dated 25.12.2016, page 68).

Is not the parliamentary system fundamentally defective when a political party is able to control both government and parliament, because of majority membership of parliament, and results in a docile parliament? (Article 6).

Why do we spend lakhs of crores of public money to maintain parliament whose members have become enemies of democracy and are lacking in accountability and an ethics of care for *aam admi?* (Articles 15, 19 and 20).

Why should we have a distorted parliament with majority of crorepati members who favour the rich?

Why should we not abolish parliament which has been spinelessly tolerating breaking of promises by government more than thousand times, without the dignity expected from the august supreme body, instead of exercising its responsibility of having a check on functioning of government?

Why should we foolishly continue to give all powers to politicians who are not qualified in the art or science of governance, have many disqualifications and have become enemies of democracy? (Article 19).

Why should we not get rid of political party system which is more a hindrance than help to democracy? (Article 20).

Is the need for a thorough change of the present system of democracy not obvious? Why should we not strive for a comprehensive democracy which ensures that people can live happily with good quality of life and dignity under peaceful environment and carry on their activities without hindrance?

Can we depend on government and political parties to really take interest in bringing in reforms which are suicidal to the greedy and selfish interests of some influential political leaders and powerful individuals and groups?

How can we motivate society to develop the will for a thorough change which is absolutely necessary to create a true and vibrant comprehensive democracy, without looking for guidance or models from other countries?

Should we not wake up and act in a peaceful manner to usher in true and vibrant comprehensive democracy?

Many more crucial questions can be added.

"The important thing is not to stop questioning"

– Albert Einstein

Article 26

Basic Needs

Article 25 emphasized the need to have a comprehensive democracy with many sub systems to overcome the misconception that democracy is required for governance only.

To systematically develop comprehensive democracy, we should recognize the basic principles and needs it has to satisfy. Thereafter, holistic action has to be taken with determination and commitment to satisfy these needs and principles. While doing so we should (a) think out of the box for innovative ideas and (b) prevent influential persons and power mongers from interfering to protect their vested interests.

Article 25 spelt out the basic principles. This Article spells out the basic needs of comprehensive democracy.

A comprehensive democracy ought to have:

1. ***Collective leadership:*** Historically, democracy was thought of as an alternative to despicable monarchy in which all power was concentrated on one individual. In the type of democracy which was developed, power was shifted to elected representatives of people. But, power often became concentrated on one leader of these representatives who became a sly monarch. Thus the process of developing true democracy was aborted. To avoid such sly monarchy and effectively complete the vision of democracy true collective leadership is absolutely necessary.

2. ***Efficient sub systems:*** In addition to governance sub system, other sub systems should be established for each of the

other aspects which ensure that people can live happily with a good quality of life and dignity under peaceful environments and carry on their activities without hindrance. At present, sub systems other than governance have hardly received any attention and should be developed after proper studies, dialogues and debates. For example, absence of a proper "Religion sub-system" has often led to disturbance of peace, loss of brotherhood, conflicts and even war. Comprehensive democracy ought to have a suitable professional authority to remove aberrations in religious activities and give proper sense of direction without interfering in true practice of any religion. This authority should carry out necessary studies, debates and dialogues. The emphasis should be on properly following religious principles to ensure that people can live happily with good quality of life (including spiritual development) and dignity, under peaceful environments.

3. ***Professional management:*** There can be no doubt that most efficient management can be provided only by professionally qualified and experienced persons, without hindrance from non-professionals. To ensure that each sub-system functions efficiently, suitable professional management should be ensured and concurrent checks and balances should be provided.

4. ***Concurrent control by people:*** At present, elections are conducted once in five years to provide voice to people through their representatives. This indirect method has completely failed (Articles 1 to 4). This should be replaced by the half yearly meetings suggested in Article 18. In these meetings, authorities of each sub-system, should inform people either directly or through their local leaders (without any exceptions), about their achievements as well as problems faced and future plans. People should give their assessment of the extent to which their needs and aspirations have been met. This direct method of ensuring that each sub system is answerable to people once in six months is far superior to giving

indirect voice to people through elected representatives once in five years. An important advantage is that during these meetings, people will become aware of problems faced by the sub system and will be able to make reasonable and pragmatic demands only.

5. ***A mechanism to ensure systematic changes in the system:*** Through the frequent and direct control mentioned above, people can give frequent feed backs about how far each sub-system has satisfied their needs and aspirations. But, most of them do not have capacity, inclination and time to suggest changes needed in sub-systems to (a) ensure that their needs and aspirations are fully met and (b) adjust to rapid changes occurring in the country and the world. Such ideas and visions can be provided by a section of intelligentsia which is in touch with people and global changes. A mechanism has to be set up to encourage flow of ideas and visions from people (particularly from intelligentsia), to analyze these and to present useful ideas to authorities of each sub-system. This approach also makes intelligentsia feel much more involved in democracy than at present.

6. ***Independent authority to regulate and expand media activities:*** Media failed to systematically put continuous pressure on government to solve problems faced by people and the country and to provide an avenue or platform for interested people to freely spread and absorb positive ideas about democracy and development (Article 16). Media was not adequately involved in activities other than governance. A professional body should be created to regulate and expand media activities, without hindrance from government or any sub system, power mongers and commercial interests. This body should also, directly and indirectly, make people more knowledgeable and involved in all aspects of comprehensive democracy so that they can participate

more effectively in six monthly meetings. Corporate bodies or influential organisations of any sub system should be debarred from owning or controlling media to gain power to influence management of any sub system and mislead people to serve their selfish interests.

7. ***Adequate opportunities and services to aam admi:*** Vested interests often indirectly curtail opportunities and services to common people. For example, commercial enterprises, by providing costly sophisticated services which can be used only by the rich, have diverted attention away from providing affordable education and health care of good quality to common people. Honest journalists are hindered in their activities. Sportsmen have very little say in sports matters. Many talented people in the fields of arts and entertainments are bypassed because of vested interests which blow up persons of their choice only. All these lead to frustrations among people and hinder proper development of these fields in a democratic manner. Therefore, full attention has to be given to provide adequate opportunities and services to people in all fields in a democratic manner.

8. ***Full focus on prosperity, dignity, peace, humanity and happiness:*** The single track concentration on GDP growth has resulted in at least 100 shocking and shameful situations (Article 15). Inclusive prosperity is conspicuous by its absence. Hardly any attention has been given to ensure that people live happily with dignity and peace. Comprehensive democracy has to give highest priority to a humanitarian approach to provide prosperity, dignity, peace, and happiness to maximum number of people. While growth of economy of the country is desirable, it is not essential for fulfilling the aim of comprehensive democracy. For instance, in 2016, Denmark which topped the list in Happiness

Index had a very low rank of 167 for growth rate. Switzerland which was ranked second in Happiness Index also had a very low rank of 162 for growth rate.

9. ***Provide speedy justice with transparency:*** Justice sub system needs a thorough overhaul (Article 11). Common people find it extremely difficult to get justice even after many years. The conservative "court system" of justice which questions the legal knowledge of judges and their ability to take a fair decision themselves without help from lawyers unnecessarily pushes up cost of getting justice and causes delays. All these lead to prolonged suffering and worry. Lack of transparency in judgments is another serious problem. Lakhs of people are not satisfied with court judgments and appealed to HRCs (Article 10).

NHRC miserably failed by refusing to examine lakhs of complaints against human rights violations.

A justice sub system which can provide speedy affordable justice with transparency (Article 11) and avoid human rights violations (Article 10) is an absolute necessity for comprehensive democracy.

10. ***Reduce inequalities:*** For many years we have given only lip service to equality even though it is envisaged in the Constitution. This hypocrisy continues because this idea is utopian and can never succeed. We have to be pragmatic and fix limits for all inequalities, without removing incentives for striving for betterment.

11. ***Accept change as a part of evolution:*** Historically, human race has come a long way from living in caves and walking on bare feet to living in multistoried buildings and traveling by aero planes and even planning to travel to other planets. All these happened because of some persons who boldly strived for change despite majority of people opposing change. It is significant

that after some time, those who opposed changes quietly took advantage of these changes and benefitted from these changes. Even more important, though drastic changes were opposed more forcefully and with scepticism, these were the ones which benefited most. It deserves to be repeatedly emphasized that all eminently worthwhile changes in the past were considered as drastic or impossible changes and were vehemently opposed and ridiculed when these were initiated. These repeated experiences over centauries emphasize the need to accept change, even drastic ones, as a part of evolution.

Those who oppose scrapping of present system of democracy which has failed miserably may argue that many modern countries are having similar system of democracy. This is so because they were not bold enough to think out of the box and try better methods despite having serious internal problems and demands or were not allowed to do so by vested interests. According to a celebrated academician, "governments all over the world have reached a point where they can do nothing at all for the society" (Article 22). This situation can be tackled only by thinking out of the box and boldly making drastic innovative changes where and when necessary.

Moreover, the above comparison shows an inferiority complex that we will only copy others. Even when change is badly needed, we are not prepared to use our ingenuity to set an example for others to follow. It is pertinent that there were times when India had set examples for others to follow. Why this drastic deterioration? Should we not strive to overcome this? May be, adoption of comprehensive democracy will be our guiding star for other needed changes!!

"Over the past sixty odd years there have been 98 amendments to the Constitution. Even this is not the full story. Hidden within there are changes that have been made to over 230 Articles we swear by." (The Times of India dated 01-03-14, page 20). Those who oppose change of democracy because the Constitution has to be amended ought to remember that we have already made more than 230 changes in our sacrosanct Constitution!!

Another argument may be that changes will upset stability. This belittles the need for evolution and the fact that historically stability has existed only for short periods of time. Otherwise, we would have continued to live in caves and walk bare foot!!

A relevant question to those who oppose change is: Are they prepared to live, eat, work, travel and enjoy life as their ancestors did? If not, opposition to change, after enjoying benefits of change, is hypocrisy.

Instead of opposing changes on any pretext, what change is required and when should be studied objectively and decision taken with an open and constructive mind.

Needed action: Without further waste of time, people with vision among politicians, social activists, legal experts, religious leaders, authors, celebrities in different fields, the media, teachers, doctors, engineers and younger generation etc. ought to take keen and sustained interest to thoroughly study all aspects of developing comprehensive democracy and start a peaceful movement to make it a reality. Organizers of the peaceful movement have to constantly keep in mind that any radical and crucially needed reform will meet fierce resistance from the entrenched vested interests in India and possibly other countries also. But they should not lose hope and should be guided by the fact that India got independence by a peaceful movement, against a mighty empire, which had to face many intermittent obstacles which postponed attainment of success.

As a prerequisite for kick starting the badly needed comprehensive democracy, mass awareness mobilization and healthy dialogues, discussions and debates should be undertaken to arrive at a broad consensus. Then a new ***Constituent Assembly should be set up to discuss this consensus and finalize changes in the Constitution.***

These urgent steps form the peaceful way to develop comprehensive democracy before violent protests against our sinking democracy (e.g., by Maoists) spread widely and rock the country. If we do not make joint efforts now to build a better India with comprehensive democracy, posterity will blame us for our callousness which led to anarchy and chaos.

Mahatma Gandhi (who successfully fought for independence against a mighty empire) has shown us that extraordinary changes can be made when ordinary people come together to do extraordinary things.

Swami Vivekananda exhorted us: "Arise, awake and sleep not till you reach your goal."

Outline of a Doctrine for Comprehensive Democracy

Introduction

Facts, observations, analyses and suggestions highlighted by the elaborate studies and discussions in the preceding articles form the basis for this outline. Article 24 provides a quick review of important aspects from earlier articles for easy reference to understand the background and/or justification for the statements made in this outline. For more details original articles have to be studied.

The present system of democracy has an election system which produces a void parliament and fifteen fundamental weaknesses (Article 14). What is worse, it is based on nine absurdities (Article 23). These are explained in brief below:

An MP or MLA elected by people is considered as a representative of people. But, to really represent people they have to be elected by more than 50% of the electorate. ***Claim of most MPs and MLAs that they are representatives of people is void*** because they had support of much less than 50% of the electorate only. Consequently the ***parliament and assemblies they formed were void.*** It is shocking that EC and SC overlooked this important defect despite having the relevant data to judge which candidates had secured votes of more than 50% of the electorate. Sad to say, even after election system completely failed, EC did not adopt any other method to exercise its responsibility under the Constitution to elect representatives of people.

Shockingly, professionally qualified, trained and experienced officers at top levels are supervised and controlled by persons who have not been assessed to have (1) required qualifications, (2) intellectual capacity to develop the required functioning efficiency, (3) special training and (4) adequate working experience!! Though this practice is obviously illogical and against the principles of management, it has continued for years *because no one has questioned this absurdity.*

For higher education, bright students prefer fields such as engineering, medicine, management, commerce etc. The duller students who could not get admission for these preferred courses often become politicians and later on supervise and control the more intelligent persons and have the last laugh!! As a result, the bewildered former tend to fear the latter (politicians) and develop an inferiority complex and type of mental slavery (to the latter) despite topping in intelligence. *This second absurdity also has not been questioned.* Why?

Political leaders used two clever strategies: (1) they cleverly isolated professionals from the power structure at the highest level so that they do not have strength to fight or question absurdities, (2) using the gift of the gab, they mesmerized people to start hero worship and to get deeply involved in their political fights. This way they cleverly succeeded in diverting peoples' attention away from absurd situations.

Brilliant top level officers had spent enormous amounts of time, efforts and money for acquiring the basic qualifications, faced competitive selection, underwent special training and worked for many years to gain experience. But these brilliant and experienced officers were not allowed to use their expertise freely for efficient functioning because of being controlled by unqualified politicians.

Ironically, they were not even given a chance to prove their worth because of fear that they would have proved their superiority in efficient functioning. Allowing this cunning strategy is the ***third absurdity.*** This deliberate wastage of professional expertise is a mockery of the system of selection and training of professionals. This is the ***fourth absurdity.***

Root cause for not questioning these contemptible situations is that the unqualified political leaders, by becoming heroes using the gift of the gab, fooled people to believe the ***fifth absurdity*** that, though unqualified, they had the <u>super human capacity</u> to effectively supervise and control professionally qualified, specially trained and experienced persons, that too in a variety of disciplines.

Political leaders also claimed that their supervision and control was necessary to ensure that professional managers listen to peoples' voice. The obvious and effective method to overcome this was to give these brilliant professional managers the necessary additional training. Ignoring this is the ***sixth absurdity.***

Instead, politicians diverted attention to the election system which they had cleverly created so that they can claim that they represent people. But, this turned out to be a contemptible hollow claim because most of them did not get support of more than 50% of the electorate which was required to become valid representatives, even after managing mocked support through influenced voting (Article 2). Why was this obviously startling revelation of contemptible hollow claim ignored? Because, blind hero worship of politicians prevented people from opening their eyes to this ***seventh absurdity*** of hollow claim also.

The ***eighth absurdity*** is the belief that voters, among whom large proportions are illiterate or inadequately educated, have the capacity to judge and elect persons who can perform functions of governance efficiently!!

In the absence of this judging capacity, blind hero worship influenced election and political leaders with the gift of the gab gained. This has continued for years ***because no one questioned this ninth absurdity.***

A <u>fundamental weakness</u> of parliamentary system of democracy is that parliament cannot be an independent pillar of democracy (as it ought to be) because the political party which controls government also controls parliament, having majority of MPs (Article 6). This basically defective system results in a servile parliament which allows dictatorial attitude in the party and the government and defeats the very purpose of having parliament as a pillar of democracy. There are more than thousand instances of government continuously ignoring parliament (Articles 6 and 22).

In addition, parliament totally failed to represent people because (a) large majority of MPs have support of only less than 35% of electorate (often much less) and shockingly resulted in a void parliament (Article 2) and (b) majority of MPs were rich crorepatis (Article 2). Because majority of MPs are very rich parliament's ability to speak for the poor is seriously curtailed. Shockingly, everyone including EC and SC have accepted these atrocious situations. Moreover, propriety and efficiency of parliament are doubtful when MPs are elected by people who do not have the knowledge and expertise needed to select efficient persons with specialized qualifications and experience to enact laws, make policies and govern the country. These situations form the <u>second fundamental weakness</u> of the present system of democracy.

People who elected them did not have the knowledge and expertise needed to select efficient persons with specialized qualifications and experience to enact laws, make policies and govern the country. This lack of knowledge and expertise among people (the selectors) becomes deplorable when large numbers of them (often the majority) are illiterate or do not have even a moderate level of general education. Just imagine what will happen to patients if surgeons are selected by such people; or to dams, bridges and houses if engineers are selected by such people; or to delivery of justice if judges are selected by such people; or to students if teachers/professors are selected such people; and so on!! Selecting top managers of government by such people is bound to have similar <u>atrocious consequences</u>. It is significant that such calamities have not occurred only because multiple professionals responsible for governance have been selected by specialized institutions manned by highly qualified selectors with many years of experience. In sharp contrast, political leaders who have to supervise these expert professionals are selected by people without requisite knowledge and expertise!! This <u>ridiculous mockery is the third fundamental weakness of present system of democracy</u>.

Successful governance of a country requires multiple professionals with specialized qualifications and experience working at the top levels without hindrance. But, functions of policy making, enactment of laws, planning and implementation of projects and overall governance have been usurped from qualified professionals by politicians who have not been assessed for the required qualifications and experience. This topsy-turvy situation is a <u>fourth fundamental weakness</u> of the present system of democracy.

While people are not competent to select efficient governments they throw out inefficient governments after they caused them prolonged pain and suffering. Inability to get rid of bad governments before such long gaps is a <u>fifth fundamental weakness</u> of the present system of democracy.

The election system miserably failed. It not only failed to elect true representatives (Article 2) but also threw up some challenging situations which it could not tackle. Three examples are given below:

1. Number of times a political party which had higher share of votes (showing higher peoples' support) had a lower share of elected representatives as happened in the recent assembly elections in Karnataka in which a party which had a 2% higher vote share (peoples' support) got 26 representatives less than the party with lower vote share. This is a mockery of the support given by people which ought to be a backbone of democracy. Repeatedly overlooking this important fact exposes a major defect of the system.

2. A spate of political defections in number of states led to confusion and disruptions in functioning of democracy. There were allegations that large amounts of money have been paid by the party in power at the centre to manipulate these defections. Election Commission did not verify the facts and take further action, if necessary. It did not also try to remove loopholes in the system, if any, which stood in its way to verify and stop such corrupt practices.

3. Recently, CBI became unusually super active and filed large number of cases mostly against political opponents of government. The opposition parties claimed that the government

is misusing CBI for a political witch hunt to spoil their image and have focused on the selection of the state, victim and time chosen for these attacks to give credence to their claim. They also claimed that Incometax Department and Enforcement Directorate joined to discredit them. EC failed to verify whether there was such misuse of power and take action, if necessary. It did not also try to remove loopholes in the system if any to stop such antidemocratic practices.

These defects constitute a <u>sixth fundamental weakness</u> of the present system of democracy.

A <u>seventh fundamental weakness</u> of the present system of democracy is that there is no system to assess efficiency of performance of political leaders in highly responsible positions every year as is regularly done for the qualified professionals involved in governance. Lack of such crucial assessment is obviously illogical and risky when these leaders did not have the required qualifications and experience and can make serious mistakes. Moreover, by contrast, it makes a mockery of the education and training given to qualified professionals and the assessment of efficiency of their performance. This is an <u>eighth fundamental weakness of the present system of democracy</u>.

It is also not realized that the illogical situations explained above are actually proclaiming loudly that politics is a strange profession which can be practiced by anyone, even without basic education or required qualification or true popular support or facing assessment of their work. Yet, shockingly, politicians have been given the responsibility of managing government, even when their claim that they represent people was hollow also (Article 2). Thus political leaders need neither education, nor required qualification nor true popular support to hold high positions without assessment of their work – a completely farcical situation!! Acceptance of this highly illogical and absurd situation about this profession is a <u>ninth fundamental weakness of the present system of democracy</u>.

Even more damaging, people have even welcomed politicians (often gladly) to occupy any position (including highly responsible positions) without having requisite qualifications or true popular support and without being assessed for their efficiency in performance. Why is it that people are so gullible and do not ask any questions? People behaved like slaves when under British rule for about 200 years and, sadly, are not able (or not even inclined) to come out of the slavish mentality to rulers even after 70 years of independence!! This is a <u>tenth fundamental weakness</u> of the present system of democracy.

Political leaders, instead of helping people to come out of this slavish situation, took advantage of it and, by becoming heroes using the gift of the gab, fooled people to believe in number of absurdities about the system without questioning these (Article 23). For instance, they fooled people to believe that even without required qualifications they had the <u>super human capacity</u> to effectively supervise and control professionally qualified, specially trained and experienced persons, that too in a variety of disciplines!! Absence of efforts to get rid of absurdities is a <u>eleventh fundamental weakness</u> of the present system of democracy.

By their callousness and repeated, uncontrolled and selfish activities, politicians also ***became enemies of democracy*** (Articles 19 and 20) – Article 19 has given six solid reasons). This is a <u>twelfth fundamental weakness</u> of present system of democracy.

The parliament they formed did nothing to overcome at least 100 shameful and shocking situations faced by the country (Article 15). This is the <u>thirteenth fundamental weakness</u> of present system of democracy.

To complete the shock, parliament also brought disgrace on itself because of lack of guts to punish government for breaking promises to it and lack of dignity by spinelessly tolerating such disrespect by government. Articles 6 and 23 pointed out more than thousand instances of lack of guts and lack of dignity of parliament. This is the <u>fourteenth fundamental weakness</u> of present system of democracy.

Lastly, because of mental slavery to politicians (Article 23) people were so dumb and callous that they tolerated being governed by suspected criminals (Article 2), justifying the remark that "A nation of sheep gets a government of wolves." This is the <u>fifteenth fundamental weakness</u> of present system of democracy.

Some additional faults are:

Judicial system has failed miserably and has basic defects (Article 11). Moreover, lakhs of complaints about human rights violations were dismissed by NHRC without examination because of a faulty regulation which has continued for many years even though NHRC had powers to amend it (Article 10). Government formation and its working have resulted in a subtle form of dictatorship (Article 5). This is strongly supported by the observations in Article 15 (items 95 and 96) that deterioration from flawed democracy to pseudo democracy has occurred. Journalists and media owners are afraid to criticize government. Both have resulted in serious death blows to democracy (Article 16). These are supported by the fact that the system has deteriorated from flawed democracy to pseudo democracy and the rank of Indian democracy has consistently "dropped in the past four years, with marked concentration of powers in the hands of one individual" (Items 95 and 96 of Article 15, Articles 21 and 22). There are at least 27 instances of hypocrisy of government about zero tolerance to corruption and undoubtedly corruption is widespread now and increasing (Article 9). Intolerance and people taking law into their hands are leading to chaos and anarchy (Article 21). Antidemocratic approach has become quite common. Social media displaced in depth studies, discussions and debates and resulted in disrespect to parliament and experts. It also spread hate and violence (Article 22). MPs and ministers not only did not have required qualifications but also have many disqualifications for democracy (Article 19). The political party system has no real advantages but many disadvantages and is more a hindrance than help to democracy (Article 20). Present democracy is restricted to governance only and does not focus on many other aspects which have influence on having a happy life with peace and dignity (Article 18). This has to be replaced with a comprehensive democracy to fully meet needs and aspirations of people. The new system cannot be built correctly without discarding the old system which has many basic faults and fundamental weaknesses and is based on nine absurdities, besides developing dictatorial tendency during the past few years.

Government has scant respect for parliament. During a period of 10 years, promises given during replies to questions in parliament or discussions on bills and motions were broken 1,024 times (Article 6). This speaks volumes about (1) government's disrespect for parliament and gross lack of credibility, (2) the latter spinelessly tolerating disrespect more than thousand times without the dignity expected from the august supreme body of democracy and (3) failure of parliament to exercise the responsibility of having a check on functioning of government.

To sustain a vibrant democracy, ministers and all officials at all levels of management infrastructure should have a mind set to comply with democratic principles and have proper perceptions about (a) democracy and (b) different aspects of management of democracy. But, there is no uniformity in mind set and perceptions within the infrastructure and it cannot function as a well-knit unit with full focus on democracy.

To conclude, the present system of democracy has a fundamental defect (Article 6), has 11 basic faults in the management infrastructure (Articles 7) and fifteen fundamental weaknesses (Article 14) and is based on nine absurdities (Article 23). Election system also has failed miserably. Therefore, there is <u>absolutely no doubt that present system of democracy is a pseudo democracy</u>. The first step for replacing this pseudo democracy is ***abolition of election system and parliament which have failed miserably.*** State Assemblies also should be abolished because these have similar defects.

As stated earlier, the election system failed miserably to elect true representatives of people (Article 2). Moreover, it threw up some challenging paradoxes which it could not tackle (Article 4). Therefore, instead of election system, the half yearly meetings (Article 18) which will ***enable people to participate directly and more effectively in sustaining democracy*** should be introduced. These will automatically take care of the weaknesses of people pointed out earlier.

President of India is a nominal figure head who applies rubber stamp to decisions taken by Council of Ministers.

Besides huge salary, enormous amounts are spent for having and maintaining a palatial residence (which also occupies large area of prime land) and for providing supporting establishments, services and security – all this enormous wastage for a rubber stamping nominal figure head who does not serve any real purpose under a democracy!! Other functions performed by President can either be abolished as merely ceremonious/ symbolic or entrusted to suitable personalities. It is crystal clear that there is absolutely no justification for continuing the position of President and it should be abolished. For similar reasons, the positions of Vice President and Governors of states also should be abolished. An additional reason for these abolitions is that titular heads like President, Vice President and Governors are remnants of fanciful monarchy and against the principle of collective leadership (Article 26).

All these abolitions together will save lakhs of crores of public money every year which can be used to remove poverty and provide benefits to people. Moreover, large areas of prime lands and buildings will be released for public use.

This outline of the doctrine for comprehensive democracy has come out with some innovative ideas to overcome the basic faults, fundamental weaknesses and absurdities mentioned earlier.

While concluding this lengthy introduction to fully expose the atrocious situations, it has to be reemphasized that present concept of democracy considers that democracy is needed only for governance and overlooks many important aspects which have influence on living happily with a good quality of life and dignity under peaceful environment (Article 18). To correct this fundamental mistake a comprehensive democracy (of the type detailed below) is essential.

Because absence of comprehensive democracy is a global reality we have to act without looking for guidance or models from other countries. It can and should be built up in stages. When we develop comprehensive democracy people from many more countries will welcome our efforts with admiration.

A Constituent Assembly (CA) should be set up to discuss and finalize all details of comprehensive democracy for amending the Constitution.

Comprehensive democracy

The following broad definition of comprehensive democracy, which includes its aim, is suggested:

Comprehensive democracy is a system which ensures the aim of people living happily with good quality of life and dignity under peaceful environment and carrying on their activities without hindrance.

This definition does not specifically mention about need for proper governance, health, education, employment or enterprise, prosperity, justice etc. because these are essential to live happily with a good quality of life and dignity under peaceful environment and carry on activities without hindrance. These can be taken care of while spelling out details of comprehensive democracy. While growth of economy of the country is desirable, it is not essential for fulfilling the aim of comprehensive democracy. For instance, in 2016, Denmark which topped the list in Happiness Index had a very low rank of 167 for growth rate. Switzerland which was ranked second in Happiness Index also had a very low rank of 162 for growth rate.

Outline of doctrine of Comprehensive democracy

1. Present democracy, by definition, makes the fundamental mistake that it gives attention to governance only. Comprehensive democracy considers governance as a sub system and includes many other sub systems (aspects) which have influence on living happily with a good quality of life and dignity under peaceful environment and carrying on activities without hindrance (Article 25). The organization which will manage this comprehensive democracy should be titled as *National Comprehensive Democracy Authority of India* (NCDAI) instead of Government of India. As the chief policy making, legal, executive and Information authority of NCDAI a Management Assembly (MA) should be constituted as detailed in paragraph 4. To ensure proper use of socio-economic, religious, cultural and other activities to serve the aim of comprehensive democracy, it is essential to establish some subsidiary authorities (Wings) under NCDAI, in addition to the "Governance Wing" (GW).

2. This Article outlines some Wings as illustrations. These should be developed further by an Expert Group or Groups (EG) created for this purpose by CA. EG should consider the need for independent Wings for activities (including those of present governance) not covered by the Wings suggested hereinafter. This series of articles have given number of suggestions for improving democracy. EG should study all these and suggest how all suggestions relevant to comprehensive democracy among these are taken care of by various Wings.

3. Creation of Wings and allocation of responsibilities between them should be formulated by EG and approved by CA. This allocation should be reviewed at suitable intervals by MA to adapt

to changes in management needs and in socio-economic, religious, cultural and other environments.

4. Each Wing should be headed by a Chief Professional Authority (CPA) on the subject dealt with by the Wing. CA should nominate CPAs of all wings from eminent professionals of different disciplines. All CPAs together should form the MA along with other eminent persons nominated by CA. To avoid dominance by CPAs who field executive power, the number of nominated members should be about 1.5 times the number of CPAs. Vacancies in and additions to MA (consequent on retirement of some members or adding more Wings and corresponding number of nominated members when necessary) should be filled in by MA from list of suitable persons prepared as stated in paragraph 14, failing which by open selection. Unlike in parliament, because there is no change of all members at fixed intervals, majority of well qualified and experienced members of MA will be continuing at any time. Equally important, CPAs, being part of MA (unlike in parliament), are involved in all decisions by MA and will be morally committed to decisions by MA. They should be given power to work independently so that they can fulfill their responsibilities and commitments without any hindrance.

5. While CPAs are empowered to independently plan and implement the plans approved by MA for their Wings, Management Council (MC) should ensure coordination of activities of different Wings and national interest without infringing on the powers of CPAs. To start with, MC should consist of three CPAs selected by CA for a three year period. After three years, every year, MA should replace one of them by rotation with another CPA who did not get a chance till then, for three years. Similar replacement should be made when a

CPA leaves due to retirement or resignation. For these changes seniority and merit should be considered. All decisions of MC should be on majority basis. MC should collectively represent India in all matters, with assistance of concerned CPAs. This will ensure collective leadership emphasized in Article 26 and avoid one individual dominating over others like a crafty monarch and denying much needed multidisciplinary approach also.

6. In the context of comparing with monarchy, it is important to recall that one advantage of a monarchy (or a pseudo democracy with a dictatorial leader) is that decisions are taken quickly unlike under collective leadership. The chances of delayed decisions will be very small under the suggested comprehensive democracy because each CPA is empowered to take decisions and can independently take quick decisions. Only MC and MA have collective leadership. However, as an extra precaution, CPA of Lokpal Wing (paragraph 74) should be given the responsibility of enquiring into complaints of delay in decision by any Wing, MC and MA.

7. To ensure efficient management, CPA and second level officers of a Wing should be professionals with qualifications and experience in the subject dealt with by that Wing and training in management. They should be assisted by officers with similar qualifications and experience. For this, suitably qualified persons should be given special training by following procedures similar to that given for civil or military services at present. CPA and officers of all Wings should be given additional training so that they work with (1) uniform perceptions about (a) comprehensive democracy and (b) different aspects of management of comprehensive democracy and (2) a mind set to comply with principles of comprehensive democracy (Article 7). To start with, CPA and second level officers of all Wings should be nominated by CA and given training

in management. Vacancies in and additions to CPA and second level officers of any Wing should be filled in from list of suitable persons prepared as stated in paragraph 14 or by promotion, failing which by open selection. Persons newly appointed to first and second levels of any Wing should be given training in management. Some checks should be provided to ensure that CPAs follow the principles of democracy (paragraphs 11 and 12).

8. In addition, each Wing should be provided with services of common cadres to provide supporting services e.g., Indian Administrative Service (IAS) (for administrative matters), Indian Administrative & Accounts Service (IA&AS) (for accounts and audits), Indian Statistical Service (ISS) (for statistical work and to monitor and evaluate programmes) and Indian Economics Service (IES) (for Wings which plan activities related to economy). They should be given additional training so that they will work with (1) proper perceptions about (a) comprehensive democracy and (b) different aspects of management of comprehensive democracy and (2) a mind set to comply with principles of comprehensive democracy.

9. This additional training for all cadres will ensure that all of them will work as a unified group with (1) proper perceptions about (a) comprehensive democracy and (b) different aspects of management of comprehensive democracy and (2) a mind set to apply principles of comprehensive democracy.

10. To give voice to people, half yearly meetings (Article 18) should be conducted regularly by "Democracy Wing" (DW) for well planned compact groups of villages and urban wards/resident welfare associations. All Wings should regularly brief DW about their achievements, problems faced by them and their future plans

for communicating these to people during these meetings. DW should organize these meetings and take follow up actions. DW should have adequate staff to complete one round of meetings within six months for all these groups. For this, a cadre with graduates in social welfare with vision and training in mass communication is required. It is likely that expenses for maintaining this large number of "democracy" officers will be much less than the amount saved by abolition of (a) large number of MPs and MLAs with much higher emoluments and perquisites, (b) election system, (c) parliament and assemblies and (d) President, Vice President and Governors.

11. In these meetings, people should be informed (by DW) about achievements of all Wings during the preceding half year, problems faced by them and their future plans. During these meetings, they should also advice people about how they can cooperate with them to achieve better results and also help to maintain peace and social harmony in the area, besides striving for national integration. People should tell if any Wing (including DW) did not meet any of their needs and aspirations. Those who conduct the meeting should ensure that all these are done properly. These interactions will ensure that (a) all Wings are answerable to people at half yearly intervals and (b) people become aware of problems faced by Wings and will not resort to trivial/unreasonable agitations. (People can also observe and make wise selection of efficient local leaders who can put forward their views in future, out of local leaders who attend these meetings.) Reports of these meetings should be sent by block offices of DW to DW headquarters immediately. DW headquarters should analyze these quickly and send to each Wing portions relevant to it so that it can take corrective actions needed. Copies of these reports to each Wing and consolidated statements prepared by DW about problems faced and future

plans as stated by each Wing should be sent to MC and MA for information and necessary action. This will ensure that all are kept informed once in six months about what has been done and has still to be done to meet needs and aspirations of people as well as problems faced by Wings and their future plans. With passage of time, officers and people will become so accustomed with these meetings that these will become more systematic, pertinent and useful. Both will also develop a sense of commitment to a common purpose, good relationship and mutual respect, which are lacking at present. People will also overcome mental slavery to politicians and become more confident about their ability to contribute and cooperate for the success of comprehensive democracy. These will be unimaginable, fantastic and praiseworthy changes. ***This is the way to ensure a truly vibrant and efficient comprehensive democracy.***

12. Through this direct interaction, people can give frequent feed backs on extent to which each Wing has satisfied their needs and aspirations and also appreciate problems faced by Wings. But most common people do not have capacity, inclination and time to suggest changes needed to (a) ensure that their needs and aspirations are fully met and (b) adjust to changes occurring in the country and the world. Such ideas and visions can be provided only by a section of intelligentsia which is in touch with peoples' problems and changes within and outside the country. "Visions Wing" (VW) with a cadre with vision and suitable qualifications should encourage free flow of ideas and visions from intelligentsia to it, analyze these and present useful ideas to each relevant Wing for necessary action and to MC and MA for information. This will also result in intelligentsia feeling much more involved in democracy than at present – an eminently worthwhile change.

It is important to ascertain ideas and visions about improving DW also which plays a crucial role for success of comprehensive democracy.

13. Activities of DW (representing common man) and VW (representing visionary intellectuals) will help MA (with representatives of both professionals and eminent social activists) to evolve a suitable ideology for the country, keeping aims of comprehensive democracy in view. This may be Gandhism or socialism or communism or capitalism or modifications of any of these to adjust to changes in environment/circumstances after its initiation many years back or a combination of two or more of these.

14. Based on analyses of flow of innovative ideas and visions from intelligentsia, VW should continuously prepare/update a list (and details) of eminent contributors who have repeatedly come out with innovative ideas and visions. They are likely to be most suitable for filling up vacancies in MA as well as CPA and second level officers of Wings. VW should send relevant lists (and details) to MA whenever necessary for selection and appointment.

15. Reasons similar to those mentioned in the "Introduction of this article" for abolition of parliament justify abolition of state assemblies also. Their abolition will save enormous amounts wasted on this ineffective system. An additional advantage is release of vast areas of prime lands and buildings for public use.

16. With abolition of state assemblies, should there be state governments? Having central and state governments will create many problems. For example, grouping of subjects for governance as "central," "state" and "concurrent" leads to conflicts and provides

avenues for shirking responsibilities or blaming each other. Sharing of revenues creates disharmony. Interstate disputes are quite common. Disagreements and dissatisfactions among central and state officers lead to contradictions and delays. Vast differences in size of states create many problems (Articles 12 and 13). Lack of uniformity in policy making and managerial activities by states will contradict "one nation one line of command" principle and also work against national integration. For example, if a motor vehicle registered in one state is driven in three other states on tour or work, additional life time tax will be demanded by these three states also!! This is not only atrocious but will also lead to harassment of citizens and raise the question "Is India one nation?" Abolition of state governments will automatically solve all these and many other problems.

17. After abolition of states, to provide a hierarchical chain for efficient management, the country should be divided into five regions with fairly equal population – north, south, west, east, and central. Each region should be divided into suitable number of zones, each zone into districts, each district into taluks and each taluk into blocks, all with fairly equal populations at each level. While some Wings of NCDAI may need offices at all levels, others may need offices at required levels only. For example, GW and DW will need offices at block and suitable higher levels but VW, Law Wing (see paragraph 21) and Tax Wing (see paragraph 25) may need office at national or regional level only.

18. Activities of DW and VW will establish a very efficient and truly democratic system to ensure that people's voices (both down-to-earth and visionary) are heard once in six months by all Wings, MC and MA. This system has seven major benefits in addition to the fantastic general benefits mentioned in paragraph 11:

19. (1) provides half yearly checks by people at block/ward level on functioning of all Wings, (2) makes people appreciate problems faced by each Wing and drastically reduces agitations, (3) actively involves intelligentsia in democracy, (4) gives ideas to all Wings for planning and implementation with involvement of people (both down-to-earth and visionary), (5) avoids inefficient and superficial central and state planning bodies without actual current field experiences, (6) saves enormous amounts spent on the present system and (7) releases large areas of prime lands and buildings for public use.

20. Giving voice to people within blocks/wards (paragraphs 10, 11 and 12) is equivalent to having a federation of blocks/wards giving effective voice directly to people within blocks/wards every six months and covering all aspects (sub systems). This is far superior to a federation of states which gives only indirect voice to people by electing their representatives once in five years and that too for governance sub system alone. The proposed system has the flexibility to work as federations of districts or zones or regions, if necessary for any Wing.

21. Instead of parliament and assemblies, MA should enact laws for the country. "Law Wing" (LW) with cadre of law professionals with vision should draft laws for whole country in consultation with concerned Wings and based on reports from DW and VW which will reflect peoples' needs for law and problems with current laws and submit these to MA. LW should provide legal advice to all Wings. It should also review laws every year to modify laws if necessary and delete obsolete laws. MA should enact laws and take suitable action on these based on annual reviews.

22. Practice of preparing annual budgets, which lead to large time gaps in approving plans (in a fast changing world),

should be stopped. Each Wing should prepare plans (including staff and fund requirements) in consultation with DW, VW and Plan Priority Wing (PPW) with a cadre with vision and suitable qualifications (paragraph 24). It should be empowered to submit its plans to MA any time. MA should meet every month (if needed) to approve plans and allot funds strictly according to a priority list for new projects for utilizing available funds prepared by PPW in consultation with all Wings. Thus, each Wing will have timely budget approval for each project. This ensures full independence and all new plans will be approved and executed without delay.

23. To ensure that activities reflect what people want, any plan submitted to MA should certify that recommendations of DW and VW (which reflect peoples' views) have been taken into account. If not, reasons for omission should be given. If MA is satisfied with the reasons it should proceed further. If MA rejects any certified plan, grounds for this should be communicated to people by DW during half yearly meetings so that people are educated about these reasons. If large numbers of these block/ward level meetings are unhappy with the rejection despite knowing the reason, MA should reconsider the matter or explain the situation in more detail to people through DW. This will prevent a "dictatorial" approach by MA.

24. The above procedures ensure that each Wing plans and executes plans which satisfy principles of democracy, without any interference or delays. But there has to be a system for allocation of funds between plans for different Wings. PPW should manage this system by preparing and updating a priority list for new projects for utilizing available funds, in consultation with all Wings and getting it approved by MA. This has to be a continuing process as

described in paragraph 21. PPW should be concerned with plan priority for allocation of funds only and will not interfere with actual plans by CPAs.

25. "Tax Wing" (TW) with a cadre with vision and suitable qualifications should draft proposals for taxes for whole country as and when required. Taxing should be simplified (e.g., by selecting suitable periods for subject groups instead of a one year period for all). Most important, if earned income and wealth are taxed, people feel that they are being robbed of their hard earned money. This feeling often motivates people to be dishonest and **creates a nation of dishonest people** who avoid tax and create black money. Moreover, direct taxes damage happy life because these lead to harassment and stress for majority of tax payers. To avoid these some people bribe tax collectors. This leads to wide spread corruption and harassment of honest people. **Direct taxes on earned income and wealth should be abolished to** (1) avoid creation of national shame *(a very important moral justification)* (2) respect the feelings of people which is paramount in a democracy and (3) eliminate black money and corruption – all praise worthy creditable achievements. **To overcome these shameful situations, Indirect taxes should be the main source of revenue for NCDAI.** While people have no control over direct taxes on income and wealth which are forced upon them by government, they can reduce indirect taxes, (like goods and services tax) without becoming dishonest, by spending less on goods and services. If this leads to loss of revenue, this should be explained to people and the rates should be increased. All this will also reduce the harm done by unchecked consumption. Finally, it is important to note that **abolition of election** and **direct taxes** (two main sources of corruption) and **introduction of half yearly meetings** will lead to a vibrant democracy – an outstanding achievement.

26. For many years we have been doing only lip service to equality. Equality is utopian and can never be achieved. MA has to be realistic, accept that inequalities are natural and fix suitable limits for inequalities which can still provide incentives for striving for betterment. "Inequalities Wing" (IW) with a cadre with vision and suitable qualifications should work out limits for inequalities in income, ownership of land and living space, profit, wealth, expenditures on special events like marriage etc. for approval of MA. To illustrate, IW should fix emoluments (salary plus perquisites) for lowest level of work and set upper limit for emoluments for any work at eight times this minimum emoluments. *(For example, if lowest emolument is Rs. 15,000 per month, highest will be Rs. 120,000 per month – without tax reduction vide paragraph 24 – which will not satisfy greed but is more han sufficient for a family to lead a decent life and save some money and comparatively high enough to provide incentives for striving for betterment).* This approach will help the poor because top level will opt in self interest for good emoluments for lowest level instead of the other way now. For some activities with age-related short efficient life (e.g., sports and games, dancing, acting, heavy labour etc.) a higher minimum limit should be fixed so that they can save for their future.

27. Similarly, IW should fix lower and upper limits for ownership of land and living space. As per latest census, around 1.77 million homeless people live along roads, on railway platforms and under flyovers!! (The Times of India dated 25.04.15). In contrast, some rich persons live in palatial mansions which occupy hundreds of acres of land or in huge multistoried buildings. How can they justify that they need this? Why are they so heartless about millions of homeless fellow countrymen who are compelled to live

along roads, on railway platforms and under flyovers while they enjoy posh comforts? IW should ensure that there are no homeless people.

28. There are many more instances of astronomical inequalities due to lack of any limits on income and wealth. For example "world's richest 100 persons earned enough to end extreme poverty for the world's poorest people four times over" (Deccan Chronicle dated 20.01.13). Their average annual income in 2012 was 2.4 billion US dollars which is more than 5.2 million times the annual income of a poor person ($460 @$1.25 per day)!! – an unimaginable and astronomical inequality. Nearly half of global wealth is owned by only 0.7% of people (The Times of India dated 29.11.17). India has the dubious distinction of being the second most unequal economy in the world with 57 dollar billionaires controlling 70% of the country's wealth. A Vice chancellor spent Rs. 1.14 lakhs for an imported name plate!! (Times of India dated 20-06-15, page 5). Some persons lavishly spend crores to buy a car. Number of rich persons (millionaires and even billionaires) has increased rapidly during 2015 to 2017. Crorepatis increased by 23.5% in 2015 (Deccan Chronicle dated 21.12.17, page11) and the number of super rich grew by 12% in 2017 (The Times of India dated 14.02.18, page 21). In 2017, while India has 101 dollar billionaires, 96% adults have wealth below $10,000 (India Today dated 29.09.17). Vast majority of people has to struggle for basic necessities of life and has been forced to live without dignity. Millions are suffering from poverty, hunger and lack of shelter at night while the rich live in palatial bunglows/flats, squander money and waste food. Fixing of limits for wealth will reduce these gross inequalities and also lead to enormous amounts of money (excess wealth) becoming available to NCDAI for public use.

29. Inequalities in profits also are often colossal. This is more so when brand names are used to hike profits hundreds of times higher than for the same unbranded articles in the questionable pretext of far better quality. What is most cruel and disgusting is that huge profits are heartlessly availed of for crucial medical "supports" required to sustain life. IW should fix limits for profits after thorough studies.

30. Fixing limits for inequalities in income, ownership of land and living space, profit, wealth, special expenditure for marriage etc. will result in a fantastic and unimaginable social change – a *praise worthy* achievement. This will also set limits for greed and lavish spending to show off wealth. The former will respect the caution by Mahatma Gandhi (Father of our Nation) that "*Nature has enough to satisfy everyone's need but not enough to satisfy man's greed.*" This will also respect the caution by the *Pope that "greed is destroying earth."* Equally important, we do not have to continue with the hypocrisy of giving lip sympathy to equality. These are praise worthy moral achievements.

30a. In 2017, "India slipped 21 places in the World Economic Forum's Global Gender Gap Index to a lowly 108 out of 144 countries" despite a decade of slow but steady progress on improving parity between the sexes. "At the current rate of progress the global gender gap will take 100 years to bridge, compared to the better rate of 83 years last year." (Deccan Chronicle dated 03.11.17, page 11). India is ranked 111 out of 189 countries on women in Parliament, as reported by the Inter – Parliamentary Union. In a report on the "State of World's Mothers." India is 4th worst even among 80 less developed countries. Global Nutrition Report 2017 placed India at the bottom with maximum number of women with anaemia in the world. More than half (51%) of women in reproductive age have anemia. During last 50 years, number of women left out from electoral roll increased fourfold from the already large 15 millions to 68 millions – showing deterioration instead of improvement!! This is gross undervaluation of right of women to vote. Moreover, there are gender inequalities in providing opportunities and services. Immediate attention should also be given to some special problems (like rape and sexual harassment) faced by females. Current focus on legal action is grossly insufficient – 93% of rape cases are still awaiting trial as trivial matters hold up cases. With such a low enforcement rate, how will enactment of new laws help? Preventive measures (e.g., holistic education suggested in paragraphs 63 and 64) should get priority. Innovative ideas should be developed by "Gender Issues Wing" (GIW). It should formulate effective innovative measures based on in depth studies of basic issues and organize dialogues, discussions and debates to help their implementation. A suitable professional cadre with vision should be created to manage GIW.

31. Any religion should serve as a guide to the path of divinity, devotion, purity within, love, peace and harmony. Instead of guiding to seek this path, importance has been given to routine superficial visits to religious institutions and practicing rituals and festivals. Dislike, intolerance and even hatred of other religions have been allowed to creep in. Instances of even encouraging these contemptible traits are not uncommon. Religious leaders are more interested in maintaining religious institutions, following conventions, and sustaining/gaining control over their followers than propagating true principles of their religion. Thus, development of divinity, devotion, purity within, love, peace and harmony, in accordance with religious principles, has been woefully sidelined. All these have resulted in disillusionment among some

people and led to instances of religious leaders losing control. As a result, leaderless and free for all atmospheres are becoming more common. It is doubtful whether honest practitioners of true spirit of religion form a majority in any religious community. It seems more likely that they form a negligible minority. Thus, ironically, religion has often led to disturbance of peace, loss of brotherhood, intolerance of other religions, conflicts and even war throughout the world. In other words, presently we are having worst effects due to not following principles of religion instead of the best from true practice of principles of religion. Even worse, religious leaders do not feel concerned about this antithesis. They ought to introspect about guiding their followers to (1) follow principles of religion to seek path of divinity, devotion, purity within, love, peace and harmony instead of giving more importance to practice of rituals and festivals and (2) strictly avoid conflicts in name of religion.

32. Assembly of large number of people to practice rituals and festivals has often led to deaths and injuries to many people in stampedes, crashing of structures etc. These have also created other problems. For example, experts say that some of these practices are a continuing threat to rivers like Ganga. Demands have been raised for sustained campaigns to solve these problems.

33. The main problem in having a logical or scientific approach is that practice of rituals and festivals are based on faith and sentiments and no one has tried to demarcate which ones are supported by principles of religion and which are continuing as practices blindly followed for many years only because no one has questioned these. Benefits from these have not been objectively assessed. It has not been realized that rituals and festivals practiced anywhere in the world by any religion are meaningless because these are practiced only by a negligible minority of world

population and no harm has come to the large majority which did not practice these. Insignificance of mantras, pilgrimages, yajnas and even Vedas was stressed by the highly respected great Hindu philosopher Adi Shankaracharya in his inspiring poem *Nirvanashatakam.* "Religion Wing" (RW) with a cadre with vision and suitable qualifications should tackle all challenging problems created by not following principles of religions and by blind faith and unquestioned sentiments. For this it should conduct in depth studies, with help of sociologists and psychologists (where necessary), to understand various problems in full and follow these up by dialogues, discussions and debates.

34. Leaders of all religions can effect desirable changes if they sincerely strive to promote peace, love, harmony and brotherhood in accordance with the principles of their religions. For example, to promote harmony and brotherhood, enlightened Hindu religious leaders can get rid of caste and other social discriminations (including untouchability) which are not based on principles of Hindu religion but on unchecked views and wrong practices continuing for many years. For this, they can make well planned visits (along with some followers) to houses of lower castes in different areas around the country, partake water and food with them and take them inside forbidden temples.

35. Religious leaders ought to be inspired by the following dignified and humane examples: (1) Devaswam Board, which administers 1,246 temples in Kerala, recently appointed some Dalits (lower caste) as priests in its temples boldly ignoring (a) the tradition of having only Brahmin priests and (b) campaigns protesting against appointment of non-Brahmins as priests. One of these new priests told the media that the institution which trained him was training people of all castes, with a broad and welcome

mind (The Times of India dated 18.10,17). (2) A Hindu temple in Kerala served food to over 1,000 Christians after they completed their prayer at a holy cross (a place of Christian worship) near the temple (The Times of India dated 31.03.18, page 10) – another example of dignity and broad mind!! (3) As another example of Kerala following its rich tradition of communal harmony, a Hindu temple will be hosting a mass Iftar dinner to about 700 local Muslims. This event is being organized with the support of all local residents irrespective of their caste, religion or politics. Eminent personalities of panchayat are expected to attend. The focus is on the spreading of the message of brotherhood and peaceful coexistence among the new generation (The Times of India dated 24.05.18, page 11). (4) A head priest at Chilkur Balaji temple carried a Dalit devotee on his shoulder into the innermost sanctum as a ritual – a gesture to emphasise equality (India Today dated 30.04.18, page 16). There may be many more unreported inspiring examples of such acts of brotherhood and harmony. Hopefully, these visionary examples will set the ball rolling for progressive improvements in inter and intra religious harmony and brotherhood.

36. Leaders of all religions should guide their followers to scrupulously avoid all parochial approaches and to ennoble themselves by getting rid of greed, hatred, jealousy, revenge and rumour mongering. They, along with some followers, should participate in programmes undertaken by other religions and even help to organize these with a spirit of harmony. brotherhood and mutual respect. Similarly, Hindu and Muslim religious leaders should concentrate attention on how tensions between Hindus and Muslims can be reduced. For instance, Muslim religious leaders should avoid issuing fatwas which create tensions.

37. As stated in paragraph 31, ironically, religion has often led to disturbance of peace, loss of brotherhood, intolerance of other religions, conflicts and even war throughout the world. A root cause of this dangerous situation is neglect of the dictum that religion is an individual's choice and wrongly considering religion as a family or community issue. To make this a reality, all children should be taught about all religions. This should be done during pre-final year at school to avoid the final year when they concentrate on examinations. Thereafter, they should be given a chance to make an informed choice of religion which should be confirmed when they attain the legal age for adulthood. They should make use of the intervening period to observe how others are practicing the religion selected by them and judge the suitability of their choice. Thus, any adult can have religion by birth and religion by informed independent choice. Undoubtedly, those who make an informed and independent choice of religion will be more committed to follow its principles with full understanding (not blindly) and will derive maximum benefit by practicing it as an individual (not community) matter. This is the way to avoid conflicts and war due to religion.

38. RW with a cadre having knowledge of all religions, should organize dialogues, discussions and debates with leaders of all religions for motivating their followers to (1) strictly follow religious principles, (2) restrict themselves to take part only in rituals and festivals which arise from these principles, (3) treat all living beings with kindness, (4) strive for welfare of all and (5) avoid treating religion as a community matter and prevent conflicts in the name of religion to ensure peace. A main aim of RW should be to make a Hindu a better Hindu, a Muslim a better Muslim, a Sikh a better Sikh, a Christian a better Christian, a Buddhist a

better Buddhist and so on so that all are better human beings with a feeling of universal brotherhood and a high level of spirituality and enjoy inter religious harmony. To be able to clarify doubts, misconceptions and dissentions during dialogues, discussions and debates, it should first carry out necessary in depth studies to provide convincing facts about all aspects. Emphasis should be on following principles of each religion to fulfill the aim of comprehensive democracy to ensure that people live happily with good quality of life with dignity, including spiritual development, under a peaceful environment and carry on their activities without any hindrance. RW should ensure that all people have equal opportunities to lead a religious life of their choice. It should not interfere with the practice of any religion but serve as a catalytical force for enlightened religious development, after removing misconceptions developed through years of ignoring religious principles. An effective RW will be able to make unimaginable, praiseworthy and lofty changes which will ensure a peaceful and happy environment in the country – an outstanding achievement.

39. Priority for GDP growth resulted in at least 100 shocking and shameful situations covering almost all crucial sectors (Article 15). Inclusive prosperity was conspicuous by its absence. Hardly any attention was given to ensure that people live happily with dignity and peace. MA should give highest priority to a humanitarian approach to promote prosperity, dignity, health, education, peace, and happiness to people. Only when this happens the country will attain its aim and glory – not by even the fastest economic growth alone. This is supported by the following facts for 2016: While India had a high rank of 12 for growth rate it had a dismal rank of 122 for Happiness Index. On the other hand, Denmark which topped the list in Happiness Index had a very low rank of 167 for growth rate. Switzerland which was ranked second in Happiness

Index also had a very low rank of 162 for growth rate. "Human Development Wing" (HDW) should ensure humanitarian developments. Happiness Index should be used to watch progress in this development. HDW should be managed by a professional cadre with vision and suitable qualifications in humanity and experience in humanitarian activities.

40. Judicial system needs a thorough overhaul to provide speedy and affordable justice with transparency (Article 11). In 2009, India had the shameful distinction of having largest backlog of cases in the world. What is worse and shocking is that government, politicians of questionable character and influential persons/organizations are responsible for piling up of many cases. SC castigated the central government "for repeatedly filing appeals on identical questions of law despite being fined earlier for clogging the justice delivery system with frivolous cases." (Article 11) Roughly, over 30 million cases are pending now. Despite huge backlog of cases, callously, government did not provide more judges and courts enjoyed long vacations!! People find it extremely difficult to get justice even after many years. Many people cannot afford to fight for justice. These lead to prolonged suffering of injustice. To mitigate these, the following procedures should be adopted.

41. Civil cases should first seek arbitration at taluk level by "Arbitration wing" (AW) with a professional cadre having qualifications in law and training in counseling. Cases not resolved by an arbitrator at taluk level should be referred by him/her to an arbitrator or a group of two or three arbitrators at district level depending upon his/her judgment about complexity of the case. This procedure will resolve many cases quickly and reduce load of unresolved cases, besides making justice affordable.

42. "Justice Wing" (JW) with a cadre with vision and qualified judicial officers and judges should take up only unresolved cases referred by AW. First, at district level, a judicial officer (or a group of two or three judicial officers as decided by JW after a preview of the case) should take up cases which come with a report by AW giving full details of the case and arbitration proceedings. Judicial officer(s) should study these cases, question both parties in a helpful manner (to overcome their diffidence or ignorance of law to bring out facts) and pass orders. Appeal can be made to High Court set up at zonal level and then to Supreme Court set up at Regional level, which should be dealt with straightaway by one or more judges as decided by that court. In this way, there is provision for study of a case once each at three levels – district, zone and region. But, as exceptions, High Court should not allow appeal to Regional Supreme Court by rich people/influential organizations (as per its judgment) because this will create serious handicaps for poorer people and thereby favour the rich. These exceptions will give benefit of doubt to the poor. Study of a case thrice (that too once each at three levels) ought to be sufficient for providing justice particularly because of the checks on quality of judgment suggested in paragraph 47. Further appeals are unlikely to improve judgment but will certainly cause long delays, besides possible miscarriage of justice for the poor who cannot afford these. Therefore these are not justified. National Supreme Court should deal with only cases with national implications or legal principles.

43. At all these levels, cases once taken up, should be (1) examined on day to day basis and (2) disposed off by judicial officers/judges without court hearings. These two procedures will reduce delays and help to clear cases quickly. Another basic

justification for this "court less procedure" is that judicial officers/ judges with qualifications and experience are fully capable of taking proper decisions without prodding or interference by lawyers. In other words, court system demeans qualified and experienced judges because it questions their capability to independently study all aspects of cases and provide justice. Under the conservative court system, many people will not be able to seek justice because they have to spend enormous (sometimes even astronomical) amounts to engage lawyers. Moreover, a major cause of long delay is large number of adjournments given by courts mainly because of lawyers (refer Article 11 for details). Most important, a basic and ironic defect of the court system is that lawyers are constantly engaged in fighting for their clients (even criminals) and not for justice!! In other words courts have to constantly face lawyers who are fighting against justice (as a part of their contract) and avoid being trapped by them.

All these can be avoided/reduced under the "court less system." Thus, the new procedure suggested will not only speed up justice but also make justice affordable to people (unlike at present) by reducing cost immensely – both praise worthy achievements.

44. With abolition of court system for civil cases, civil case lawyers can find regular employment in the wide spread cadres for arbitrators at taluk and district levels) and judicial officers and judges at district and higher levels (refer to paragraph 46 for assured scope for employment). This will give immense short term and long term relief to lawyers most of whom face irregular income and uncertain future at present – particularly to junior lawyers who now find it extremely difficult to start practice and/or are paid poorly by senior lawyers who generally exploit them.

45. Court system (with judges and lawyers) at district, zonal, regional and national levels also should be part of JW. It should be used only for criminal cases for which further investigations are necessary. Once a case is taken up it should be heard daily to the extent possible. Because of these there will be drastic reductions in volume of pending cases, postponements (and their durations) and quick disposal of criminal cases (unlike at present). Moreover, there will be drastic reduction in number of under trials, including honest persons, languishing in jails for many years – a shameful inhuman situation at present. To make justice affordable to more people, justification for some advocates demanding exorbitant fees, not comparable to those in other professions (even with superior qualifications and nature of work), should also be examined and corrective steps taken till limits to inequalities are introduced (paragraph 25).

46. To speed up justice, adequate numbers of arbitrators, judicial officers and judges should be provided on priority basis by MA and vacations to judges should be abolished. While government claimed lack of resources for appointing more judges, there were innumerable instances of wastage and wrong priorities (Article 11). Thus, meager allocations made were due to low priority and not lack of resources. MA should give highest priority for release of adequate funds to AW and JW because providing affordable quick justice is most important. If necessary, part of the enormous savings from abolition of parliament, assemblies, Election Commission, President, Vice President and Governors should be used to provide affordable quick justice.

47. Lack of transparency and miscarriage of justice are serious problems (Articles 10 and 11). To avoid these, orders by judicial officers/judges should give clear and precise reasons for judgment.

These should be regularly checked for a sample of cases of each judicial officer/judge by judges specially designated by CPA of JW, to avoid miscarriage of justice.

48. NHRC failed miserably to examine lakhs of human rights violation complaints because NHRC (procedure) Regulations 1997 did not permit it to review court judgments. This restriction should be removed. Then NHRC will have to examine lakhs of complaints about denial of justice by judges (Article 10). Therefore, NHRC should be restructured to replace judges with eminent human rights activists and lawyers. NHRC should be renamed as "Human Rights Wing" (HRW).

49. Effective functioning of democracy requires an alert media with broad vision which functions as a watch dog of democracy, informs people about the state of affairs and provides platforms for public debates. Media in India needs to improve its functioning in all these aspects. Media failed to put adequate pressure on government to solve problems faced by people and the country and to provide platforms for interested persons to freely spread and/or absorb positive ideas about development (Article 16). Moreover, media has not been sufficiently active in provoking and encouraging debates about saving the democracy and arriving at consensus on possible solutions. Editorials did not focus adequately on the sinking democracy and how to save it. Printed media did not adequately encourage journalists and social activists to publish articles discussing need and/or suggestions for improving democracy. Innovative ideas were lacking and its value system was also defective. It chose wrong priorities and became commercialized also. What is most damaging at present is that the media scene in India is catastrophic because of the fear among journalists to criticize the Government. Editors' Guild of India recently condemned

"the erosion of right to practice free and independent journalism because of "inability" of media owners to withstand pressures from the political establishment as well as frequent "blocking or interference" in broadcast of content critical of the government." Obviously, this also curtails employment opportunities for honest journalists. All these have dealt serious death blows to democracy (Articles 16 and 23). "Media Wing" (MW) with a cadre with vision and qualifications in mass communication and journalism should take adequate steps to overcome all deficiencies pointed out in Articles 16 and 23. It should also ensure that these do not recur. It should regulate and expand media activities with proper sense of direction and innovation and without commercial interests and hindrance from power mongers and corporate bodies. It should make people knowledgeable about all aspects of comprehensive democracy so that they can participate effectively in half yearly meetings and also extend their full cooperation for the success of comprehensive democracy. For all this, in addition to its activities, it should also encourage and support newspapers, periodicals and TV channels which follow its policies. Corporate bodies and vested interests should be debarred from owning or controlling media to gain power to influence any Wing and mislead people to serve their selfish interests. Under comprehensive democracy, MW need not fear to criticize GW or any other Wing because it is not dependent on any other Wing. Moreover, the half yearly meetings with people should be made use of to tackle any unusual developments.

50. "Health Care Wing" (HCW) should provide to all citizens total health care, which includes curative, preventive and promotional health care, with sense of equity and justice. Current health care system failed to do so. It also differentiated between

the rich and the poor even in concepts for providing services. In a report on the "State of World's Mothers," India is 4th worst even among 80 less developed countries (Article 15). Global Nutrition Report 2017 placed India at the bottom with maximum number of women with anemia in the world. More than half (51%) of women in reproductive age have anemia. India retains the dubious distinction of topping the list of nations with most premature births. On infant mortality rate, India is ranked 126 out of 175 countries. Malnutrition is widespread and alarming. According to WHO, 50% of Indian children are either underweight or stunted. These show the need for special attention to improve health of women and children. Innovative and committed approaches are needed to make health services more effective so that it can provide total health care to all. HCW with a cadre with vision and suitable qualifications should give high priority for this.

51. A democratic country has to continuously strive to ensure delivery of total health care to all its citizens, with a sense of equity and justice. For this innovative and committed efforts have to be made with a sense of vision, mission, direction and human approach to make health services more effective so that it can provide total health care to all. While this has been recognized long time ago, it is unfortunate that only lip service has been rendered to promotional health care. Even the curative services in vogue focus more on giving relief (often temporary) from suffering due to specific health problems than on providing total cure for all health problems with a holistic approach by utilizing the best treatment options available from different systems of medicine. Innovative research is needed to select and accept these best options. The overall approach should be to provide affordable total health care of best quality possible to maximum number of people

(particularly the marginalized and weaker sections of society) near to their homes, with a sense of humanity, equality, responsibility and commitment.

52. Because public health services have failed to satisfy most people, large number of hospitals and clinics have been started as business enterprises. These often provide services with an eye on huge profits. Playing with peoples' health to make money is very cruel. For example, *"Almost 44% of the 12,500 patients for whom surgery was recommended were advised against it by their second opinion consultants,"* as reported by a study. Malpractices such as ordering costly diagnostic tests when not needed, earning cuts and commissions, inflating patients' bills and accepting freebies are quite common. Because general awareness about these malpractices is low, their services are wrongly labeled as of high quality. High voltage health marketing and misuse of paid research findings has led to their fancy services becoming more and more fashionable and catchy. This has further led to demands for multiplying such institutions with fancy heath care, without questioning whether such costly fancy care is actually needed for or relevant to bulk of health problems faced by people. These and other aberrations have to be studied in depth before planning services of good quality to people who cannot afford to pay high prices.

53. One approach to improve public health services is to make Primary Health Centres (PHCs) centres of excellence in a phased manner. For this, to start with, select some PHCs and provide them with all facilities for good quality of curative, preventive and promotional health care. In addition, wherever possible, philanthropic and business oriented health institutions should be encouraged and helped to set up and run such centres of excellence to provide total health care in more and more rural and urban

areas and thereby ensure faster spread of such centres of excellence throughout the country. Setting up these centres of excellence with provision of better facilities for diagnosis and treatment are likely to overcome the hesitation among doctors to work in PHCs.

54. While all these services should be provided free to the Below Poverty Level cardholders, affordable low amounts should be charged for consultation, diagnostic tests and medicines from the remaining poor and all middle class persons. The upper class who can afford to pay should be charged at a higher rate which is less than that of private hospitals. All these rates should be flexible and fixed locally taking the economic situation of the area into account.

55. This system has many advantages: People can avail of health services of good quality near their homes at affordable expenditure. Replacing free services with a pragmatic differential payment system for services will lead to recovery of at least a substantial part of expenditure of PHC on providing services. Once people take recourse to preventive and promotional health care, the number of patients who need curative services and the staff required to provide these will decrease progressively. All these together will result in substantially decreasing the cost of running the PHC. Important "bye products" of total health care are increase in productivity of people due to reduction in absenteeism due to sickness and increased fitness and vigour for work.

56. Serious attention has to be given to increase the overall budget for health care. All "pennywise and pound-foolish" approaches should be strictly avoided for (1) developing the centres of excellence (remodeled PHCs) to overcome the present step motherly approach to rural health care and (2) carrying out appropriate health service research. Priority has also to be given to

provide total health care (curative, preventive and promotional) to millions of people suffering from common diseases, instead of low (or no) priority at present. It has not been realized that freedom from common diseases will (1) make millions of people happy most of the time, (2) lead to increase in productivity of people due to reduction in absenteeism due to sickness and increased fitness and vigour for work and (3) increase popularity of health centres.

57. Number of systems of medicine has been providing health care to the satisfaction of many people for many years. There are general indications that one system was able to cure a disease that another could not. These observations have been reported for different systems and different diseases by some observant patients. Based on these, one could set a long-term goal of an "ideal holistic health care system" in which any person with a health problem can approach the "family health provider" (hospital or doctor) who will treat him/her if the health care system which it practices has the best possible care for that health problem. If not, he/she will be referred to a provider practicing another system which has the best possible care for that health problem. This will ensure delivery of the best health care that is appropriate for the problem. Practitioners of different systems of medicine will accept this selective approach, only when they have convincing information on the comparative strengths and weaknesses of each system vis-à-vis each health problem. But no serious attempts with an open mind have been made to scientifically study this aspect so that these systems of medicine could be made to supplement each other, for providing maximum benefit to maximum number of suffering people.

58. HCW should focus on all these and come out of the rut. CPA and second level officers of HCW should have qualifications

in at least one of the different systems of medicine and public health and training in management. Those working in curative health institutions under HCW should have a different cadre with qualifications and experience in the relevant system of medicine. They can be promoted to top levels in HCW after acquiring qualification in public health and training in management.

59. Innovative approaches are essential for ensuring health of people because even best treatment alone is not sufficient for good health. Promotional health care which will help people and will reduce need for curative care deserves high priority. "Health Promotion Wing" (HPW) staffed by a cadre with experience in health promotion activities should focus on these. HPW should promote innovative ideas with a sense of commitment. It should work in close collaboration with HCW.

60. Our education system has fundamental defects. It is mainly oriented towards getting employment for making money. Even for this, skill training is grossly inadequate. More importance is given to passing examinations than to developing analytical/logical thinking and spirit of making experiments to develop knowledge and its applicability. Often, theory alone is taught first and its application later (if at all) instead of sandwiching theory and application in suitable stages in an intelligent manner. Students have to waste time and efforts to acquire some types of knowledge which are not even indirectly relevant to their future needs. Attempts to dovetail aptitude with selection of fields for education and skill development are scarce. This has often resulted in the calamity of round things being squeezed into square plugs. For example, research and development (R&D) jobs are often taken up by persons without any aptitude for or interest in these but only to earn a salary. This results in slow or no contribution to R&D.

It is a matter of serious concern that quality of some schools (mainly government) was so bad that they could not attract enough students and had to close down.

61. Finding faults with others is a national negative habit because it is seldom followed by positive ideas about finding solutions to the problems which are the subject of criticism. It has not been realized that, on the one hand, this negative habit has caused serious consequences to both national and personal issues and on the other hand, criticism in any form is a type of assessment of efficiency of activities performed. What is essential is to train students to avoid negative criticism only, that too with prejudice, but systematically carry out positive and constructive criticism in an objective manner. This training will lead to creditable achievements. Ignoring these is a serious lapse in the education system.

62. Multiple failures in education have posed challenging problems in many fields. Most Indians could not develop the proper mind set and aims as well as productive habits required for social and economic developments which will benefit people. Insufficient exposure to behavioural norms have resulted in public health problems such as open defecation, throwing garbage in streets etc. Failures in education also include high drop out rates, child marriages, deficiencies in population control and lack of hygienic practices affecting their heath and that of children. Intolerance, violence (especially destruction of public properties), lack of respect for laws and ignorance of social responsibility have roots in defective education. Indifference to communal harmony and inability to realize the importance of dialogues and debates to solve problems arise from defective education. India's demographic advantage of having a young population has not only been watered

down but converted into a serious unemployment problem by defective education producing enormous number of unqualified youngsters. It is important to carryout studies which can help to clarify all such matters and make necessary changes.

63. Most important, no thought has been given to have a holistic education to generate good citizens with character, health consciousness and true practice of religion. Such holistic education with vision will lead to healthy changes in peoples' approach towards many problems and mitigate some serious problems (e.g., rape and harassment of women, conflicts due to religion and caste, mass/indiscriminate shooting and killing by perverts, alcoholism, smoking, drug addiction etc.). These changes in peoples' approach will result in a happy life of good quality with dignity under peaceful environment and carrying on activities without hindrance – an outstanding achievement.

64. To make holistic education a reality and to overcome all basic defects (paragraphs 60, 61, 62 and 63) "<u>Education Wing</u>" (EW) should conduct in depth studies to develop a system of education which wraps up all the above aspects. It should have a cadre of professionals with experience in research and development of education and training in management and having proper vision and commitment. EW should give highest priority for progressively setting up adequate numbers of schools and other education institutions of good quality with adequate number of qualified staff with vision for efficiently implementing the new system of education throughout the country as quickly as possible. For success of the new education system, balanced composite developments to ensure adequate numbers of schools and other education institutions of good quality with adequate number of qualified staff with vision should be ensured.

65. Child safety and development are matters for serious concern. Sexual abuse of children is alarmingly high with 50 cases being reported every day. Raping and murdering children are quite common. NCRB data shows that instances of child rape increased by 82% in 2016 compared to the previous year. Overall crime against children has also increased (The Times of India dated 02.12.17, page 16). It is shocking that only 1% of those accused under the Protection of Children from Sexual Offences Act of 2012 has been convicted. In connection with a PIL which alleged that 1,17,480 children had gone missing between January 2008 and January 2010 and of them 41,546 were yet to be traced, SC remarked that "No body seems to be concerned about missing children. This is the irony." Another alarming fact is that selling of children as slaves by poor families is quite common. Child labour continues to be a problem though illegal. Malnutrition is widespread and alarming. According to WHO, 50% of Indian children are either underweight or stunted. Education of children leaves much to be desired. Funds provided for health and education of children are thoroughly inadequate. Holistic education suggested in paragraph 63 and 64 is likely to help in proper development of children. Child Safety Wing (CSW) with a cadre with vision and suitable qualifications should carry out in depth studies and engage in dialogues, discussion and debates to solve these serious problems. It has to work in collaboration with HCW, HPW and EW to provide better health and education to children.

66. Unemployment has been a major problem for years. What is worse, it has been deteriorating at an alarming rate over the last few years. Against a need to generate about 10 million jobs every year, only 1,55,000 were created in 2015 and 2,31,000 in 2016. Of the latter, 122,000 were generated in the last quarter

of 2016 and shows that recent efforts are leading to an increased rate. Yet, number of jobs created in 2017 may not exceed 500,000 which is only a dismal 5% of the target. Current methods are grossly insufficient. <u>Employment and Labour Wing</u> (ELW) with a cadre with vision and suitable qualifications should explore innovative methods to overcome this damaging situation. A basic defect in planning is the almost total dependence on creating jobs in industries. Instead, ELW should adopt a needs matching approach with vision which will give top priority to creation of jobs in other sectors which are suffocating for want of workers to expand their badly needed activities. For example, education sector needs more teachers; health sector needs more doctors and paramedical staff; construction of national and state highways and district roads need more workers etc. Water management (paragraph 67) will need many workers of different types. This "needs matching" approach will not only create jobs but also lead to laudable improvements in many other sectors. For this, ELW has to develop advanced planning with vision in consultation with sectors which need workers.

67. Acute shortage of water is a serious problem. Shockingly, while many areas are suffering from drought, large scale wastage of water continues. Frequent floods are causing serious damages to life and property, besides huge wastage of precious water. Current methods to solve these problems are thoroughly inadequate. A need matching approach with vision is essential. <u>Water Management Wing</u> (WMW) with a cadre with vision and suitable qualifications has to carry out in depth studies in order to plan and execute innovative projects to store and utilise water. For example, a series of large reservoirs can be constructed in (1) suitable hilly areas with heavy rainfall to store rain water, (2) the upper reaches of rivers which are usually flooded, in order to prevent floods by storing

excess water and using it to produce electricity. Irrigation canals can be built from these reservoirs to drought affected areas. These reservoirs and surrounding hilly areas can be made into places of tourist attraction. Fish cultivation in these reservoirs can provide food. Boating arrangements can attract tourists and make profits. Irrigation canals from these lakes to drought affected areas can solve problems due to drought to a large extent. Growing trees on both sides of these canals can enlarge "forest" cover. All these will provide enormous multiple benefits year after year: (1) Prevent huge loss of (a) life and properties due to floods and (b) crops due to drought, (2) Provide jobs to large number of people, (3) Produce electricity which is in short supply, (4) augment fish production and (5) Increase revenue. High priority and adequate funds should be given to this matching approach with vision which will lead to unimaginable fantastic achievements.

68. Defence Ministry is responsible for safeguarding the country from attacks by other countries. For this, there is a professional military establishment consisting of army, navy and air force under the ministry – a civilian establishment. Under the principle that professionals should be freed from non-professional supervision to maximize efficiency, a National Defence Wing (NDW) should be created in place of the ministry. NDW should be headed by a three member National Defence Committee (NDC) consisting of top officers of army, navy and air force. This committee should be chaired in rotation each year by army, navy and air force. This set up will help to overcome problems faced by the military establishment in having adequate numbers of all modern equipments required to have an efficient set up. With abolition of the civilian ministry, frictions with nonprofessionals as at present will be avoided. Disputes between

army, navy and air force about funding priority will be routinely solved by PPW with approval of MA (Paragraph 24). Other disputes should be solved by MC.

69. NDW has to perform the following four functions:

(1) Defend the country when attacked, (2) Negotiate with forces of other countries to overcome/rectify adventurism by them and/or prevent war, (3) carry out attacks (like surgical strikes) to teach other forces a lesson for indulging in provocative activities and (4) conduct a war if necessary. Decision (3) should be taken only with the consent of CPA of External Affairs Wing (EAW). Decision (4), should be taken only with prior approval of a five member war committee (WC) consisting of the Chairman of MA, members of NDC and CPA of EAW.

70. One of the most important expectations from comprehensive democracy is that people can have a peaceful life of good quality with dignity in a peaceful environment and be allowed to carry on their activities without hindrance. At present, these expectations remain a woeful dream in many ways. Most people do not benefit from the law and order machinery. Police have earned a reputation of being corrupt in dealing with problems faced by people. People are even afraid to go to a police station with a genuine complaint. A general impression is that persons with money or influence can get away with any crime. In fact, people are even afraid of the protectors of law. Police have earned the reputations of being "criminals in uniform" and "armed militia of politicians." Democracy also requires equality in application of laws. Violations of this requirement are far too common mainly because of political interference. To solve these problems the police establishment should not be under a civilian establishment as at

present but function as an independent Internal Security Wing (ISW) under a police officer.

71. To overcome lack of trust between police and people, ISW should build up good relationship between police and people. For instance, the entire area of a police station should be divided into as many sub areas as number of constables in the police station. Each constable should have frequent interaction with the people living in the sub area allotted to him/her by forming a "Police People Interaction Club" (PPIC). PPIC should regularly meet once a month and whenever there is a special need. In these meetings people should inform the constable about security problems they are facing and ask the constable to inform the police inspector so that action can be taken to solve the problems. In the next meeting the police inspector should inform people about the status of the required actions and reasons which are standing in the way if action is not complete. People should make use of the half yearly meetings to question ISW about these and ask for expediting proper action to solve the problems.

72. In the PPIC meetings, the police inspector should tell what people can do to improve security and request for their cooperation. PPIC should also be used by the police inspector to improve awareness of laws among people and to arbitrate disputes if any by residents of the sub area.

73. All such interactions by ISW will lead to mutual understanding of the problems faced by both groups and also make police "friends of people" instead of "criminals in uniform" and "armed militia of politicians" as at present. This will be an **outstanding achievement.**

74. Even well organized systems need checks and balances to ensure that unexpected failures are identified and corrected. Attempts to have Lokpal (ombudsman) for this purpose have dragged on so far (Article 9). Moreover, Lokpal cannot function efficiently without investigating agencies under its control to ascertain facts. Therefore, "Lokpal Wing" (LPW) headed by Lok Pal should have not only a cadre with suitable qualifications, vision and commitment but also have Central Vigilance Commission and Central Bureau of Investigation fully under its control. It should have power to investigate transparency in functioning of all Wings, MC and MA. It should also have the responsibility of questioning long delays (explained in paragraph 6).

75. India has cultural diversity. I have not come across a definition or compact description of Indian culture. Probably, these are not possible because of extreme diversities. The situation becomes more complex because when changes are suggested these are often not accepted due to blindly sticking to tradition, free for all attitudes in the absence of proper leadership and non-acceptance of a sense of discipline. Moreover, superstitions and obsolete practices form part of almost all cultures. Attempts to overcome any of these problems are opposed in name of tradition, forgetting that many traditions had short lives since Stone Age. These changes in tradition were part of evolution which was and is absolutely necessary. It is important to reach a balance between traditions and progress to evolve a national consensus on accepting suitable changes to have dynamic Indian cultures which can adapt progressive changes from time to time. A serious obstacle is absence of leaders who can apply their minds to overcome the total confusion which prevails in the cultural scene. To tackle these challenging problems, "Culture Wing" (CW) should first carry

out comprehensive studies of the diverse cultural situations in the country and then study how (1) unscientific and emotional cultural practices and superstitions can be reduced and (2) changes in culture can be attuned to progress from time to time. Thereafter, it should organize necessary dialogues, discussions and debates to evolve a national consensus on suitable dynamic Indian cultures and create a climate for acceptance of necessary progressive changes from time to time. This will be an excellent and creditable achievement. CW should be staffed by a cadre with vision and knowledge of different cultures and their superstitions and obsolete practices.

76. National integration is essential to develop best possible democracy for the whole country (Article 12). "National Integration Wing" (NIW) with a cadre with vision and qualifications in sociology and mass communication and experience in the field should plan and implement multiple innovative approaches for national integration, with determination and commitment. For example, NIW should encourage, facilitate and provide financial incentives for (1) inter zone/region migration, (2) inter caste, inter religion and inter zone/region marriages, (3) "know your country" education trips for school children and college students and (4) a national script to be used by all languages (for justification for these see Article 12).

77. Entertainment and recreation not only make people relaxed and happy but also have profound influence on mind development – good and bad. For example, unintentionally, mind development is seriously perverted when providers of entertainment thoughtlessly introduce themes which tend to show how evil succeeds repeatedly during major part of the entertainment programme or show that villains successfully continue their evil acts time and again and enjoy making good people (particularly women) continuously

suffer and cry. The fact that these have profound bad influence on mind development especially of children has not received adequate attention from them. They close their eyes to the fact that there are many instances of criminals learning tricks from entertainment programmes. Objections raised are scoffed at by claiming right to freedom of expression, forgetting that they also have the responsibility to prevent disastrous short term and long term mind development by their actions. It is pertinent that, while use of such oft repeated themes requires a kind of talent which is quite common and mediocre, use of better or innovative themes requires special talents of a different kind which is not so common. In other words, freedom of expression is often misused as a shelter for mediocrity because of inability to develop special talents. Such misuse of freedom of expression should be exposed and condemned. Another problem is that many talented people are bypassed because of vested interests which blow up persons of their choice only. This hinders proper development of these fields in a democratic manner and leads to frustrations. "<u>Entertainment and Recreation Wing</u>" (ERW) with a cadre with vision and having experience in the field should organize dialogues, discussions and debates to solve these problems. For making convincing dialogues, discussions and debates, it should carry out elaborate studies to collect relevant facts about harmful effects and also collect views of experienced social psychologists. It should give high priority to encourage and support (1) development of innovative talents and (2) entertainment and recreation activities that promote good mind development.

78. Development of sports and games has been faulty. The fact that these have good influence on developing character and good quality of life has not received adequate attention. It is shameful

that India with more than billion people has performed badly in Olympics and international competitions in most sports/games. Even much smaller and poorer countries have performed better. Systematic attempts to identify talents and give them training and develop well equipped facilities for this are grossly inadequate. The need for income and financial security during old age for sportsmen who can have only a short period of quality performance has not received enough attention. Many parents do not encourage children because even top performers often lead pitiable life after short period of active sports/games. Premier institutions for sports/games are managed by outsiders. They have diverted attention to unhealthy commercialization of sports and games. "Sports Wing" (SW) with a cadre with vision and having experience in the field should apply its mind to solve various problems in developing these activities on sound lines.

78. Activities in arts, crafts, music, dancing and literature have influence on having good quality of life. For convenience of reference these may be grouped under "Arts." "Arts Wing" (ARW) with a cadre with vision and having knowledge and experience in these fields should develop and encourage these activities, after well planned studies followed by dialogues, discussions and debates to solve conflicts/problems.

80. "Panchayat Wing" (PW) with a cadre with vision and suitable qualifications should organize and maintain village level activities under comprehensive democracy through Village Panchayats. It should have constant dialogues with DW to maintain the necessary links. For any special activity it should work in collaboration with the Wing responsible for it. PW should also guide and prepare villagers to make the half yearly meetings at block level meaningful and effective. Panchayats at block, taluk and district levels should avoid clash with DW activities at block level.

81. Each Wing should carry out concurrent monitoring of its activities using data maintained by it. "Monitoring and Evaluation Wing" (MEW) headed by an ISS officer with vision should check these monitoring reports and give guidance whenever necessary. It should also independently evaluate functioning of all Wings once a year. For this, it should be staffed by ISS and IES officers. Evaluation should be based on necessary special studies in addition to available data.

82. Efficiency of each CPA should be assessed every year by MA (not by MC which consists of CPAs only) after examining monitoring reports of the Wing, evaluation reports of MEW for the Wing and peoples' assessment and views about that Wing prepared by DW and VW. Efficiency of staff of each Wing should be assessed by CPA every year based on suitably prepared confidential reports for that Wing's activities. Punishments should be given for gross or repeated inefficiencies – by MA for CPA and by CPA for its staff. The latter can appeal against this single authority decision to MC and then to MA.

83. All offices should avoid paper work which requires large quantity of stationery and lot of storage space. "Computer Wing" (CRW) with a suitable professional cadre should organize paperless office system and keep a watch on it. CRW should train all officers and subordinate staff in computer usage and provide hardware and software support.

84. Following office procedure is suggested. Instead of opening a paper file for any subject, concerned official should open and number a computer file, type relevant notes and send it by email to next higher level after attaching relevant documents. Letters received by post should be copied and attached. Official at receiving level should either ask for more information from

lower level or make notes and forward it by email to next higher level. Wherever necessary, the notes should quote precedents and relevant points of law. This procedure should be continued up to decision making level, which will then have notes made by all lower levels and attached documents for study. It should take decisions and inform concerned individual or office through email. This will ensure secrecy and reduce time gap between taking decision and communicating it. If the decision can be communicated only through post, copy of outgoing mail should not be kept in paper file because it is available in the computer file. This procedure is not only quicker but also ensures that decisions made are not tampered with and prevents leakage of information from lower levels because decisions made are available only with decision maker and files are not passed up and down through messengers as at present. Security lapses similar to what happened in Petroleum ministry can be ruled out. This procedure will also help delivery of quick service to people, besides saving on cost of stationery and postage stamps and storage space for paper files. After the matter is closed, decision maker's file with all notes, attachments and orders should be maintained in pen drives or CDs and preserved safely for future reference.

85. At present, government has ministries of finance, home (administration), agriculture, commerce, trade, industry, communications, external affairs, defence, different transport systems, etc. mostly controlled by IAS officers. Above paragraphs have given some examples to emphasise the need to carve out independent Wings controlled by professionals. Taking a cue from these, EG set up by CA (paragraphs 2 and 3) should study in depth the need to replace some ministries by suitable necessary Wings or merged with suitable Wings or scrapped if not necessary.

All these Wings should have CPAs with qualifications and experience in the relevant fields and management training. To satisfy the principles and needs of comprehensive democracy, EG should suggest modifications in the aim, structure, functions and staffing of these Wings (if necessary) and of new Wings and get approval of CA. Aim, structure, functions and staffing of all Wings should be reviewed at suitable intervals by MA to adapt to changes in management needs of comprehensive democracy necessitated by changes in socio-economic, religious and cultural environments.

86. More details have to be taken care of. These can and should be finalized after detailed discussions by EG, keeping in mind needs and principles of comprehensive democracy and the important suggestions given in all these articles, and approved by CA.

87. Comprehensive democracy outlined above has many advantages including the following 27 outstanding advantages:

1. People can live happily with good quality of life with dignity under peaceful environment and can carry on their activities without hindrance because all aspects (sub systems), which have influence on these, are taken into account (not governance alone as at present) – An eminently worthwhile achievement.

2. Maximum efficiency can be achieved because all activities are independently managed by suitable professionals without hindrance from non-professionals.

3. Needs and aspirations of people will be satisfied as fully as possible because once in six months people can question the relevant Wing responsible for any action needed to satisfy any need or aspiration.

4. These checks also lead to more efficient and effective functioning of all Wings.

5. Once in six months people become aware of problems faced by each Wing and will not resort to unjustified agitations.

6. Intelligentsia gets opportunities to be much more actively involved in democracy than at present.

7. All plans will reflect peoples' views and needs because every plan has to be certified by DW and VW which are aware of peoples' views and needs.

8. Delays in sanctioning and execution of plans will be drastically reduced.

9. This system is more decentralized and effective because direct checks are exercised by people once in six months at block/ward level instead of having only a check on electing their representatives once in five years for indirect intervention on their behalf at state level.

10. Because of abolition of states and provision for people to regularly exercise their voice directly at block level, the present day disruptive demands and agitations for creating more states in different parts of the country will be automatically solved.

11. National integration and uniform laws and taxes for whole country will eliminate parochialism and lead to the feeling of being an Indian.

12. All inequalities will be drastically reduced and enormous amounts of unutilized money available with the super rich will become available for developing and maintaining MA and all Wings of NCDAI – unimaginable and outstanding achievements.

13. Greed which is causing much harm now will be drastically reduced – another unimaginable and outstanding achievement.

14. Quality of education, health care and religious and cultural practices will be vastly improved.

15. Rape and harassment of women, shooting sprees by perverts, other crimes, road accidents, alcoholism, smoking, drug addiction etc. will be drastically reduced by holistic education which will produce citizens of good character, discipline and commitment to good quality of life.

16. Disharmony and conflicts due to religion and caste will be drastically reduced – an outstanding achievement

17. Delay in providing justice will be drastically reduced and justice will become more affordable – a praiseworthy achievement.

18. Miscarriage of justice will be drastically reduced because of regular checks on judgment – an outstanding achievement

19. Violation of human rights will be drastically reduced because lakhs of violation complaints will be examined instead of being ignored as at present – a worthwhile achievement.

20. With abolition of direct taxes, the country does not have to bow down in shame for dishonesty and creation of black money and respect for the feelings of people, which is paramount in a democracy, will be restored – a praiseworthy achievement.

21. Abolition of election and direct taxes which are the main roots of corruption and the half yearly meetings at block level will lead to zero corruption – another praiseworthy achievement.

22. Lokpal with investigating agencies under its control will provide checks on transparent functioning of all Wings.

23. Defence of the country will be in professional hands working without hindrance from nonprofessionals.

24. Will create a climate for acceptance of necessary progressive changes in culture from time to time – a praiseworthy achievement.

25. Abolition of election removes an unrealizable responsibility thrust on people and frees them from mental slavery to politicians – an outstanding achievement.

26. Abolition of parliament, assemblies and offices of President, Vice President and Governors will save enormous amounts of money and release vast areas of prime land and buildings for public use.

27. This outline of democracy has suggested innovative solutions to overcome the basic faults, fundamental weaknesses and absurdities which led to the present pseudo democracy – an outstanding and praiseworthy achievement.

88. Despite so many outstanding advantages some people will oppose change on their own or under pressure from others. Two relevant questions to them are: (1) Are they prepared to live, eat, work, travel and enjoy life as their ancestors did? If not, opposing change and then enjoying benefits of change is hypocrisy; (2) Are they prepared to get rid of their inferiority complex and use their ingenuity to set an example for others to follow? They should also answer some more relevant questions in the discussions under "Accept change as a part of evolution" in Article 26 before opposing the change to comprehensive democracy.

89. It is pertinent that government has been sitting for more than ten years on poll reforms suggested by Election Commission.

Moreover, under comprehensive democracy outlined above, GW will only be one of the Wings of NCDAI and will miss its present superiority and dominance. Therefore, it is naïve to depend on government to develop the comprehensive democracy despite so many outstanding advantages.

90. This series of articles clearly shows that all citizens, organized groups and statutory institutions, besides government, are responsible for development, maintenance and further growth of democracy. All of them should wake up and act if they sincerely want a true and vibrant comprehensive democracy.

91. ***Action needed:*** To demonstrate that they are keen to have a comprehensive democracy which ensures the aim of people living happily with good quality of life and dignity under peaceful environment and carrying on their activities without hindrance, people should demand setting up of a new Constituent Assembly to (1) discuss and finalize all details of the comprehensive democracy outlined in Article 27 and (2) appoint interim governments at the centre and in all states comprising of qualified and honest experts selected by it to govern the country during the period between dissolution of the current parliament and setting up of all Wings of NCDAI. ***Another step which can be done effortlessly is to click NOTA option in coming elections.***

92. Without further waste of time, people with vision (particularly among the young) should take keen interest, study all aspects of developing comprehensive democracy and lead a peaceful movement to make it a reality. Organizers of the peaceful movement have to constantly keep in mind that any radical and crucially needed reform will meet with fierce opposition from the entrenched vested interests in India and possibly in some other countries also. On the other hand, they should not develop a

defeatist mentality and should be constantly guided and inspired by the fact that India got independence by a peaceful movement against a mighty empire which had put up a series of obstacles and taken many cruel and violent steps. It should be specially noted that these could only delay attainment of success. With adequate precautions, commitment, determination to fight against all obstacles and patience success can be achieved and will confirm the invincibility of peoples' power. Creation of mass awareness and support for a peaceful movement to create the comprehensive democracy outlined above, with professionals in charge of all activities, has become easier now because "65% Indians say a system in which "experts" rather than elected officials make decisions would be good" (India Today dated 06.11.17, page 9). It is pertinent, encouraging and reassuring that creation of mass awareness will ensure that peoples' power will be forthcoming to take adequate steps and precautions needed from time to time for success of the peaceful movement.

93. Therefore, as a prerequisite for kick starting this peaceful movement, these visionaries should act to (1) create mass awareness by suitable dialogues, discussions and debates on Articles 24 to 27 and (2) arrive at a preliminary general consensus about advantages of comprehensive democracy. They have to take special care to ensure that they do not get bogged down by any point other than advantages of comprehensive democracy or distracting details, deliberately and cunningly focused upon by opponents. Then the peaceful movement should demand setting up of a new Constituent Assembly to (1) discuss and debate this consensus and all pertinent back ground details given in this series of articles, (2) work out full details of the comprehensive democracy (taking into account suggestions in these articles also) and

(3) make changes in the Constitution to make the comprehensive democracy a reality.

94. These steps form the peaceful way to develop the comprehensive democracy before violent protests against our sinking democracy (e.g., by Maoists and regional groups) spread widely and rock the country and result in a violent revolution which is already looming in the horizon. It is pertinent that a violent revolution will make changes under stress of violence and hurry. These will be forced upon people bowed down by fear of frenzied violent mobs. This will be a crushing blow to democracy for many years and will indefinitely postpone the time when people can live happily with good quality of life with dignity under peaceful environment and carry on their activities without hindrance. This likely calamity adds to the urgency of starting the peaceful movement for comprehensive democracy immediately. If we do not make such joint efforts now to build a better India with comprehensive democracy, posterity will blame us for our callousness which led to disintegration, anarchy and violence.

95. Swami Vivekananda had exhorted us: "Arise, awake and sleep not till you reach your goal."

96. Let our joint efforts be guided by the following exhortations also:

1. *Have vision:* A blind person asked Swami Vivekananda: Can there be anything worse than losing eye sight?" He replied: "Yes, losing your vision!"

2. *Have an ethics of care:* "Having an ethics of care for suffering millions will not clash with your legitimate self interests and will make you happy."

– Anonymous

3. ***Learn from history:*** "Never forget that a small group of thoughtful committed citizens can change the world; it is the only way that ever does."

– Margarat Mead

4. ***Prevent evil to triumph:*** "All that is necessary for the triumph of evil is for good men to do nothing."

– Edmund Burke

5. ***Conquer silence:*** "Our lives begin to end the day we become silent about things that matter."

– Martin Luther King Jr

6. ***Dream, think and Act:*** "Dream, dream, dream. Dreams transform into thoughts, and thoughts into action.

– A.P.J. Abdul Kalam

7. ***Have courage:*** All our dreams can come true, if we have the courage to pursue them.

– Walt Disney

8. ***Innovate:*** "I dream of things that never were, and ask why not?"

– Robert F. Kennedy

9. ***Work and Dedicate:*** "Few things are created and perfected all at the same time. It takes effort, work, and dedication to achieve your goal.

– John Dillon

10. ***Be bold:*** "Boldness has genius, power and magic in it"

– Goethe

11. ***Use will Power:*** If there is a will there is a way.

— A proverb

12. ***Develop proper attitude:*** Attitude is a little thing that makes a big difference.

— Winston Churchill

13. ***Make efforts:*** "There can be efforts that fail but there should <u>not</u> be a failure of efforts.

— Anonymous

14. ***Act when time has come:*** There is one thing stronger than all the armies in the world, and that is an idea whose time has come.

— Victor Hugo

15. ***Use power of people:*** Mahatma Gandhi (who got us independence from the mightiest empire by leading a non-violent movement) has shown us how even unbelievable changes can be achieved when ordinary people come together and use their hidden power to do extraordinary things.

16. ***Progress is a result:*** There is nothing mysterious about progressing. It is doing instead of doubting, and working instead of wishing.

— Gerald Findle

17. ***Deserve Victory:*** Victory belongs to the most persevering

— Napoleon Bonaparte

HEEDING THE ABOVE EXHORTATIONS
LET US RESTORE OUR VISION
AND BE BOLD ENOUGH TO DREAM, INNOVATE AND ACT
FOR ACHIEVING EXTRAORDINARY CHANGES
WITH A WILL TO DEVELOP THE COMPREHENSIVE
DEMOCRACY

Abbreviations

AMR	–	Anti-microbial resistance
ARW	–	Arts Wing
AW	–	Arbitration Wing
BJP	–	Bharatiya Janata Party
BRICS	–	Association of Brazil, Russia, India, China & South Africa
CA	–	Constituent Assembly
CAG	–	Comptroller & Auditor General of India
CBI	–	Central Bureau of Investigation, India
CEO	–	Chief Executive Officer
CIC	–	Central Information Commission, India
CM	–	Chief Minister of a state
CPA	–	Chief Professional Authority under NCDAI
CRW	–	Computer Wing
CSW	–	Child Safety Wing
CVC	–	Central Vigilance Commission, India
CW	–	Culture Wing
DoPT	–	Department of Personnel and Training
DW	–	Democracy Wing

DySP	–	Deputy Superintendent of Police
EAW	–	External Affairs Wing
EC	–	Election Commission
ED	–	Enforcement Directorate
EG	–	Expert Group(s) set up by CA
ELW	–	Employment and Labour Wing
ERW	–	Entertainment and Recreation Wing
EW	–	Education Wing
GDP	–	Gross Domestic Product
GIW	–	Gender Issues Wing
GW	–	Governance Wing
HCW	–	Health Care Wing
HDW	–	Human Development Wing
HRC	–	Human Rights Commission
HRW	–	Human Rights Wing
IAS	–	Indian Administrative Service
IA&AS	–	Indian Administrative and Accounts Service
ICS	–	Indian Civil Service
IES	–	Indian Economics Service
IMR	–	Infant Mortality Rate
ISS	–	Indian Statistical Service
ISW	–	Internal Security Wing

IT	–	Income Tax Department
IW	–	Inequalities Wing
JW	–	Justice Wing
KSHRC	–	Karnataka State Human Rights Commission
LPW	–	Lokpal Wing
LW	–	Law Wing
MA	–	Management Assembly under NCDAI
MC	–	Management Council under NCDAI
MEW	–	Monitoring and Evaluation Wing
MGNREGA	–	Mahatma Gandhi National Rural Employment Guarantee Act
MLA	–	Member of – Legislative Assembly
MP	–	Member of Parliament
MW	–	Media Wing
NCDAI	–	National Comprehensive Democracy Authority of India
NCRB	–	National Crime Record Bureau
NDC	–	National Defence Committee
NDW	–	National Defence Wing
NHRC	–	National Human Rights Commission
NIW	–	National Integration Wing
NOTA	–	None Of The Above

NPA	–	Nonperforming Assets
PHC	–	Primary Health Centre
PM	–	Prime Minister of India
PPIC	–	Police People Interaction Club
PPP	–	Private Public Partnership
PPW	–	Plan Priority Wing
PW	–	Panchayat Wing
R&D	–	Research & Development
RPA	–	Representation of People Act
RSF	–	Reporting without frontier
RSS	–	Rashtriya Swayam Sevak Sangh
RTI	–	Right to Information Act 2005
RW	–	Religion Wing
SC	–	Supreme Court of India
SHO	–	Station House Officer in charge of police station
SHRC	–	State Human Rights Commission
SW	–	Sports Wing
TW	–	Tax Wing
UPA	–	United Progressive Alliance
UK	–	United Kingdom
UPSC	–	Union Public Service Commission of India
UN	–	United Nations

UNICEF	–	United Nations Children's Emergency Fund
UNDP	–	United Nations Development Programme
USA/US	–	United States of America
VHP	–	Vishva Hindu Parishad
VW	–	Visions Wing
WC	–	War Committee
WHO	–	World Health Organisation
WMW	–	Water Management Wing

www.ingramcontent.com/pod-product-compliance
Lightning Source LLC
Chambersburg PA
CBHW051432250726
48655CB00001B/18